DERIVATIVES
in the
STOCK & MONEY
MARKETS

Greg Peel

DERIVATIVES
in the
STOCK & MONEY
MARKETS

**A plain English guide to the mysterious
world of the financial markets**

LANSDOWNE

Published by Lansdowne Publishing Pty Ltd
18 Argyle Street, Sydney NSW 2000, Australia

First published in 1999 by Lansdowne Publishing Pty Ltd

Author: Greg Peel
Cartoons: Mick Tate
Design: Sarah Collins
Author photograph: Monte Luke Photographics

Publisher: Deborah Nixon
Editorial Coordinator: Joanne Holliman
Copy editor: Caroline Beaumont

National Library of Australia Cataloguing-in-Publication Data

Peel, Greg, 1962– .
 Derivatives in the stock and money markets : a plain English guide
 to the mysterious world of the financial markets.

 Includes index.
 ISBN: 1 86302 659 2

 1. Investments. 2. Stock exchanges. 3. Hedging (Finance)
 4. Financial institutions. 5. Banks and banking. I.
 Title II Title: Plain English guide to the mysterious
 world of the financial markets.

332.642

Set in Sabon on QuarkXPress
Printed in Australia by McPherson's Printing Group

Acknowledgments

There are many people to whom I am indebted for their assistance, support and encouragement during the writing of this book. There are some I must acknowledge directly.

I extend my wholehearted thanks and gratitude to Richard Jenkins, whose support has been instrumental in bringing a nice idea into publication.

Many thanks to Jonathon Coultas for always being available for consultation, assistance and red wine. Thanks also to Stephen Ewington and James Benjamin for providing constant encouragement and help when needed.

Lastly, thank you to Sarah Mills for her support, Mark Gardiner for his assistance, Kate Forsyth for imparting her knowledge and Craig Evans for his graphical skills.

ℭ

Greg Peel was born in Sydney and presently lives in The Rocks. After graduating with a Bachelor of Business degree from the University of Technology, he joined Macquarie Bank as a trainee in 1986.

During Greg's nine years with Macquarie he was involved in principal trading of futures, options and the derivatives of currencies, bonds, commodities, stocks and stock indices, both locally and offshore. He resigned in 1994 as a director of Options Trading in order to pursue his own trading opportunities. In 1998 he joined the boutique fund manager, Triton Asset Management, as a director.

Derivatives in the Stock & Money Markets is Greg's first book.

Contents

What is the stock market? Everyone has an idea, but do they really know? How does the money market work? What about foreign exchange? This chapter introduces these concepts along with a look at other financial market places. There are no tricks.

A farmer and a baker take us into the world of futures. It is a world of hedging and speculating, of exchanges, margin calls, leverage and liability. You will see into the futures.

Computers can be unleashed onto the market with often devastating effect. Arbitrage is all about the attempt to make something for nothing, particularly in the stock market. How does this happen?

Options form the basis of most derivatives traded in markets around the world. There is possibly no more powerful tool. But just how does an option work? A share warrant is a type of option. We will look at options without labouring on any mathematics.

The option to sell is just as important as the option to buy.

Contents

Introduction

On a postcard day in Sydney many years ago I was invited to attend a lunch at one of the city's premier seafood restaurants to celebrate the twenty-first birthday of a university colleague. The view was spectacular, and the thought of tucking into a bit a overpriced lobster at someone else's expense was just enough to top it off. Being single at the time I was seated next to the mother of the birthday girl's best friend who turned out to be a most charming lady, although I had the feeling I'd been put there for the purpose of babysitting one of the oldies, being a mature twenty-four myself. Nevertheless, we were only into the bread rolls when the question I always cringed about was inevitably asked:

'So Greg, what do you do for a living?'

Futures traders in the mid-eighties did not attract quite as much disdain, at the time, as they often do today (for one thing Nick Leeson, the 'man who brought down Barings, was still a mere office clerk). A life of glamour, excitement and money was the image in the minds of at least those people who had actually heard of the occupation. This did not, however, alter the fact that ninety percent of those people who had actually heard of the occupation had next to no idea of what a futures trader actually did.

'I'm a futures trader.'

I silently hoped that my fellow guest would simply respond with something fittingly gracious like, 'That's nice,' and then we could go on enjoying the meal. It was not that I wasn't proud of what I did for a living. On the contrary, it was just that a complete explanation took a bit of time and effort and this was an opportunity for me to forget work and engage in the typically frivolous and entertaining conversation that early twentysomethings are good at.

'Oh wonderful! Does that mean that you try to predict the future?'

Sigh. The standard misconception. It's surprising how many people assume that futures traders must have crystal balls. I hoped to put a quick end to the query.

'No. It's just like trading the stock market, and could you pass the butter please, gosh, what a nice dress.'

'Oh...thanks. So your job is, like, using graphs and things to tell people what future prices will be?'

Oh dear. I could see that she just wasn't ready to leave it alone. Now I knew I was in for a long lunch.

That was at the beginning of my career. I was to go on and spend nine years as a *derivatives* trader for a well-known Australian bank (one that most would refer to as a 'merchant' bank although it actually had a trading licence). But at that stage we didn't really use the word *derivatives*. I traded futures. I traded options on futures. I traded options on the Aussie dollar and on the gold price. I traded stocks and stock options. I even 'program' traded, and all the while I never had a client, I was simply making money for my bank. To this day I don't believe my mother has a clue what I do for a living.

In actual fact, everything I had ever traded was, in strict terms, a *derivative*. Nobody outside of the financial market (and not really a hell of a lot of them inside the financial market) really paid much attention to futures and options and such in the mid-eighties. The stock market was going to the moon and that's all anyone cared about.

It might have been that most people were happy to go on in life not really having to worry about what a futures contract was, what a call option was, or how foreign exchange worked. Moreover, it was unlikely that anyone outside the financial markets could give two hoots about something called 'portfolio insurance' or something called 'program trading' or something called 'stock index arbitrage'. It just wasn't that important in the average person's life.

Until October 1987. In one day, the Dow Jones index in New York fell 508 points—the biggest market 'crash' since the 'crash of '29'. Not to be ever accused of mimicking Wall Street, the All Ordinaries index in Australia fell...516 points. Suddenly the market was affecting everyone, even if it was just a case of being bombarded with doom and gloom predictions on the nightly news. After the initial shock, those who hadn't jumped from a thirtieth floor window immediately pulled out the fingers of blame and wildly started pointing. A suitable scapegoat was quickly found in the form of 'program trading'. The headlines screamed: 'COMPUTERS BLAMED IN STOCK MARKET FALL'. At least that took the heat off the human beings. We learnt that 'Institutional investors commonly use computer-driven program trading to hedge their huge stock portfolios. In a falling market, they can use a technique called portfolio insurance to sell stock index futures contracts instead of actual shares of stock to minimise losses.' And that 'Some critics of portfolio insurance claim it drove the stock prices down on October 19...by triggering the large 'sell' orders on the Chicago Exchange.'[1]

So, did this mean that our lives were turned upside down by a bunch of computers that sold these things called 'futures'?

Washington got in on the act and formed a 'presidential task force', headed by a Mr Brady, that produced a report which 'blames the automatic trading programs of these groups for generating large sell orders' and says that 'the use of both "portfolio insurance" and "stock index arbitrage" pushed the market down. With both techniques, computers can generate trades that result in orders to sell huge amounts of stock under certain circumstances.'[2]

Just what did those recalcitrant computers think they were up to, hmmm?

The argument of who was to blame has never really been resolved. A sensible approach suggests that classic herd mentality (and a good helping of greed) sent everyone rushing into the market, and when the tide turned they were climbing over themselves to get out. The use of computers had exacerbated the crash by removing the human ability to say, 'Now hold on there one minute, let's just put things in perspective before we all get carried away.' Two things were absolutely certain, however, and that was that the market would never again pay scant heed to what was going on in the *stock index futures* market, and that words like 'program trading', 'portfolio insurance' and 'arbitrage' had very much become part of the vocabulary.

1 Sydney Morning Herald, *23rd November, 1987*
2 Sydney Morning Herald, *11th January, 1988*

Realising, rather abruptly, what effect futures trading could have on a falling market was all right for those in the financial markets themselves, but this was still cold comfort for the mums and dads who had lost their life savings in one fell swoop. What *are* futures?

And that was not all. After the dust had settled a little in October, it began to become apparent that another perilous instrument had sent more than one trading operation to the wall with a distinctive *splat*. Options. Options on stocks, for example BHP (losses from which Robert Holmes a Court significantly felt the effects) and options on futures. One small but influential futures options trading outfit, when contemplating a $55 million loss at the time, had believed it statistically impossible for the market to fall so far in one hit, and when it collapsed on the day, they maintained that 'the computer was unable to sell futures contracts fast enough'[3] (there's that damned computer again). If the proportion of those investors who could honestly say that they understood what was going on in the futures market was not large, then the proportion of those who honestly understood how options affected the stock market was minuscule. But the options market quickly became the fastest growing market in the country, and the world.

What *are* options?

And all of this led, in ensuing years, to a sort of 'reds-under-the-bed' style of paranoia amongst market participants and financial journalists. Every time the market moved down more than a couple of points there were cries of 'program trading!' or 'futures arbitrage!' and the institutional investors in Australia would scurry off to hide behind the legs of the Australian Stock Exchange, peek out wide-eyed and point accusingly. They stopped just short of shouting 'Burn them! Burn them!' and the journos were happy because they found a new excuse for everything. Why was the market down today? Futures selling. Why was the market up today? Unwinding of futures selling. Don't worry, the junior journos who wrote the daily market report didn't know what it meant either. They usually got their information from those sources who didn't actually use futures but were sure that futures *must* be responsible. At least it beat being quoted as saying that the market was up today because there were 'more buyers than sellers' (a popular, tongue-in-cheek phrase used when one really has no other idea).

Then, if all else failed, market movements became 'options related'. 'XYZ Ltd moved sharply today on the back of an "options play".' Or, 'Volatility in the market was due to "option expiries".' On and on it went.

Mind you, sometimes these assessments were actually true but, having worked as an options trader at the time, I can safely say that this was rare. The formula was easy: blame options, and *no one knows what we're talking about anyway*. Least of all Joe (or Josephine) Average Investor.

As we moved into the early nineties things tended to settle a bit. For one thing, the market started to head back up from whence it came. 'Stormin" Norman Schwarzkopf did more than his fair share to help as the Gulf War finally brought renewed strength to world stock markets. This thing called 'program trading' started to push markets *up* rather than *down* (and institutional investors became conspicuously non-critical of something that pushed the market *up*) and options seemed to become quite useful rather than scary. Joe (or Josephine) Average Investor would not have been aware of anything being too untoward.

Let's bring the clock forward now to February, 1995 and BANG everything's in turmoil again. Some spivvy, overpaid barrow-boy and 'rogue' has, through fraudulent trading, brought down Barings Bank in London. One billion dollars. Bankers to the *Queen* no less. How could it happen?

It will come as no surprise that Nick Leeson, the aforementioned 'rogue', was a *futures* broker. And yes, he lost all that money trading in the futures and options markets. Nick was in charge of Barings' Singapore business specialising in the Japanese index futures which are traded in Singapore. How could it happen? Quite easily as a matter of fact. Nick claims[4] that it all started when he tried to make back some money lost on an error. Errors are a regular occurrence in the fast-moving futures market. Someone bought when they should have sold on a client's order—that sort of thing. So Nick bought futures in anticipation of a rise in the market believing he could make back the money lost on the error and no one would be any the wiser. The market went down. So he bought more futures and still the market went down. He had no trouble hiding the position within Barings' existing accounting system but he did need an excuse to keep asking for more cash. So to fix this problem he created false trades with clients and also sold 'put' options to generate some income. (Put options make money when the market goes down, rather than up). Eventually there was an earthquake in Kobe, Japan and the market 'fell out of bed'. Not only did his futures collapse in price but the price of the options he had sold rose sharply (thus providing a loss-loss situation). Soon it was all over and Barings was gone.

The shock waves around the world were intense. In the UK, in

4 Leeson, N., Rogue Trader, *Little Brown & Company, London, 1996.*

particular, the chalk-striped brigade were choking on their kippers left, right and centre. And there were those culprits once again—futures and options. Had nobody *learnt*?

By 1995, an insidious new word had crept into the common person's vocabulary—*derivatives*. The Barings situation was, to observers, another in a long line of derivatives disasters. Futures and options are two instruments that come under the banner of derivatives. Once upon a time they were considered complex, but nowadays they are referred to as 'vanilla', meaning plain, run-of-the-mill sort of things (some people even use the expression 'plain vanilla' which always makes me cringe). Derivatives in the '90s had stretched well into the 'chocolate whirl with hundreds-and-thousands' level of complexity and this is where a lot of players had come to grief. Many of these deals were private arrangements between two parties and not visible transactions occurring on, say, a futures exchange, where regulatory and credit-control factors are in place. We only ever hear about the deals that have gone awry and not the thousands of transactions occurring around the world every day that prove beneficial to all concerned. It's only ever the negative side that hits the press and so the average newspaper reader is forgiven for thinking that *derivative* equals *disaster*.

So far I might have given the impression that derivatives are peculiar to the stock market. This could not be further from the truth. Derivatives are employed in any market: interest rates, foreign exchange, metals, commodities and so on. Have you encountered someone with an option to buy a house? Have you been offered wine futures? Derivative disasters, occurring in all sorts of markets in past years, have led to the notoriety of the instruments.

In 1989, the London borough of Hammersmith and Fulham thought they were on a sure thing in a series of interest rate swaps but managed to lose $6 billion. The banks that were on the other side of the transactions came out hurting when a court ruled that the borough was never authorised to trade exotic derivative products in the first place. In 1993, mighty German commodities conglomerate Metallgesellschaft, one of the most highly respected in its field, lost $2 billion in oil derivatives. In 1994, US corporate giant, Proctor & Gamble, used derivatives to speculate on US interest rates and lost $200 million. They subsequently sued Bankers Trust, from whom the derivatives were purchased, for giving them bad advice. Not to be outdone, Bankers Trust decided to sue them back. Eventually the

Americans, sick and tired of people being burnt by these *derivative* things, called a House of Representatives inquiry and asked George Soros, an influential funds manager, largely blamed for the European currency crises of the previous year, to 'please explain'. They were hell bent on regulating the things. George suggested that regulation was not the answer, and probably nigh on impossible, but monitoring of exposures created by derivative positions was definitely a good idea.

Fast forward to 1997. October 1997. Every year since the crash of '87 investors have become very nervous around about October. This is because the crash of '29 also occurred in October, as did the 'crashette' of '89. So '97 was not going to be an exception. And as the tenth anniversary of the crash of '87 came and went without too much panic there were storm clouds building over Asia. When the clouds burst the following week, a wave of currency collapse swept through the region and a stock market crash of about half the extent of the one ten years before hit the US and, subsequently, Australian markets. Asian governments dived into panic mode and started laying blame on anyone from foreign exchange speculators in particular, to the Jewish people in general. Just when everyone thought it was going to be the beginning of the end once more, the markets turned around the following day and 'crashed' up. This was unprecedented. What followed was possibly the most volatile period of stock market trading ever experienced as, one by one, Asian countries collapsed and rebounded and collapsed again, swinging by huge percentages each day. The Australian market, although not as wildly erratic as those of its adopted northern cousins, sustained levels of volatility not experienced in ten years.

Again a period of calm descended, but not for long. One year later, a new form of organisation hit the headlines and shocked the world. The *hedge fund*. When Russia defaulted on its government debt, and Brazil's economy looked set to collapse, it suddenly became apparent that one of the biggest hedge funds in the world had gone under in a sea of leveraged exposures. Long-Term Capital Management was bankrupt with $200 billion US dollars of positions—a situation that could have brought down some of America's biggest and oldest investment banks and ultimately required a rescue package from such saviours as the Union Bank of Switzerland, Europe's largest bank, which had lent billions to Long-Term. Again there were accusations made. Again that word *derivative* was prominent.

As the roller-coaster ride continues it is apparent that derivatives, first cited as a cause of the crash of '87, and the subject then of calls for regulation, are alive and well and unregulated more than ten years later.

So: *What on earth are derivatives?* We've seen news reporters speak the word with a facade of understanding. We've read newspaper reports that throw it in with an air of nonchalance. 'Losses in the first quarter were sustained when a derivatives transaction went against the company.' *What's a derivative?* 'It's a…you know…just a derivative.' *Uh-huh*. We've read of 'derivatives' and 'futures-related buying' and 'option plays' and 'interest rate swaps' and 'gold hedging' and any number of other expressions that obviously one needs a degree in finance and several years experience to understand. *Doesn't one?*

No. Not really. The financial market, like any other field of endeavour, uses a lot of jargon which sounds impressive but is really quite straight-forward. If your doctor told you that you had been diagnosed as suffering from acute coryza you'd be checking that your life insurance was up to date before you discovered that 'coryza' meant you simply had a cold. But that doesn't mean you can write your own prescriptions—that's where the doctor's degree comes into play. Similarly, most of the products and strategies used in the financial markets can be readily explained if put into everyday language, if common or garden analogies are used, and if the reader is not dismissed offhandedly as a complete fool. And then, of course, they extend into regions where years of experience and maybe a degree in mathematics are required to fully appreciate the intricacies, but then we'll leave that to people who trade derivatives for a living.

This book attempts to show that some of the mystique of derivatives, and indeed financial markets in general, is easily shattered. Futures, options, warrants, interest rate caps, foreign exchange and other financial products are explained in everyday terms. No longer should you need to say, 'Oh, well, I've never understood all that stuff anyway'. We will look at what the benefits and pitfalls are in derivatives trading from the point of view of both the small player and the big and nasty player. And for future reference, the book concludes with a glossary of the jargon introduced along the way.

1. Let's Start at the Very Beginning

What Does 'Derivative' Mean?

The Macquarie Dictionary's definition of the word 'derivative' is: 'derived ...not original or primitive; secondary.' And the definition of the word 'derive' is: 'to receive or obtain from a source or origin'. The bottom line is that a derivative does not stand alone but is in some way related to something else. A financial derivative is related to one or another of the financial markets such as the stock market, interest rate market, precious metals, foreign exchange, oil, any number of commodities, and then some. The market to which the derivative instrument is related is called the *underlying* market. When there is a change in the underlying market there will also be a change in the price of the derivative instrument, but the direction and magnitude of that change can vary greatly depending on what sort of derivative instrument we're talking about.

Before attempting to understand typical forms of derivatives, it's a good idea to briefly examine some of those underlying markets which may have an effect, even if indirectly, on our lives, and which also produce the greatest volume of related derivative transactions.

The Stock Market

If you were to do a spot survey of the person-in-the-street and ask them what a financial market was, the most frequent response you'd get would be something like 'Um...shares 'n' stuff'. The stock market (or 'share market') is probably the most recognisable and tangible form of financial market. Virtually everyone's heard of BHP, Kerry Packer and the 'stock exchange'. When one thinks of investing some money, maybe a nest egg that's been building up in the bank account, or maybe a bit of an inheritance from a relative who was considerate enough to pass away, one thinks of shares.

So what are shares?

When you buy a share, you are literally doing just that—buying a share of a particular company. When Johnno down the road invites you to put up half the money for his new lawn-mowing business in exchange for half the profits, he's inviting you to buy a fifty percent 'share' of the business. If Kerry Packer wanted you to invest in Publishing and Broadcasting Ltd you probably wouldn't get a phone call from him but you still have the same opportunity. The difference between 'Johnno's Beaut Mowing Service' and PBL (apart from matters of scale) is that Johnno's is a private company and Kerry's is a *publicly listed* company. To buy a share of a private company, the present shareholders would have to be willing to sell to you. To buy a share of a publicly listed company, you simply have to come up with the money and ask a stockbroker to make the purchase for you. 'Publicly listed' means that the company is one of hundreds 'listed' on the stock exchange in which the general public may invest.

There's more than one reason why a company would decide to go public but by far the most frequent one is in order to raise capital so that the company can afford to go about the sort of business its executives have in mind. They want your money. Capital raised by issuing shares is called *equity*. The company might have otherwise chosen to have *borrowed* money from someone and this is known as *debt* (we're all familiar with that word). When you invest money in a company by buying shares you are expecting, or at least hoping, that the company will be successful. Success will be reflected in growth of the company (and therefore the share price going up) and healthy dividend payments to shareholders (your cut of the year's profit). When someone borrows money from you, you expect them to ultimately give it back, even if the borrower was unable to use that money effectively. When you invest in a company and that company proves to be unsuccessful, you may legitimately lose all of that money. That is the danger in buying shares.

The reason we say you buy 'shares in' a company, and not 'a share of' that company, is because the amount of capital that the company is trying to raise is conveniently divided into nice neat parcels of round figure amounts, often $1.00, to make it tidy and easy for everyone. These parcels are called 'shares'. Therefore, you might buy 1000 shares in Westpac Bank, for example. Incidentally, the names 'share market' and 'stock market' are interchangeable and it is equally correct to say, 'I own shares in Westpac' or 'I own stock in Westpac'. To confuse the issue, the companies listed on the stock exchange are also referred to as 'stocks'.

It is possible to buy shares in a publicly listed company at the time that the company decides to issue those shares (known as buying 'on issue'). It is also possible to buy those shares at any time after the company has been listed and has commenced trading on the stock exchange. In fact it often happens that if a stock is popular, and therefore highly sought after at the time of issue, you may apply to buy the stock, but you may not get any. Moreover, a company in which you have just decided to invest, may have listed long ago. You will then need to buy that stock in the *secondary market*. The secondary market is where buyers and sellers get together to buy and sell shares in stocks that have been listed some time in the past. When the company originally listed, it issued a *finite number of shares*. Unless the company decides otherwise, that number will remain the same. This means that in order for you to buy shares in the secondary market someone else, who had purchased them previously, *must want to sell them*. This is where the stock exchange comes into play.

The stock exchange is where you go to buy and sell shares. But it's not like any other market. In fact *you* don't go there at all—they wouldn't let you in. In order for you to trade on the stock exchange, you must retain the services of a registered stockbroker. It's the stockbroker's job to buy and sell on your behalf, which he or she will do with other stockbrokers who are representing other buyers and sellers. They're not unlike real estate agents. And, like real estate agents, they will charge you a commission, known as *brokerage*, for the privilege of transacting your business. Mind you, the role of the stockbroker is also to advise you, provide you with research, account for your transactions and generally keep you up to speed with the goings-on of the stock market.

Bids and Offers

Accepted jargon varies from one market to another. Many people are familiar with the jargon of the real estate market where you 'put in an offer' to buy a house at a price that you are prepared to pay. If the house goes to auction you 'bid' the price you're prepared to pay. In the stock market (and other financial markets), the 'bid' is the price someone is prepared to pay for a stock and the 'offer' is the price at which someone is prepared to sell that stock. If your broker tells you that XYZ is $10.20 bid and $10.25 offered, you must pay $10.25 to buy XYZ because that is the price at which someone will sell. Similarly, if you are selling XYZ, you must sell at $10.20 as that is the price that someone will pay.

When you decide to buy your shares, you will have to pay the price at which someone is prepared to part with them. So the original issue price of the share, say $1.00 as previously suggested, has absolutely no bearing on the price that you may now have to pay. Because the stock exchange acts as a central clearing house for all buy and sell orders, you are guaranteed that you will buy your shares at the lowest available price at the time, and similarly, a seller is guaranteed of the highest available price. When your *bid* is the same as the seller's *offer,* then a trade will occur. This price could be much higher or much lower than the initial issue price. I suggested previously that if a company is successful and grows in value then its share price will rise. This is not an automatic function. A share price will only ever rise as long as there is someone prepared to pay more for that share than the previous buyer.

Earlier I said that only stockbrokers are allowed into the stock exchange. This is still true, but since 1990 it no longer involves actually entering a specific building. You don't have to be too old to recall frequent television news footage of a pack of blokes with numbers on their ties screaming and yelling at two or three young guys who strode up and down a catwalk chalking numbers on to something that resembled the destination board at Central railway station. This was the stock exchange. The young guys were registering bids and offers against the hundreds of stocks listed on the exchange as they were yelled out from below. When the prices matched, the relevant brokers would find each other on the floor and exchange tickets representing the traded shares. The process is similar today, except that the exchange has been computerised and so brokers sit in their offices all over Australia in front of a computer provided by the exchange and transact business directly. Not unlike the Internet really.

Every day, prices of individual stocks will rise and fall depending on the level of enthusiasm, or desperation, of buyers and sellers. Not every stock will trade every day. Some may stay at the same recorded price for weeks because no one's particularly interested in either buying or selling. This is rarely true of those companies with the largest capitalisation. Capitalisation is determined by multiplying the share price by the number of shares on issue (and therefore the biggest company is not necessarily the company with the highest share price). The biggest companies are known as the 'blue chips'[5] and will trade in large volumes on most days. The movement of a share price on any given day will be influenced by factors that affect that

5 *The expression 'blue chip' relates to casino gambling chips. Traditionally, the chips of the greatest denomination were the blue ones.*

company specifically, or by factors that affect the market in general. In order to gauge market sentiment and determine whether, in general, the market was positive or negative on the day, it is not necessary to look up every stock price and tote up the wins and losses. A measure of the general daily movement of a stock market is provided by a *stock index*. In Australia this is called the All Ordinaries Index. The AOI was originally a measure of all the ordinary shares listed on the Australian Stock Exchange. Ordinary in this case is not in the sense of 'strewth, these shares are pretty ordinary' but rather it implies standard shares and not preference shares or some other form of share (which will be addressed later). Today, not every stock is included—only those which satisfy the exchange's criteria of size (capitalisation) and liquidity (frequency of turnover of shares). Typically, stocks satisfying these criteria number between two and three hundred.

The AOI is a *capital-weighted index*. When the index was introduced in 1979 it was initially set at 500 and each stock contributed to a percentage of that number depending on the capitalisation of that stock. (The AOI was preceded by the Sydney All Ordinaries and the Commercial and Industrial index which take us back to 1875).[6] The biggest stocks were the greater percentage of the index and when a big stock moved in price it had the greatest effect on the movement of the index. A lowly capitalised stock would only represent a small percentage of the index and therefore would only have a small effect on the movement of the index. Being a capital-weighted index, the AOI takes into consideration that a change in the price of a stock itself increases or decreases the capitalisation of that stock (remember that capitalisation = price x number of shares on issue). Thus the percentage contributions of each stock to the index do not remain static, but rather fluctuate with price. A list of the top stocks appear regularly in newspapers. Below is a sample of how the stocks are listed.

ASX 100 Sector		ASX Code 25			As at – 3/12/98			
ASX			Extra	Index	AMV	– % All Ords –		Avg. Daily
Code	Company		Code	Price ($)	(A$m)	30-Nov	30-Oct	Turnover ($m)
AAP	AAPT			3.73	484.60	0.10	0.09	0.43
AFI	Aust Found			2.79	1882.23	0.40	0.41	0.95
AGL	Australian Gas Light			11.84	3851.58	0.82	0.83	6.17
AMC	Amcor			6.94	4445.98	0.95	0.96	11.50
AMP	AMP Limited			20.62	11087.31	2.37	2.29	50.28
ANI	Austn Nat Ind			1.02	805.93	0.17	0.17	1.25
ANZ	ANZ Bank			10.51	16180.46	3.45	3.16	55.70
APF	Advance PF			1.45	664.28	0.14	0.15	0.85
ARG	Argo Inv			3.30	466.40	0.10	0.11	0.26
ARL	Austrim Limited			0.00	0.00	0.00	0.12	0.01

6 For information regarding the composition and calculation of the AOI, refer to the Australian Stock Exchange's monthly publication Companies on the Australian Stock Exchange Indices.

When you watch the news tonight and you hear: 'To finance news now and the stock market responded positively to comments made by the Treasurer this morning. At the close of trade the market was up 15 points to 2478,' you will know that it is the AOI to which the newsreader is referring. The most famous stock index in the world, and by far the most influential, is the Dow Jones Industrial Average. The Dow is an index of the 30 most highly capitalised stocks listed on the New York Stock Exchange. The NYSE is located in New York City on the corner of Broad St and Wall St. When the comment is made that 'Wall Street rallied strongly today,' it actually means that there was a strong rise in the Dow Jones index. The movement of a stock market anywhere in the world often hinges on the movement of those 30 stocks in New York.

And that's the stock market. It is a place where we can part with some of our hard-earned cash in order to invest in the potential success of a company over which, as a small shareholder, we have no control. Fortunes are made and lost every year in the stock market. Perhaps a concept that is closer to home to most people is that of borrowing money rather than investing it. Let's have a look at that.

The Money Market

An expression that is loosely used and frequently little-understood is 'the money market'. It can be uttered with any amount of qualification from hushed reverence to bitter disdain and will usually evoke knowing nods from the listener, even though the listener's understanding of the money market might only stretch to those people in suits who get off the train at the CBD. And they're the ones who are seen clogging the city pubs while throwing down vodka and tonics by the crate-load on a Friday night (bastards). Even the more informed tend to lump all financial activities from the stock market to foreign exchange to gold trading under the banner of *the money market*. The reality is that these more informed people are not wrong, it's just that from inside the financial markets the expression 'money market' is used to refer to specific activities relating to money, specifically in the form of debt, and nothing else. It does not include stocks or commodities. Strictly it includes foreign exchange, but most organisations run a separate FX department, and for the purposes of this chapter, I shall visit foreign exchange under a separate sub-heading. What this leaves us with is a market purely involved with *interest rates*.

The application of interest rates dates back to when Gronk was happy to lend Ug ten rocks until another orange ball appeared from behind the volcano as long as Gronk got eleven rocks back in return. Suffice to say the process of borrowing and lending dates back to time immemorial. Today, Joe (or Josephine) Average is very up to speed with the concept of borrowing. This is evident in his (or her) home loan, car loan, credit card, other credit card, holiday loan, department store charge card, money that was borrowed from the in-laws to get the business through a slump etc. All of these loans attract *interest*. (Well, maybe the in-laws are more accommodating). When you borrow money from a bank, building society, credit union or loan shark, the interest you pay is the *cost* of that money. The *rate* of interest, almost invariably quoted on a per annum basis even if you're borrowing for one month, will vary depending on the purpose of the loan and the amount and time required. The interest rate is quoted as a percentage of the amount borrowed. The structure of repayments and the compounding effects will vary, but I do not intend to go into that sort of detail here. I do, however, suggest that anyone with any sort of loan should make sure they fully understand the structure of their loan and their ultimate obligations.

What a lot of people don't realise is that Joe (or Josephine) Average also often *lends* money to the bank or building society etc. This doesn't mean that a representative of Westpac rings them out of the blue and says 'Mate, d'you reckon you could spare us a tenner till our profit results come through?' Lending is what you are effectively doing when you *deposit* money in an account of some sort. This deposit might attract a small amount of interest like a savings account, a larger amount of interest like a term deposit, or maybe no interest as in some cheque accounts. Whichever the case, the amount of interest you can earn from lending money to the bank will always be less than the amount you will pay when borrowing money from the bank. 'Scoundrels!' you say. 'Thieves!' And although this is an oft heard response these days, what people sometimes fail to realise is that a bank is a commercial business and the difference between deposit and loan rates is its profit margin, and that competition between banks and other financial institutions should work to keep this margin as tight as possible. Those who are still not happy, have the opportunity to buy shares in the major banks and thus share in this profit. In fact most individuals have already indirectly invested in the banks via their superannuation or other funds which place money in the banking sector.

Individuals are not the only entities who borrow from or lend to the banks. All businesses from the corner store to BHP have daily dealings with a financial institution. The cash flow cycles of large organisations, ie the timing of payments and receivables, result in those organisations on any given day having shortfalls or surpluses of serious amounts of cash.

Before the 1950s, this was a problem. Banks were restricted to longer-dated periods of lending, and overdraughts were just too expensive and limited for serious short-term financing. There were corporations briefly sitting on large amounts of cash, while simultaneously others were briefly in need of large amounts of cash and the banks could do little about it. This led, decades ago, to the birth of the *money market*. Dealers in the money market stood as intermediaries between corporations. Those with a surplus would put money on deposit with a dealer, and those with a shortfall could then borrow from that dealer. A slight difference in interest rates provided the dealer with a fee. This activity of dealing or 'broking' loans and deposits eventually extended to the level where the dealers themselves acted as principals. Thus the first 'merchant' banks were established.

Merchant banks had the short-term (less than 14-day) lending market sewn up until 1984 when the government deregulated the banking industry, thus lifting the restrictions on the major trading banks. In response, most merchant banks quickly lined up to be approved as trading banks.

Today, the money market (also known as capital markets) is a thriving, frenetic market place patronised by banks, merchant banks, dealers, corporations, insurance companies, credit unions, funds managers, building societies and more who turn over millions of dollars daily in the process of borrowing and lending. When a bank lends money today, a large proportion of its available funds would have come out of the money market. The amount of time for which loans and deposits can be arranged varies across the board from overnight to ten years or more. 'Cash' is deposited and borrowed for very short periods of time. For longer periods of time, there exist different means of borrowing money. These appear in many and varied forms and include such instruments as bank bills, treasury notes, promissory notes, certificates of deposit, government bonds, semi-government bonds, debentures and so on. Rather than spend an eternity examining each instrument and their little idiosyncrasies, we'll select two for closer scrutiny that are sufficiently representative of the whole bunch—bank bills and government bonds.

A 'bill of exchange' is an instrument that dates back into antiquity and its development is linked to the trading of goods over great distances. It is effectively an agreement to pay back a debt incurred when goods were purchased after a certain period of time (which was initially linked to the time it took to get the goods from A to B). The bill would pass from one party to another and then could be passed to a third, and so it eliminated a need to transport large amounts of currency such as gold. The cost of money, or the interest rate applicable to the time period, was built into the bill in the form of a *discount*. This means that the money lent at the beginning was less than what would be owed at the end. Bills have always been used within Australia for import and export purposes, but only since the sixties have they been legitimately used for domestic financing. Some bills are accepted by banks and are thus known as 'bank-accepted bills' or more simply 'bank bills'. These typically have a duration of 90 days and no longer need have an underlying trade of goods of some sort for the bill to exist in the first place.

A bond is a 'fixed interest security', issued with a longer-dated maturity period, often ten years. The purchaser of a bond is effectively lending money to the issuer in return for a fixed interest rate or *coupon*. The stream of interest payments made to the bondholder over the period is not dissimilar to that of dividends paid to shareholders, except that dividend amounts are rarely fixed. This leads to a constant comparison of the yield (return on investment) of the stock market and the bond market. While corporations can issue bonds, the most popular form of fixed-interest investments are bonds issued by the government. Governments have been borrowing money from their citizens for centuries in order to cover the cost of wars or, more recently, budget deficits. In return, citizens are usually happy to assume that the government will actually honour the loan and the interest payments.

The money market (or capital markets) is usually divided into two distinct parts: the 'short-term money market', which encompasses cash, bank bills and instruments of a similar maturity, and 'fixed interest', which encompasses bonds and other longer-dated instruments. There is no distinct cut-off point however, and the remaining time to maturity of different instruments will often overlap. Trading in the market is conducted exclusively over the telephone. Government debt did originally trade on what is now the stock exchange, but this is no longer the case.

As the daily process of borrowing and lending unfolds, it will become apparent that, on any given day, there may be an excess of funds available or a distinct lack of funds available. Funds will flow in and out of the market depending on payments made to the government (eg tax), or by the government (eg welfare). Left uncontrolled, the cost of borrowing cash could fluctuate wildly from day to day and even hour to hour. This doesn't happen too often, however, because Big Brother is watching. Each day the Reserve Bank will trade in all sorts of instruments from cash to bills and bonds and foreign currencies with the intention of borrowing (taking funds out of the market) when there is a surplus and lending (injecting funds into the market) when there is a deficit, thus instituting a smoothing effect. This is called the Bank's *open market operations*. The Reserve Bank is the banker to the government and participates in the money market by dealing directly with a handful of authorised or official dealers who in turn deal with everybody else. The Reserve Bank deals mainly in short-term instruments (as well as issuing bonds and printing bank notes for the government) with the intention of influencing the daily cash rate known as the *11am rate*. The 11am rate, so-called because cash borrowed overnight must be repaid by 11am, influences all short-term interest rates in a flow-through effect into 90-day bill rates and so on into time. This effect begins to wane as we move towards two or three years maturity and is non-existent at the ten-year point. Fixed interest securities are not beholden to the short-term fluctuations of availability of funds but rather reflect prevailing economic conditions and the government's longer-term economic policy.

When the Reserve Bank controls the cash rate it does so with a specific target rate in mind. If the economy is sluggish the Bank might decide to give it a spark by *lowering rates* (also known as an *easing* of monetary policy). The theory is that more people will seek to invest in various ventures if they can borrow money cheaply. Therefore, the Bank does not attempt to borrow the excess funds required to square up the cash in the system and rates will fall in order to clear out the excess. (In reality, the Reserve Bank need only *announce* that it is lowering rates and the market will do the rest.) This is what occurs when it is reported on the news that 'the Reserve Bank today decided to lower interest rates by half a percent'. The most visible effect of these movements is the often (but not always) immediate move by the banks to lower their various lending rates, the most watched of which is the home loan rate. Those who have a floating (variable) home loan rate will enjoy lower monthly payments, at least for a while. Those with a fixed home loan rate will probably curse as they cannot participate given that their rate is 'fixed' for some period, usually one, three or five years. The reverse is true, however, if the Reserve Bank decides that the economy is growing too fast, possibly leading to excessive inflation, and so it raises interest rates (*tightens* monetary policy) and all floating interest rates go up. The Reserve Bank therefore has a very powerful role to play in the economic activities of all Australians and so it acts independently of the incumbent government. (Is that scoffing I hear in the background?)

To say that rates will be raised or lowered, depending on the growth or lack thereof of the economy, is to simplify matters somewhat. There are a myriad of economic factors taken into consideration by the Reserve Bank and a number of different objectives that can be attained through monetary policy. But this is enough for another book altogether.[7] It is possible for individuals to invest in the activities of the money market via a *cash management trust*. These are an alternative form of investment usually with the easy access of a savings account (just don't ask them for 'cash' as they don't keep any) providing unspectacular returns at a very low risk.

That takes us to some point of appreciating the markets of equity (stock market) and debt (money market) as it relates to our own little world, or more specifically, country. What happens when we turn our attentions to matters offshore?

---

7 For a more in-depth look at the workings of the money market in
   Australia and the influences of economic policy, I recommend the
   latest edition of Edna Carew's Fast Money—The Financial Markets
   in Australia. (Carew, E., Fast Money 4, Allen & Unwin, Sydney, 1998.)

Foreign Exchange

Walk around any major city in Australia and you see them: 'Bureau de Change', 'Cambio', 'Wechsel'. In fact, walk around any city in the world and you see them. Little booths adorned with little flags adjacent to numbers with many decimal points displayed in bright red LED, and signs in several languages, but never English. Why are they never in English? I think it's because we just decided that 'bureau de change' will do for us too. Bit like 'kindergarten'. The closest most Australians ever get to the dynamic world of foreign exchange is wondering whether they should change their $1,000 of holiday spending money into US dollar travellers' cheques *now* or in two-months time while they're at the airport just before departure. Frantically they scour the business section of the newspaper looking for clues. Those without holiday plans can still observe Swedish backpackers emptying their coin pouches at the 'bureau' hoping to change enough Krona for a bus ticket to Cairns.

The concept of foreign exchange is a fairly simple one—each country has a different currency, usually, but not always, with a different name, and almost never exchangeable one-for-one with the Australian dollar. When you go overseas you need to swap your cash for their cash and then convert everything you wish to purchase back into Aussie dollars in your head, using the appropriate ratio, so you can always tell whether your about to be ripped off blind. Over the period of your average overseas holiday or business trip, you are unlikely to notice any difference in that ratio from one day to the next. It may transpire, however, that when you return to that same country two years later that the ratio of Aussie hard-earneds to the local readies is very much different to what it used to be. It means that over the period the *exchange rate* has changed.

An exchange rate does not simply exist because countries choose to call their currencies by different names, some of them pretty damned silly. Exchange rates are a measure of the relative value of the currency of one country against the currency of another. These rates will change readily over time to reflect a change in the perception of that relative value. The important question then is: what provides a currency with its value?

A country cannot simply print more and more bank notes when it feels it wants to buy something overseas. If that were the case, we'd all be driving Mercedes. The recipient of our money overseas, who may have provided us with a service (holiday) or goods (stereo) or who might be receiving dividends from an investment (Japanese-owned golf course), has to be happy that our money is actually worth something to him (or her). In order to evaluate a currency, the recipient will take into consideration the reserves of gold and other currencies held by the reserve bank of that country, the money owed to foreign creditors, the stability of the government, the extent of resources (natural and human), the state of the economy, whether a war is about to break out etc. Of course each recipient doesn't individually ponder these factors for each transaction—the collective ponderings of the foreign exchange market do that for him (or her) in setting the ratio of Aussie dollars to another country's 'whatevers' every day.

To better appreciate a currency's value, let's imagine that there was not a common currency for all Australians but that each person or family created their own currency (ie printed up their own money). The paper money is necessary to overcome the limitations of the barter system where sometimes it's a bit hard to try to swap a bit of house-painting for half a cow, or a motor mower for one thousand postage stamps. The difficulty is, however, that each family's currency will not necessarily be of equal value.

Now let's consider three families who live on the same street. On the large corner block is the mansion of Percival Rolan-Innet and his family. The house has been the family home for generations (although it's empty in summer when they all head down to the beach house after the annual trip to St Moritz). The Rolan-Innets have extensive pastoral holdings and mining interests and Percival spends most of his time sitting on a number of boards of large corporations. If you peer through the wrought iron gates you can usually see the chauffeur polishing the Bentley, purchased new many years ago by Percival Snr. The currency of the Rolan-Innets is the 'toff'. The daily inflow of currency to the coffers of the Rolan-Innets from their extensive corporate dealings ensures that rarely do they need to print many toffs for their own use. Therefore, the toff is a valuable currency.

Further down the street in a modest, partially renovated federation cottage lives Bruce White with his wife and two young kids. That's Bruce out the front washing the Commodore, which is provided by the accountancy firm where he works. The Whites have managed to pay off half their mortgage and have some money invested in a balanced fund. Bruce's wife, Jane, is doing her MBA part time and they usually get away with the kids up the coast once a year. The currency of the Whites is the 'collar'. Bruce and Jane are very careful not to use their printing press too often.

In the middle of the street is an unfortunately ugly, blonde-brick block of flats. A two-bedroom flat on the ground floor is rented by Danny Dunnuthen, his girlfriend and their five children. When Danny gets out of bed, he's occasionally able to pick up a bit of labouring work but it's never regular. The rather battered and unwashed Datsun 180B parked outside is Danny's, although strictly he still owes money on it. As he's moved six times in the past two years, the finance company doesn't know where to come to repossess it. When Danny's not working, he never goes much further than the pub down the road. It seems these days that Danny has to print off more and more of his currency, the 'useful'.

You own the grocery store at the other corner of the street. Owning a grocery is a bit of a hassle because you are constantly having to accept all sorts of different currencies from different people. Unless a customer has something to barter with (you didn't mind swapping all those free-range eggs for that lady's weekly shopping the other day), you have to know the person in order to decide how much of their currency you will accept for, say, a litre of milk. In fact that's the situation you're faced with at the moment because standing at the register, each with a litre of milk in their hands, are the Rolan-Innet's housekeeper, Jane White and Danny Dunnuthen.

The currency you accept has to be used by you to restock the shelves, pay the lease and keep you comfortable. Your creditors are very fastidious in considering the type and amount of currency you pass on to them and so you must be careful to wisely evaluate each bank note that's placed in your hands. You're more than happy to accept the Rolan-Innet toffs. Around here they're as good as gold and have been for as long as anyone can remember. The toff is basically the benchmark for all other currencies—solid as a rock. Anyone will sell you anything for a few toffs. For a litre of milk you charge the housekeeper half a toff (fortunately the Rolan-Innets mint their own half-toff coins).

The Whites are fairly new in the neighbourhood but everyone knows them to be a hardworking, frugal couple with potential to go places. Their commercial sensibility is evident in the fact that there are very few White collars floating around. You happily charge Jane two collars for her milk.

You've a good mind to refuse Danny Dunnuthen. Two weeks ago you charged him fifty usefuls for a packet of cigarettes only to hear that he hadn't worked all fortnight and simply printed up another batch. The cigarette company charged one hundred usefuls to replace it. Given Danny's lack of earning capacity and all those mouths to feed, the Dunnuthen useful has got to be on a downward spiral. They can no longer be worth the paper they're printed on. You decide to charge Danny two hundred usefuls. He doesn't have enough and leaves, you suspect, to print off some more. When he comes back you'll charge him three hundred.

A currency exchange snapshot, quoting other currencies in terms of the toff which is used as the benchmark, would suggest that there are eight collars to the toff and 400 usefuls to the toff. Or to put it another way, the collar is trading at T 0.125 and the useful at T 0.0025. Given all the hassle, it's just as well we have a common currency isn't it?

This is not the case, of course, in the global community. Our little example is an analogy for the world's daily operations. Bear in mind that exchange rates are not simply a reflection of the comparative wealth of two countries, but must also take into account the amount of currency that is out there (in its many forms, of which cash is only one). The toff can be loosely compared to the British pound of days gone by or the US dollar of today. The US dollar is the benchmark for other currencies. The US has a large and wealthy population and a fair share of resources and stability. It is the US economy that the world follows. The collar is not unlike the dollar of Australia or New Zealand. These are two countries with small but stable economies, small but sufficiently affluent populations and lots of natural resources. The useful, on the other hand, would equate with the currency of a resource-starved, populous country with little stability and even fewer prospects. An African or Eastern European country may be an example. The constant printing of the useful is a response not unlike that of the heavily borrowed South American countries where inflation rates of hundreds of percent are not unusual.

There are two words that I have used to date which are very influential in foreign exchange terms—*economy* and *inflation*. The state of the economy, of which the level of inflation is one indicator, is reflected in various factors such as the level of economic growth, unemployment, foreign debt and the *interest rates* of a country (as you recall from the last section). The rate of inflation is a measurement of a reduction in spending power. It is evident in the change of the price of a litre of milk from one year to the next. Inflation is caused by various factors including the overly rapid growth of the economy, when new-found wealth causes increased spending thus pushing up prices, and the printing of currency, which dilutes the asset backing of each dollar, thus rendering each existing dollar lower in value. The rate of inflation accounts for one portion of an interest rate. (This makes sense when you consider that if you borrow money for one year, the interest you pay needs to take into consideration the reduction of spending power of that money over that period). Some indication of the state of the economy is provided by the other portion (known as the *real* rate). Shorter-term rates are less affected by inflation and economic initiatives as they are by the immediate availability or lack thereof of short-term funds. It is in longer-term rates such as bond rates that the country's economic health and wellbeing are reflected. A high bond yield (high rate) will attract overseas investment provided the country is a sound and stable one, and provided that high inflation is not the main reason for a higher rate. Investors will need to exchange into the local currency, ie 'buy' the local currency, in order to purchase the bonds and this will have an upward influence on the exchange rate. Remember, however, that an exchange rate is a *relative* measure. If your country is performing well and attracting investment from around the world, an exchange rate may still move down if the other country against whom you are measuring has an even better-performing economy.

Despite the fact that I suggested that short-term interest rates have little bearing on exchange rates, this is not quite true. Changes in short-term rates will have an immediate short-term effect on exchange rates.

A simple example will give you an idea on the relationship between short-term interest rates and exchange rates. Two countries, Smithland and Jonesland, each have interest rates of 10% at which you can either borrow or deposit. The exchange rate of the S dollar to the J dollar is:

1:1 (or S = 1.00 J).

Due to economic developments, the Smithland rates fall to 5%. If there were no change to the exchange rate, you could do the following:

(1) Borrow 100 S dollars (at 5%).
(2) Exchange them into 100 J dollars (at 1:1).
(3) Deposit the J dollars (at 10%) and receive 10 J dollars.
(4) Exchange 110 J dollars back into 110 S dollars (1:1).
(5) Pay back the 100 S dollars plus 5 S dollars interest.
(6) Bank 5 S dollars.

This is a riskless transaction that you could do till the cows came home. However, before you could blink, the market would adjust the exchange rate from 1:1 to 1:2 (S = 0.500 J) and the 10 J dollar interest you receive will only convert to 5 S dollars. Profit = 0. Once again, it just goes to show that there's no such thing as a free lunch. You may also now begin to appreciate why exchange rates want to constantly move up and down and up and down again. It's all these 'push me-pull you' effects of the economy and interest rates and inflation and…if you're going to ask about chickens and eggs, forget it. I don't know either. Let's move on.

The Australian dollar is amongst the ten most actively traded currencies in the world. The standard measure of the AUD[8] is against the US dollar. At the time of writing one AUD was worth .6267 USD. Another important currency for Australia and the world is the Japanese yen and so the AUD/JPY rate is often noted by the media. A more global measurement is given by the AUD's value against the *trade-weighted index*. This is an index of the currencies of Australia's major trading partners.

The exchange rate between Australia and any other country is of vital importance to exporters, importers, companies with overseas investments and overseas companies which invest in Australia (and holiday-makers). There is no *ideal* exchange rate. In fact, there is a push-pull of opinion between, for example, the exporters of coal, who favour a lower exchange rate in order to make Australian coal more competitive in the world market, and the importers of television sets, who prefer a higher exchange rate in order to make foreign TVs more affordable in Australia. What both parties have in common is that they are constantly changing money from one currency to another. The exporter receives payments in, say, yen and must convert them back into Australian dollars. This is called selling yen and buying Aussie. The importer must pay the supplier in, say, Korean won, and so must first convert into won from Aussie. This is called buying won and selling Aussie. Any party with a need to exchange currencies must first contact a foreign exchange dealer at a bank.

Foreign exchange dealing is conducted by banks and foreign exchange brokers (who themselves deal with banks). Hundreds of millions of Australian dollars change hands *every day*. However, not every transaction includes a corporation or investor on one side and a bank on the other. Banks also deal with *each other* and this is known as *interbank* dealing. The reasons one bank may deal with another are many and varied and include

---

8 *This is the foreign exchange dealer's code for Australian dollars.
US dollars are USD, Japanese yen are JPY and so on.*

The Myth of Holiday Money

I have often been asked by acquaintances, in my supposed capacity as a financial markets expert, what I think the Aussie dollar price will do before they go on holidays. To many this is of great concern. The last thing they want to do is exchange currencies at unfavourable levels.

Consider, say, that you're planning to change $2000 in spending money at some time before next month. If the dollar were to move by one cent (.6264 to .6164) which would not be too unusual, then you would be down by $20 US which is about $25 Aussie. If the rate were to move by ten cents in that time which would be absolutely extraordinary, you'd be out of pocket $200 US against the maybe $5000 you're spending all up.

My advice to my acquaintances is, forget about it and enjoy your holiday.

off-loading deals done previously with a third party and dealing on behalf of some other area of the bank. However, the majority of interbank deals are simply *speculative*, which means that the foreign exchange dealers are betting on the movement of the exchange rate during the trading day. A dealer will usually start and finish the day with a clean slate having made or lost thousands on the day's exchange rate movement. The market, however, is open twenty-four hours a day so that when the daytime dealer goes home, either a night-time dealer takes over or an offshore office kicks in. The twenty-four hour day is usually divided into three eight-hour shifts of Sydney-London-New York and back to Sydney. (If you ever see someone wearing a T-shirt and board shorts and looking baggy-eyed and unshaven while drinking schooners at 8am, chances are they're either a bum or a night-shift FX dealer). *Whaddaya mean what's the difference?*

The reality of interbank speculative dealing is that it accounts for about 90% of the daily turnover. That's right—90% of hundreds of millions of dollars is just punting by foreign exchange dealers from all around the world. At the end of the shift, nearly all positions are back to zero and half the players have won and half the players have lost. 'That's outrageous!' you say. 'All those overpaid cowboys simply toying with our Aussie dollar.' But in actual fact there are great benefits in letting the cowboys loose. Without the speculators, there would be no *liquidity* in the market. An exporter looking to change his yen into Aussie would have to find an importer looking to change his Aussie into yen. And then haggle about the price. Again there is no central exchange like the stock exchange (the FX market, like the money market, is conducted over the telephone). The daily activity of the speculators ensures that both importer and exporter can exchange currency at almost the same price at any time for any reasonable amount.

The reason that speculators are able to play casinos with our Aussie dollar is because the dollar 'floats'. This means that government is happy to allow market forces to determine exchange rates rather than the government deciding what the various exchange rates should be. Prior to 1983, when then Treasurer Paul Keating 'floated' the dollar, Australia had set its exchange rates by various means which usually involved 'pegging' our currency to something else like gold or the pound or the US dollar or a basket of other currencies. This 'pegging' meant, in more recent days, that the exchange rate was shifted once each day (also considered to be a 'dirty float'). Given that the market anticipated the government's every move each day, it seemed pointless not to allow the currency just to float altogether. Occasionally some market aberration sends the Aussie rushing up or rushing down in a mad panic and it scares the pants off everyone. At this point, the Reserve Bank will usually step in and start buying or selling the currency in order to restore stability. This, as well as interest rate movements, is a means by which the Reserve Bank can 'control' the currency (and in so doing render the float just a little bit 'dirty' still). The scariest post-float panic occurred one day in 1986 after Mr Keating had made his infamous 'banana republic' speech. In a matter of hours, the Aussie plunged from 0.6335 US dollars to 0.5730 and then bounced back to 0.6175 before we all had to start hoarding bread. Not so much of a float as a surf carnival.

As the majority of major currencies float even the 'bureaux de change' need to adjust their exchange rates daily. So next time you're in a foreign land and need to visit the little booth with the little flags and glowing red numbers, you can take a moment to reflect on the ebb and flow of economic policy and interest rates, and the cut and thrust of the foreign exchange dealing room, and the exporters and the importers, and the cowboys, and the hundreds of millions of dollars changing hands every day before you smile and say, 'How many Albanian leks do I get for twenty Australian, please luv?'

Commodities

The last of the underlying markets we are going to be introduced to are the commodity markets. The good thing about commodities is that they are not just numbers that represent the cost of money, or the relative value of money, and nor do they involve a mere certificate of ownership representing a portion of a company that might actually *do* something useful, but nevertheless is still just a price in a newspaper as far as we're concerned. Commodities are things that we can see, touch and consume. The Concise Oxford defines a commodity as a 'useful thing; article of trade'. Simply, commodities are things which we can put to some use and are thus prepared to buy and sell. The most highly traded commodities, those that lure not just producers and consumers into the business of buying and selling but also banks, brokers and speculators, are metals, oil and food.

Metals are divided into two camps—*precious*, being gold and silver, and *base*, being copper, lead, zinc, tin, nickel, aluminium, platinum and so on. A simple explanation of the difference is that precious metals are made into jewellery, while base metals are used in construction and manufacturing. Gold, however, performs a role in the financial markets which elevates it to a level that is far more significant than its capacity to be fashioned into dazzling necklaces, bangles and rings. Gold requires closer inspection.

The value that the world places on gold has its origins in the most basic of human emotions. Gold is shiny and sparkling and there's not a lot of it—everybody wants some. It is also the most malleable of metals, allowing it to be easily beaten into shape, and yet it is extremely dense, which gives it its impressive weight. Gold is highly resistant to corrosion. Pure gold can be found in convenient lumps thus eliminating the need for extensive refining which is one reason why it has been mined by the most ancient of civilisations. Apart from its use since ancient times in jewellery-making, the most important role gold has played in history is as a currency. *We're back to currencies again!* Silver, the second most malleable metal, also rare and pretty when polished, has always been gold's poorer cousin.

Long before banknotes were invented, and after rocks and shells and beads became outmoded, gold and silver were fashioned into coins. The value of the coin was quite simply the value of the gold or silver it contained. This was known as a *bimetallic* monetary system, and the stability of the system was ensured by the fact that the metals were very rare and not often stumbled over. (This could not be said of the system briefly in place in Douglas Adams' *The Restaurant at the End of the Universe* where the unit of currency was the leaf. The system had to be abandoned when it eventually required stripping three deciduous forests in order to buy a peanut.)[9] Eventually paper money appeared as a matter of convenience but it was directly exchangeable for a specific amount of gold or silver. This is called *commodity money*. Today's banknotes are not exchangeable into anything, and today's coins contain nothing like their face value in metal, but they are considered legal tender by government edict. This is called *fiat money* (not only used for buying Bambinos).

The industrial revolution sparked a huge increase in world trade and also introduced the first uniform concept of foreign exchange in the form of the *gold standard*. Gold was used as the benchmark for various currencies and so a fixed set of exchange rates resulted. This system was abolished and reinstated several times due to depression and the odd world war and occasional 'floating' occurred in between. Towards the end of the Second World War, the International Monetary Fund was created to approve movements in exchange rates which were now marked to the US dollar, which in turn was marked to gold. This idea fell apart when the US government financed the Vietnam war by printing more gold-backed money than it held in gold reserves. By 1978, the US had abandoned the gold standard as had every major trading nation by the end of the decade. The seventies were a decade of high inflation, fuelled not only by the collapse of the gold standard but also by OPEC's[10] determination to raise the price of oil. In 1971, gold cost $35 an ounce. By January 1980, it had risen to $850 an ounce.

Although currencies became separated from gold, the metal remained as a 'safe haven' for investors. Gold still provided a sense of comfort and stability in times of economic difficulty and military tension. When inflation loomed, gold became a popular substitute for savings. When the world was facing a crisis in which paper money might prove worthless, there was a rush to gold. Such a feeling of crisis accompanied news of the Chernobyl nuclear accident which probably sparked fears of the end of the world.

The most recent significant rush to gold occurred on the day Iraq invaded Kuwait. This only lasted one day, however, and the price had rushed straight back to where it started by the following day. This was the beginning of a decline in popularity for the metal as the 'safe haven', and consistently lower world inflation rates have ensured a drop in the volatility

9   Adams, D., The Restaurant at the End of the Universe, *Pan Books Ltd, London, 1980.*
10 *Organisation of Petroleum Exporting Countries.*

of the gold price. It will be interesting to see if the world will face a crisis of economic confidence in the future that will send everyone climbing over each other to hoard the shiny metal again.

Despite an apparent drop in popularity, gold still gets pulled out of the ground wherever possible. Australia is the world's third highest producer of gold after South Africa and the US. The fact that Aussies love their gold can be seen in the number and popularity of 'specky'[11] gold mining stocks listed on the stock exchange. Most of the gold mined in Australia goes to Asia to be used in making jewellery. The Asians like to hoard lots of gold. Most nations keep reserves of gold in their bank vaults (in the US, it's at Fort Knox) in order to back up their currencies. In more recent times, the selling of gold reserves has not been unusual, with countries like Russia desperately needing stable foreign currency to fund their post-communist existence. This is because it costs about 27 zillion rubles to buy a peanut in Moscow.

So, although gold is a tangible substance that can be classified as a commodity, it is treated in every way like a currency. Silver on the other hand is really struggling to maintain its 'precious metal' status. Industrial uses drag silver closer to the base metal category. It is still a commodity that attracts a high degree of speculation and volatility, but its price is paltry compared to gold's (about $5 to $300). It is interesting to note that the price of the most 'precious' metal, gold, is presently outstripped by that of the industrial metal platinum (at about $350).

Base metals, you'll be pleased to know, do not act like currencies, even though they might be used to make coins. Price fluctuations in the base

11 'Specky' means speculative. These companies go looking for gold. When their geologists see even a mere glint on the horizon, gold fever strikes and the stock goes berserk. Often it's a false alarm.

metals are usually a reflection of the availability of the metal at the time rather than whether more sources have been discovered. The base metals are sufficiently abundant, and therefore low enough in price, for people not to go nuts over a new discovery of, say, lead. (Not all base metals are in abundance. Some of the sexier ones, like platinum and palladium, are more rare and this is reflected in the price).

The most important factor affecting base metal prices around the world, other than simple demand and supply, is *inventories*. That is, how much of the stuff is sitting in a warehouse ready to use. If the squirrels have been at work hoarding metal for winter thus increasing inventories, the price of the metal will fall. Conversely, if there has been a high immediate demand in metals for, say, construction, causing inventories to be reduced, the price will rise. At various times throughout history, individuals have tried to 'corner' a metals market, or in fact any commodities market. This involves buying so much of the stuff that you totally control the inventories and, therefore, the price. Most cornering attempts end in disaster. The most recent protagonist was a Mr Hamanaka from Sumitomo Bank in Japan who, without authority, bought enough copper to send the price skyrocketing. He was eventually sprung, however, and the copper price suffered all the pain of re-entry.

The commodity that accounts for the greatest percentage of world trade is oil. Oil has become essential to daily life since the invention of the combustion engine, plastic-ware and many chemicals such as paint. Every day, vast quantities of crude are pumped from just below the earth's surface by those countries fortunate enough to have a source, and sent around the world in giant, ocean-going tankers to be sold to those countries who missed out in the geographic distribution. Russia, the US and Saudi Arabia produce about half of the world's crude oil. Most of the rest is found elsewhere in the Middle East, which has helped to make oil a political tool. OPEC was created during the sixties when the price of oil began to fall and the trappings of previously unforeseen wealth appeared under threat. In the seventies, OPEC (which includes both enemies and allies of the West) tried to force up the price of oil, but this proved short-lived as oil conservation and alternative energy sources became popular. The frustrated OPEC members settled on a production quota system to maintain a stable but sufficiently high price, but even this proved to be flawed when Saddam Hussein decided Kuwait looked like a good place to build a port. Despite the US being the world's second highest producer, it is a net importer. Australia is a net exporter.

Sol had it right: oils ain't oils. Unlike gold, oil pumped out of the ground in one part of the world is not identical to the oil flowing in another part. It's similar, but still sufficiently different to mean that some crudes are used for different purposes to others, and that prices vary slightly. Nevertheless, three or four crudes are used as benchmarks for other varieties in different parts of the world. *West Texas Intermediate* from the US and *Brent* from the North Sea are two. Oil is not only traded heavily in its crude form. Refined products also do a bumper trade. These include heating oil, jet fuel, petrol, diesel, propane, kerosene and so on. All these commodities, along with natural gas and electricity, together form the *energy* market. The remaining commodities that are traded in large amounts around the world, outside of the metal and energy markets, are called *soft* commodities. These include all manner of agricultural products such as wheat, corn, cocoa, sugar, coffee, soybeans and so on, and also clothing materials such as wool and cotton. There are no tricks to understanding the trade in things you can eat and wear.

There is one important aspect of all commodities markets, and indeed most financial markets, that we do need to appreciate, and that is that although billions of dollars flow back and forth around the world each day in the trading of these markets very few transactions ever reach the point where something is handed over. That is, buyers will usually sell before they are due to take delivery and sellers will usually buy to avoid making delivery. What matters to the great majority of the market participants is simply the change in the price. Are you lost?

Say you are convinced the price of oil is going to rise. To back your judgement (and to profit if you're right) you could buy a lot of 44-gallon drums, fill them with petrol, and store them in your garage. Or you could buy a share in an oil well. Or you could simply by an instrument whose price fluctuation is linked to the oil price. Such instruments exist in all manner of commodities and financial products. What are they called? *Derivatives*. It often surprises people to learn that the dollar value of the volume of commodities and financial products changing hands every day is far, far outweighed by the dollar value of the volume of derivative instruments of that commodity or financial product changing hands every day.

Having got some sort of handle on the underlying markets, it's time we learnt something about derivatives.

2. Futures Presented

Down on the Farm

Already I've asked you to imagine yourself as a grocer. Now take a couple of steps back down the food chain and imagine yourself as a farmer. A wheat farmer to be precise. It's June and you are in the process of planting this season's crop. There is a lot riding on this year's harvest, and you can almost sense the presence of the bank manager standing beside you as you survey the sewing operation. The shining new machinery chugging away in the fields still very much belongs to the bank, as does the added acreage acquired from the neighbouring farm after the neighbours finally chucked it all in last year. The added debt burden could break you if things didn't work out this year. Your eyes turn skyward as you contemplate the wild card in your ongoing livelihood—the weather.

Last year had been a bumper crop. After years of drought which barely allowed you to harvest a crop worth enough to feed your family, the gods had smiled and the rains had come. And the wheat had grown tall and healthy all over the district and all over the country's wheat belt. The statisticians were predicting a record harvest and the pub in the nearest town was overflowing with grinning wheat farmers. Having managed to survive without calling in the bank during the drought, mainly because the scarcity of wheat had allowed you to sell your modest crop at a good price, you had seen the opportunity to make up for the difficult years and so threw everything at it. New land and sadly needed new machinery. The proceeds of the harvest would more than adequately justify the borrowings. It was meant to be a very good year.

What you had failed to pay much attention to was the fact that wheat harvests in the northern hemisphere had also been extremely good this season. In Russia and the US in particular, it appeared that records were being broken. Bread manufacturers breathed a sigh of relief when they could finally see an end to escalating grain prices. It had started slowly at first so that you didn't really notice, but as harvest time approached the trickle turned into a flood. The price of wheat around the world was collapsing. As fast as silos were filled, there was still more available. Government bodies had stopped hoarding grains for future price control. Your world had collapsed around you and there was nothing you could do about it.

The harvest in the southern hemisphere had been completed just as the price of wheat had hit a six year low. The bank was concerned about its loans. Your eldest son had to forsake the farm and look for another means of income in the town. You pulled your youngest daughter out of her first year of private school. You were now in too deep and had to bet on the next year's income in order to survive. And, although it seemed that you couldn't win either way, you planted another crop.

As you stand looking out over the ploughed fields, you estimate that the slight recovery in the wheat price in the past couple of months should provide you with enough income to keep you afloat into the next season. But harvest time is still a long way off and who knows what the weather might do…

Then there's a tap on your shoulder and, lo and behold, it's me. You are even more surprised when I tell you that I want to buy your wheat crop. You say that's all well and good but I must have my calendar upside down because the crop is only in the process of being planted now and will not be ready for sale for six months. I say I won't be needing the wheat before harvest time but I *do* want to buy it now at a price we agree on. I'll give you a deposit now and pay the rest in full at the time that you deliver me the wheat. I'm prepared to pay you $170 a tonne.

$170 a tonne is a pretty good price. You had thought that if everything went in your favour you might have got $175 come harvest time. But that's still six months away and last year's experience still scares you. $170 would pay the bills. $170 would keep the bank off your back.

'What if the price of wheat is much higher at harvest time?' you ask.

'Then that will be my good fortune,' I say. 'What if it were much lower?'

'Then I'd lose the farm.'

'Well, you can make sure that doesn't happen by fixing your price now. Then you can relax—your worries are over.'

'You're right. I'll do it.'

Congratulations. You and I have just traded a futures contract.

Futures and Forwards

In actual fact what we have just agreed upon is more correctly described as a *forward* contract. The forward contract is the predecessor of the futures contract. The simple difference between the two is that a forward contract is agreed upon privately between two parties whereas the futures contract is traded at a futures exchange. Futures exchanges have developed all over the world to bring together people like you and me. But before we get into the workings of a futures exchange, let's look more closely at the contract that you and I have just agreed upon.

The most important feature of the forward contract is the price. There is a price at which one can sell wheat *today*. This is called the *spot* price. The spot price, however, may have absolutely no bearing on a price that is settled upon for the delivery of wheat in *six-months time*. That price is simply a reflection of the amount I'm prepared to pay and the amount at which you're prepared to sell. This is called the *forward* price. In this case, it is $170.

Next we will have to have agreed upon the actual date of delivery which will be some mutually convenient date after the harvest in six-months time. This is called the *maturity date*, or *expiry date*, of the contract. It will also need to be decided exactly where the place of delivery will be.

Importantly, the contract would specify the type of wheat. I can see the wheat being planted and assume that it will be the same type of wheat that is ultimately delivered, but I must protect myself from the opportunity you may have in six-months time to buy a lower quality grain and deliver that to me, while keeping your higher quality grain to sell elsewhere.

Lastly, we will predetermine the *amount* of wheat to be delivered. I am not prepared to say to you that I will buy 'whatever you've got' in six-months time. Remember that prices of commodities are affected by the volume of those commodities available. I will need to specify *now* that I am buying x thousand tonnes at the maturity date. This puts the pressure on you to estimate the yield of your crop. And notwithstanding the room for error of your estimation, even if everything goes smoothly from now to then, there is a possibility that another disaster may befall you. The entire crop could be lost to a hundred-year flood. A plague of locusts may cut a swathe through the wheat belt. By entering into the contract you have guaranteed yourself a price with which you are happy, which you know will keep you in business. If you have nothing to deliver in six-months time you will have to go and buy x thousand tonnes from somewhere else and then deliver them to me. And it's a pretty fair bet that the price will be substantially higher.

The only thing certain in farming is the uncertainty. In fact in any market, not just the agricultural market, there is a level of uncertainty that determines that prices go up and prices go down and some people make money and some people lose it. It is the existence of such uncertainty that led to the first forward contracts and the first futures exchanges. Let's look at some history.

Of Rice and Yen

The first evidence of a type of modern futures trading can be dated back to the twelfth century. You may recall the impetus for *bills of exchange* being the sorts of distances covered by early traders and the time it took to move goods from A to B. As traders gathered at various market places in Europe, they found it a lot easier merely to lug around various samples of their wares rather than the complete inventory. Buyers would be provided with a *lettre de faire* being a contract that specified delivery, of goods at a later date when the ship arrived. The contract included the price, which was fixed then and there. By the time of delivery the new price of that commodity might be higher or lower, so the buyer might end up paying more or less now than the price at delivery time, but one presumes he didn't have a lot of choice.[12]

We move now to the seventeenth century for the first recorded use of futures contracts. The Japanese Shoguns received rents from the feudal peasants in the form of a share of the rice crop. Presumably to smooth out their cash flows, the shoguns would sell rice that was still growing or held in storage by issuing receipts to merchants who would buy ahead of their estimated rice needs. The 'rice tickets' eventually became an acceptable form of currency.[13] By 1730, an official structure had been set up governing the term, or time of delivery of the rice, standardising amounts and grades and specifying that traders must have credit with, and trade all tickets through, a clearing house.[14] This could be considered the earliest example of a *futures exchange*.

The growth of the British Empire in the late eighteenth and nineteenth centuries as the world's greatest global trading network, led not only to a developing stock market, but introduced crude forms of futures and options

12 *Teweles, R.J.,* The Commodity Futures Game, *McGraw Hill, New York, 1977.*

13 *Dominguez, J.R., Devaluation and Futures Markets, Lexington, Mass., 1972.*

14 *Bakken, H.H., 'Futures Trading—Origin, Development and Present Economic Status', in Futures Trading Seminar, Mimir, Edison, Wisconsin, 1953. Quoted by Teweles, op. cit.*

as well. But as early as 1720, the time of the 'South Sea Bubble' (one of the world's earliest stock market crashes), one could agree to buy stocks at a later date and a higher price. On-selling this agreement to someone else at a yet higher price meant that profits could be made without much outlay of funds. This activity was made technically illegal, but nevertheless continued in the centuries afterwards.

The *real* birth of futures exchanges occurred, not surprisingly, in the United States. Futures in the US grew along the lines of the twelfth century *lettres de faire* or 'to arrive' contracts. Commodity exchanges began as informal clubs and developed into highly organised operations with rules and standards that bred the true futures contract. The first official trade occurred on the Chicago Board of Trade (now the world's biggest futures exchange) on March 13, 1851, and called for the delivery of 3000 bushels of corn in the following June at one cent below the market price at the time.[15]

The beginning of futures trading in Australia came about due to a situation not unlike the one you found yourself in with your wheat. Clive Hall was a wool trader working in a woollen mill in 1951. The price of wool had plummeted, causing hardship for farmers, and it stayed that way for several months. Then, just when all looked lost, the price doubled in a matter of two weeks. Clive saw that it was obvious for both growers and buyers that some insurance was needed against wild price fluctuations. In 1953, he was able to trade on the wool market in London but this was not practical and eventually he petitioned the government in Australia. On November 18, 1959, Clive received a letter from the then Treasurer, Harold Holt, giving a futures market the go-ahead. On January 8, 1960, the founding chairman, Clive Hall, chose five firms to become the initial members of the Sydney Greasy Wool Futures Exchange, the predecessor to today's Sydney Futures Exchange.[16]

So what exactly happens at a futures exchange?

The Exchange

The futures exchange operates in a similar fashion to the stock exchange. It provides potential buyers and sellers of futures with a market place featuring standardised contracts over many and various products. The exchange is also a clearing house for all transactions and it is subject to legislation enacted to protect the users of the exchange from fraudulent or coercive

15 *Calder S., Lindsay P., Koch D.,* Futures Stock, *Horwitz Grahame,*
   Sydney, 1980.
16 *Calder S. et al, op. cit.*

activities. Each exchange is subject to varying levels of control dependent upon the country of location.

Different exchanges provide contracts over different commodities with varying levels of popularity. Rather than privately agree on a forward wheat contract, as you and I did, we could have found basically the same features of our contract available in the form of a futures contract. Futures contracts, traded on an exchange, have predetermined specifications relating to size or amount (eg x tonnes of wheat), type (eg a specific quality and breed of wheat), expiry (eg last day in March, June, September etc) and delivery (ie where and when). The table below provides the contract specifications for the wheat contract traded on the Sydney Futures Exchange. Price is determined by buyers and sellers reaching a common ground, although the exchange will control the *increment* of price movement. A contract traded on the exchange must always be traded at the best available price at the time. Therefore, 1000 contracts may not trade at $1.00 if one contract is bid for at $1.01. The one contract must be settled first. This ensures that a fair market is provided for both the biggest and the smallest users.

SFE Wheat Futures Contract Specifications*

CONTRACT UNIT:	50 metric tonnes
STANDARD DELIVERY:	Wheat of Australian Standard White (ASW) quality of minimum 9% protein (based on an 11% moisture and 5.7 nitrogen scale) delivered in store at the GrainCorp Newcastle Terminal.
ALTERNATIVE DELIVERY CENTRES:	Graincorp storage facilities at Moree, Parkes and Junee t a freight differential published by the Exchange.
QUOTATIONS:	Australian dollars per metric tonne. Tick value of $0.50 per tonne or $25.00.
CONTRACT MONTHS:	January, March, May, July, September and November up to 18 months ahead.
DELIVERY PERIOD:	The delivery period begins on the first business day of the contract month and

	ends with the close of trade on the final day of trading in the contract month.
FINAL TRADING DAY:	The last day of trading is the third Tuesday of the contract month. Trading ceases at 12.00 noon.
TRADING HOURS:	From 10.00 am to 12.30 pm on the trading floor. From 4.40pm to 6.00am (7.00am with daylight saving) on SYCOM.

*As provided by the Sydney Futures Exchange.

Note: 'Tick value' refers to the minimum price increment of each successive trade. 'SYCOM' refers to the Sydney computerised overnight market (when the floor's closed trading is conducted on computer). Also, I thought a 'tonne' was metric.

Unlike the Australian Stock Exchange, which is a computer-traded system, the Sydney Futures Exchange presently maintains an 'open outcry' trading system. This is true of most world futures exchanges, including the vast exchanges of Chicago and New York. There is a trend, however, toward automated trading systems such as that adopted by the Australian Stock Exchange. The New Zealand Futures and Options Exchange, for example, features computerised trading.

The open outcry system is so-called because it is a system based largely on an awful lot of yelling and screaming. Trading for a particular contract—let's say it's wheat—is conducted in an amphitheatre-like area called a 'pit', located on the 'floor' of the futures exchange. As with the stock exchange, *you* can't just hop in the ute and head into the big smoke from the wheat farm and expect to walk into the exchange and start selling wheat contracts. First of all, as with most things, you must contact a broker. Let's say that after I had offered to buy your wheat six months ahead, you had actually declined and said that you would try the futures exchange instead believing that you may get a better price, and that you felt safer dealing on the official exchange. What is the process?

First you would call a registered futures broker located somewhere in an office, probably in the city. The broker would advise you on the specifications of the contract and the recent activity of the market and he or she would probably offer an opinion on the likely movement of the market, at least in the short term. In order to be allowed to do this, the broker will previously have passed an extensive examination on the activities of futures markets. You will have to open an account and deposit some money. The amount required to deposit is a very important part of the futures market process and I intend to address it more fully in this chapter but in the meantime let's just say there is some money down. You inform the broker that you wish to sell 500 tonnes of wheat out to January. Given that the standard wheat contract specifies 50 tonnes per contract you will be selling 10 contracts. You wish to sell at $172 per contract. A quick check of the market monitor screen in the broker's office indicates that the market has just traded at $172, with the buyers still prepared to pay for more at that price.

The broker will then place a call to 'the floor'. A lot of yelling and screaming will occur between people wearing impossibly loud jackets and your sell order will be completed. To whom you actually sell is of no concern to you.

Lairy Jackets

If you have ever seen footage of a futures exchange you will have noticed that all the traders in the pit wear extremely loud, coloured jackets which have the capacity to make that trader look like a complete goose. This is not because futures traders like to show off. Rather, it is a means by which representatives of the same firm (thus sporting the same jacket) can quickly find each other in the crush of humanity of the futures floor which can often resemble the crowd at a grand final. It also ensures that a representative of one firm can immediately identify which other firm he (or she) has just traded with, even if the representative of the other firm is some distance away.

The jackets also double as a good place to carry notebooks, pencils, chits, calculators, chewing gum, crosswords, throat lozenges etc.

The phone then rings on the farm and the broker informs you that your transaction is complete. And the mandatory commission will have been charged.

One very important difference between the stock exchange and the futures exchange is this. When a company lists on the stock exchange for the purpose of raising capital, it begins by issuing a specific, fixed number of shares at a predetermined price. The company has a target amount of capital they wish to raise. Now, those shares may trade on the first day of listing at any price above or below the price at which the company issued the shares.

For example, a share issued at $1.00 may first trade at $1.25, reflecting the fact that the shares are highly sought after and the buyers are prepared to push up the price. In order to sell the shares in the secondary market one must have already purchased the shares on issue. So the buyers paying $1.25 are buying from people who were sensible enough to apply for shares at $1.00 on issue. Buyers at $1.25 will then be able to sell their shares at a later date to yet more buyers and so the market proceeds. The important point is that you *cannot sell shares unless you have bought them first.*[17] Why would you want to sell shares if you didn't own them anyway? Well, maybe you thought $1.25 was way too high a price to pay for this awful company, and you'd like to sell at $1.25 in the belief that you could buy back the shares more cheaply at a later date and make a profit that way. This, however, is not allowed. One reason share markets tend to rise over long periods is this simple fact of always having to buy first and sell later.

If you're following the plot here, you have probably already figured that there is no such rule in futures trading. For one thing, the wheat trade you have just completed involved you *selling* wheat contracts. Ah! you say, but in this case you are selling actual wheat at the end, and you already own that wheat. Well, you sort of own it, even though it hasn't even grown yet. This is true, but when your broker's representative in the wheat pit yelled 'Sell 10!' the buyer did not turn around and say 'Now hang on there just one minute! How do I know you've got wheat to sell? Or that you've planted wheat that might be ready to sell in six months?' The buyer couldn't care less whether you, as the client behind the sell order, have even *seen* a grain of wheat before. By selling futures contracts, you have entered into a legally binding agreement to deliver an amount of wheat in six-months time. If you don't have any wheat in six-months time then you could *buy back* your wheat futures in the market before the expiry date. The price you pay may be less, or more, than the price at which you initially sold your contracts which means that you will make, or lose, money. But either way you have avoided having to deliver actual wheat.

Open Positions

The daily turnover of wheat futures at the exchange then is entirely dependent upon...what? Is it a predetermined amount of wheat, just like the capital of a company listing on the stock exchange? No. Is it restricted by the amount of wheat that is grown in the whole country? No. World? No.

17 *There are exceptions to this rule in very select circumstances that will be made clear in a later chapter.*

There are absolutely no restrictions on the amount of wheat that is traded in the form of wheat futures in any given day. Unlike shares, there is no finite amount 'on issue'. A wheat futures contract *does not exist* until two consenting adults agree to trade one. And they can trade as many contracts as they like, even if it represents more than the total amount of wheat ever harvested in the history of mankind. The only obligation is that the wheat must be delivered at the specified date after the expiry of the contract. Every working day between now and expiry is an opportunity to buy or sell wheat contracts on the exchange. So the seller, who is holding contracts equivalent to the total amount of wheat ever harvested in the history of mankind, will more than likely buy back his (or her) contracts before expiry and thus avoid the delivery obligation. Contracts can thus either be traded to 'open' or to 'close'. A contract is 'opened' when both the buyer and the seller have no previous futures position. A contract, or number of contracts, is therefore created. If the buyer had no previous position, but the seller had already bought contracts, and was now selling them back to the market, the 'opening' and 'closing' trades would net each other out. This is also true if the buyer was buying back contracts sold previously, but the seller was selling without having previously bought. If the buyer and seller had previously sold and bought respectively, then they are both 'closing' and those contracts will *cease to exist*.

To sum up: A buyer and seller entering the market for the first time will create contracts, and a seller and buyer exiting the market will dissolve those contracts. The good news is, however, that when you wish to exit the market having been, for example a buyer, you do not have to find the person you initially bought from to sell your contracts to them exclusively. You can sell out to anyone you like. This is where the futures exchange becomes involved beyond simply providing a trading floor and a set of rules to trade by. The exchange acts as a *clearing house* which means it puts all the trades into a big pool and then dips into the big pool to close those trades out again. You couldn't care less who you buy from and who you sell to during the period before expiry. In fact you'll never know. The exchange will randomly match boughts and solds so that the futures contracts you sold were effectively sold *to the exchange* (this is called *novation*). The representatives of the brokers trading in the pits record the trades and note the buyer and seller on the 'chit'. The exchange takes its copy of the chit and keeps a running total of all the bought and sold contracts being held by each particular broker and each particular account maintained by that broker. (One of those accounts is yours). When a broker conducts a trade on behalf of a client, the broker will inform the exchange as to whether that trade was to 'open' or to 'close'. The exchange then takes all the 'opens' and all the 'closes' and nets them off. This leaves us with an amount of wheat futures contracts that are still open and this is called the '*open position*'.

Now, that probably just seemed like a lot of unnecessary rambling about the tedious details of accounting for futures trades, but there is a point. Each day the buyers and sellers come into the market and trade wheat futures. The price of those futures will rise and fall depending on the greater eagerness of the buyers or the sellers. Also fluctuating from day to day will be the open position. Before any trade has occurred in the particular contract, maybe nine or twelve months ahead of expiry, the open position is zero. As interest develops in the contract, the open position will rise to some level, fluctuate over the life of the contract, and most likely steadily decrease toward the expiry date, as those sellers without enough wheat to deliver close out and those buyers who really don't want so much wheat being delivered close out. On the day of expiry, the remaining open positions will represent amounts of *actual* wheat that will *actually* be delivered by the sellers to the buyers. The sellers won't know who the buyers are, but that's okay because the wheat needs to be delivered to a predetermined delivery point as specified by the contract. I was not joking when I said it is possible to have an open position representing the total amount of wheat ever harvested in the history of mankind. Well, all right, so I was *exaggerating*. But it is the nature of nearly all futures contracts traded in the world that, at some point, the open position represents an amount of a specific commodity far, far greater than any seller would have the capacity to deliver or any buyer the capacity to utilise. In fact it is common for open positions to exceed the *available world reserves* of a specific commodity on any given day.

If that's the case, then one can assume that most open positions must fall rapidly as expiry looms and all the buyers and sellers close out, leaving only those who actually *are* committed to the exchange of physical wheat. And one would be absolutely right. The average percentage of futures contracts, traded around the world each year that *actually* result in a delivery being made is…wait for it…three. Yes, a massive 3% of all futures trading activity is for the purpose of one party handing over a commodity to another party.

So why does all that trading activity occur in the first place?

Hedgers

Let's recap. At the beginning of this chapter you were concerned that you needed to earn a certain price per tonne, come harvest time, of the wheat you were only now planting. Too low a price would see you bankrupt. The current price is sufficient to cover your needs, but harvest is still six months off and past experience suggests that anything could happen to the price between now and then. I came along and offered to guarantee you a price *now* for your wheat which you would deliver to me in six-months time. Although it is always quite possible that you could earn *more* for your wheat in six-months time, the price I offered was pretty good and knowing that the wheat had already been sold at that price removed any further uncertainty and allowed you to relax and get on with it.

I didn't mention it before, but the reason I was keen to buy your wheat ahead of time is that I own a bakery. Low wheat prices over the past twelve months have been terrific for my business as I've been able to sell bread quite cheaply while still making a good margin. In one year, I've opened three more outlets. But I know that good things don't last forever, and the recent slight rise in wheat prices to me looks rather ominous. I have a sneaking suspicion that wheat prices are going to 'go for a run', meaning a period when the price rises steadily. Although I can't be certain, I do know that a major price rise would bring my business growth to a screaming halt. And that's something I would like to avoid if possible. It's just as well that I found you and was able to buy your wheat forward at a good price. Now I, too, can relax.

What both of us have achieved in entering into our transaction is called *hedging*. You have probably heard of the expression 'hedging your bets' and this is exactly what we have done. You're exposed to a downward movement in the price of wheat. Therefore, you 'hedge' by selling ahead to remove that exposure. I'm exposed to an upward movement in the price of wheat. So I 'hedge' by buying ahead to remove that exposure.

All day, every day around the world there are people hedging exposures to adverse price movements. Not everyone hedges. It is merely a business decision—it's not compulsory. It's not unusual to read in the press of the yearly profit report of a major company with international dealings and learn that 'profits were adversely affected by an unexpected increase in the exchange rate over the period.' These statements are usually made with an air of fatalism, as if there were nothing the company could have done about it—exchange rates are in the hands of the gods—and we're sure we'll probably pick it back up again at some later stage when exchange rates inevitably fall. This is rubbish. The company has merely made a conscious decision not to hedge its profits against adverse movements in the exchange rate, and subsequently paid the penalty. Hedging is a cost, but it is a cost that may end up saving you money, and sleepless nights. A commonly used strategy is to hedge *part* of the exposure to an adverse price movement, say half. Then you can still participate if prices move in your favour, but you will also take some loss on an adverse movement.

So who will win, out of you and I? Well, we both can, really. You're happy because you know you've saved the farm. If wheat prices rise dramatically by harvest time, then you'll probably not speak for a week and kick the dog a lot until you calm down and realise that it could easily have been the other way around. I'll be stoked because I was right and saved myself a lot of money. If prices fall further than they are now, then you'll breathe a heavy sigh of relief knowing that you won't be ruined, and I'll probably mope for a while, but at least I'll know that I can still afford to expand my business on the price I achieved by buying from you. In other words, hedging removes the risk inherent in our business, but hedging will also prevent us participating in favourable price movements beyond the level at which we decided to hedge. Nevertheless, the idea is that we are both sufficiently happy with our trade no matter what happens. Isn't hedging wonderful?

Coming back to earth, the odds, in reality, of me somehow stumbling across you and fortuitously doing a deal on the forward wheat price are pretty slim. You don't see a lot of bakers driving around the farmland hoping to find a farmer who might be interested in doing a deal. We both know, however, that we can go to the futures exchange and achieve the same result. The futures exchange is a meeting place for all the farmers and bakers of the world who are looking to hedge against the wheat price. It is also a meeting place for all the oil producers and petrol companies, all the gold producers and jewellery manufacturers, all the cotton growers and clothing manufacturers and so on who are dependent on the price of their respective commodities not moving too far in the wrong direction, and therefore they are keen to do hedging deals with each other.

Does that then mean that every transaction occurring on a futures exchange is for the purpose of hedging, and that every trade is between a producer and a consumer? No, far from it. If it were only producers and consumers who frequented the futures exchange, and bearing in mind only *some* actually choose to hedge, and then they may only hedge *part* of their requirement, then the volume of wheat traded in the form of futures contracts would be only a proportion of the amount of physical wheat that actually changed hands. But this is far from true. We know the amount of wheat represented by open positions at the futures exchange is far greater than the amount of *actual* wheat traded each year. There is obviously no need to hedge *more* than the amount of wheat one is going to produce or consume, so what do the bulk of the trades and the open positions represent?

Speculators

The simple answer is *speculation*. The bulk of trades entered into on the futures exchange are transacted for the purpose of speculating on the movement of a price between now and the time of expiry. The great thing about commodity prices is that they will rise and fall with monotonous regularity over a period of time. These rises and falls, however, do not necessarily follow any sort of pattern, and so futures provide an opportunity for the speculator to 'punt' on price movements in the hope of making a profit and then closing out before delivery is required.

It is the 'punters' in the market, those with no farms and no bakeries, who most likely have had their only close encounter with any aspect of rural life at the Royal Easter Show, who provide the great majority of the trading turnover. Wheat is a commodity with a price that fluctuates greatly, and anything that fluctuates will attract speculation. Futures traders tend to play down the point, but a futures exchange is not particularly all that different to a casino.

So, here we have a market born of the need for producers and consumers of commodities to reduce the risks involved in their businesses through the perfectly legitimate activity of hedging against adverse future price movements, and amongst the crowd, in fact forming a very large part of the crowd, are people whose only interest is to profit from the misfortune of others! Instead of trying their hand at blackjack or horse-racing, they turn to futures and the smell of a quick buck through punting on *wheat*, amongst other things.

It is undeniable that futures trading for the purpose of speculation is only one step away from a casino. One can well argue that investments in the stock market, no matter how carefully considered, are also a form of gambling. The real question, however, is 'Is this such a bad thing?'. Before we move on to examine this question more closely, it is necessary to appreciate the one most attractive feature of the futures market from the speculator's point of view.

Leverage

Remember when you first decided to hedge your wheat crop by selling futures, you had to open an account with a broker and deposit some money. I said this deposit is very important and I would come back to it later. Well, here I am. It may have struck you as strange that you as the *seller* would need to deposit money. Surely you would be *receiving* a deposit from the buyer, and at the end of the contract receive full payment? You're right in assuming that at the end of the contract you will receive full payment, but it is the nature of futures contracts that not only does the exchange withhold the deposit put up by the *buyer*, it also demands a deposit from the *seller*, which is held by the exchange until expiry. How so?

Again, if we make a comparison to the stock market, we note that when you buy shares you immediately have to pay for them. For the full amount. And when you sell those shares at a later date you will immediately receive full payment.[18] If you are buying wheat six months ahead of time it is unlikely that you would agree to pay the full amount now and then be at risk of the delivery just never happening. It makes good business sense to put down a deposit now, securing the contract, and then pay up when the wheat has actually been delivered. The futures exchange agrees with you, and thus

18 *Actually you must pay for shares within 3 days (T+3) and you will receive payment in 5 days (T+5), although this process is under review.*

the purchase of wheat futures only requires a deposit to be made initially. Interestingly, it is *exactly* this minimal deposit requirement that makes futures trading so attractive to speculators. Unlike stocks, where my capacity to have a punt is restricted to the balance in my bank account, I can trade *serious* amounts of wheat back and forward and hopefully make serious amounts of money. For this privilege, all I have to do is put up a deposit. If I take the amount of money I was going to put into the stock market and put that into *deposits* on wheat futures, then I have greatly amplified the potential profit opportunity. This is called *leverage*.

Let's look at this concept with a more specific example. Forget that you were ever a farmer and consider now that you just like to speculate on the markets. And you believe that wheat prices are going to rise. Now I can hear you thinking that if you're not a farmer, or a baker, or anyone specifically involved in the production and consumption of wheat, then why on earth would you be of the opinion that wheat prices were going to rise, fall, or do anything? That's a fair question, but the nature of speculators is that there may be a million and one reasons why a speculator chooses a particular commodity and subsequently forms an opinion on that commodity's short-term price movements. Maybe you follow charts. Maybe you look at historical price cycles. Maybe you just think that the price has fallen a long way and is due to turn around. Maybe you read an article in the paper about starving North Koreans and figured that if South Korea decided to bail out its communist neighbours, then wheat would be one commodity it would need in quantity. Maybe you dreamt about a wheat shortage. It doesn't matter *why* you have an opinion. It will only ultimately matter whether that opinion was right or wrong. Often speculators can be a good judge of a market because they *are* removed from it, and not emotionally tied up in it. It's sort of the old 'can't see the wood for the trees' effect. But there is no point in dwelling on the reasons. The point is that you are of the opinion that the wheat price is going to rise in the next six months, and you wish to back this opinion.

Using your Lever

Listed on the stock exchange (hypothetically) is a company called Wheatgrow Corp. Not surprisingly, Wheatgrow is a company that grows wheat, and its profitability is directly linked to the level of the wheat price at any time. If the price of wheat rises, the share price of Wheatgrow rises in about the same proportion. You are prepared to put $10,000 against your belief that the wheat price will rise. Wheatgrow shares are trading at $1.00, and so you decide to buy 10,000 shares.

Within four months, your predictions prove well-founded and the spot price of wheat rises from $170 to $187 per tonne—a rise of 10%. Given the close correlation of the Wheatgrow share price to the price of wheat, it is not surprising that Wheatgrow also rises 10% in the same period to $1.10. You decide that this was the rise you were looking for and so you sell out your Wheatgrow shares for a profit of $1,000. Well done.

Alternatively, you could have chosen to back the wheat price more directly through wheat futures. The deposit required for one wheat contract, representing 50 tonnes of wheat (see SFE Wheat Futures table), is $450. Investing the same $10,000 you are able to buy 22 contracts, or 1100 tonnes of wheat, at the current January futures price of $170. After four months, well before the contract's expiry, you are happy to pocket the 10% price rise and sell out your futures at $187. You have made $17 on 1100 tonnes of wheat—$18,700. I think you'd agree this is far more attractive than $1,000.

Agree! That's an 18.7 times greater profit. How long has this been going on? It is not hard to see why the futures market is a magnet for speculators. But the more cautious among you will have already jumped to the obvious question—but what if the market *fell* 10%?

If the price of wheat had fallen 10% over the period, and we had bought Wheatgrow shares, we would have lost $1,000, but still had $9,000 invested. If we had bought futures we would have lost $18,700 and consequently be in the red to the tune of $8,700. A very dangerous prospect indeed. Clearly the futures market is one of possible high rewards, but definite high risks.

Margins

The futures exchange is not silly enough to stand back and hope that its speculative participants get it right most of the time, so that it's not constantly chasing up money owed on bad trades. If that were the case, the futures exchange would have shut down about a month after it opened. In fact, the exchange will never allow any client to be in a position of owing money on a trade that's turned sour at any stage during the life of the contract. This is achieved by the exchange adopting what is known as a *margin* system. The margin system operates by making daily calls upon the clients to increase the amount of money in their account, on top of the initial deposit, whenever the daily closing price falls below a comfortable level. The further there is to run on the contract, the more chance there is that a price may fall and recover within the time. The futures exchange recognises this and so, rather than panicking when a position starts going the wrong way, the exchange simply asks the client to add a bit to the deposit to provide a better buffer. If the price continues to fall, then more additions will be required. Any time the price does an about face and heads higher, the client will cease to be called upon to add more money. In fact he (or she) may then withdraw money from the account if they so desire, as long as the original deposit remains. Each of these requests to top up the account are called *margin calls*. Margin calls are made daily, if necessary, and the client must pay up by the following day. By continually making margin calls, the futures exchange will ensure that it won't suddenly have to chase a client for money come expiry time when it is realised that he (or she) doesn't have enough to meet his (or her) obligations.

Trading Places

Do you remember the movie *Trading Places* starring Dan Aykroyd and Eddie Murphy? When the Duke brothers tried to corner the market in orange juice futures, using illicit information, they met their match. The wrong crop report was substituted and the Dukes speculated heavily in the wrong direction. When the dust settled, and the Dukes had lost the lot, the director of the exchange approached them for a *margin call*. Enough for one to have a heart attack and the other to cry out, 'Turn the machines back on!'

If you haven't seen this movie please do.

The margin system does not, however, prevent a client from reaching a point during the life of the contract where the margin call is more than he (or she) is capable of paying. If you had bought your 22 wheat contracts by utilising the only $10,000 you had to spare, then as soon as the price began to fall you would have been margin-called and not been able to pay. In the event that a client fails to meet a margin call the following day, the position is automatically closed out by the broker (whose responsibility it is to collect the margins). That is, the broker simply sells your 22 contracts into the market and your excursion into wheat futures is over. If the price turns around and starts rushing back up the next day, well…tough. By adjusting the margin requirements *every day*, the broker ensures that any loss due to a client's failure to come up with the money is minimised. A loss worn by the broker will only be due to *one day's* adverse price movement, no more.

And you have probably gathered it is the broker, not the exchange, that would wear the loss. Therefore, it is the broker's responsibility to carefully assess a client's financial position before allowing them to trade futures. If you had submitted an asset and liability form to your broker, suggesting that all you had in liquid assets was $10,000, then there is no way the broker would have allowed you to spend the entire $10,000 on an initial deposit, leaving no leeway for margin calls. It's a bit like a bank making personal loans—the bank needs to feel confident that the lending exercise is not going to turn sour on them. It is possible for a broker to be caught out by a major client failure and not have the funds to pay the margin call to the exchange. In this case, the exchange (which is a 'not for profit' organisation of participating brokers) draws upon a fidelity fund set up for such emergencies and contributed to by all member brokers. In dire circumstances, the exchange may still have to let the broker go under.

Leverage, we might conclude, is something to be treated with respect. It allows for amplified rewards, but also amplified risks. Now, coming back to our original query, why would the *seller* of wheat futures have to put up a deposit with the exchange as well as the buyer? Is it only the buyer who is at risk? If the seller of the wheat futures is a wheat farmer, and can fairly safely be expected to have the wheat ready for delivery come expiry time, then one may feel that there is little risk of the seller getting into trouble. But we know that, on average, only 3% of futures trades ever actually result in delivery, and the rest are closed out before the expiry time of the contract. This tends to suggest that an awful lot of sellers do not in fact have any wheat at all and are simply *speculating* on a fall in the wheat price prior to the expiry date. That's right. Speculation is not restricted to buying. Over any given time period, markets tend to rise and fall and so it is equally likely that there will be those who speculate on a rise in the price and those who speculate on a fall in the price. And futures provide the perfect opportunity for downward speculation. Remember that a futures contract *does not exist* until one party sells to another party, and that the seller has no requirement to prove that he can actually fulfill the contract come expiry, ie the seller is *not obliged to own a wheat farm.* What this means is, that while the buyer of a futures contract is at risk that the price may fall, the seller is equally at risk that the price may rise. As far as the futures exchange is concerned, both parties are at risk and therefore both parties must put up a deposit. So a deposit for a futures contract is not in the nature of a traditional deposit where a buyer pays something now and the rest on delivery. It is more of a form of security against financial loss. And the insurance is topped up continually throughout the life of the policy, through margin calls, as the level of risk rises and falls. The seller is margined in exactly the same fashion as the buyer.

A Casino?

The responsible attitude toward risks associated with speculation taken by the futures exchange, tends to suggest that the 'casino' label applied to the exchange is, on closer inspection, a bit harsh. Isn't it? One H.C. Emery has this opinion:

> The possibility of making quick and large gains from fluctuations in prices leads thousands into the speculative market, who have no real knowledge of its condition, and no real opinion as to the course of prices. They depend chiefly on chance for their success. Such speculation is the merest gambling in spirit. The evil is still further increased by the 'margin' system. The speculator need not have capital enough to make his purchase, but only enough to 'put up a margin' of five or ten per cent with his broker...
> Added to the natural tendency to gambling, are all the attractive and alluring circulars and advertisements put out by

commission houses [brokers] which are regardless of how many
men they may lead to ruin, so long as commissions are
forthcoming. The amateur speculator, moreover, often goes in
beyond his means, and resorts to credit to retrieve his position.
The money of others is drawn into reckless trading;
embezzlement and ruin too often follow.

H.C. Emery doesn't seem to think that futures trading is anything other than gambling but, his conclusions notwithstanding, everything he has said about ill-informed speculators who are lured into the market by brokers' enticements, and are subsequently caught out by the risks of leverage are absolutely true. And H.C. Emery made these comments in 1896.[19]

Whichever way you look at it, speculation is speculation. Draw your own conclusions. Does it, however, serve any purpose, other than allowing one side to profit and the other to lose? Let's just clear one thing up first. I have been at pains to point out that, on average, only 3% of all futures contracts actually result in delivery. It might seem logical to assume from this statistic, therefore, that 3% of all futures trading is for the purpose of hedging and the remaining 97% is for the purpose of speculation. This is not actually true.

19 Emery, H.C., 'Speculation on the Stock and Produce
    Exchanges of the United States', *Columbia University*
    Faculty of Political Science: Studies in history, economics
    and public law, Vol. VII, No.2, New York, 1896.

When you were a farmer and I was a baker and we had decided to enter the futures market to hedge our respective exposures (ie you to sell wheat futures, and I to buy them) we had accepted that I would ultimately take delivery of someone's wheat for use in my bakery, via the correct delivery point (see SFE Wheat Futures table—page 46), and that you would ensure that you delivered the right amount of wheat and the right grade of wheat to the delivery point, and in so doing we were both happy in the knowledge that we were no longer exposed to an adverse movement in the price of wheat. Now, if it's only the price of wheat that we're concerned about, then why do we need to go through all that other hoo-ha? In other words, why don't we just sell and buy futures contracts respectively and then, just like a speculator, close them out before the expiry date once the risk of adverse price moves has abated. That way you don't have to worry about whether you have grown exactly the correct grade of wheat and whether you have grown enough wheat. Nor do you have to put up with the hassle of delivering your wheat to where the exchange tells you. You can sell it to whomever you choose, when you choose and where you choose, but you will still have hedged against the price being below the level of break-even for the farm. Similarly, I can buy whatever type of wheat I want, from a more convenient location, but still I will have effectively paid a price for that wheat that I wanted to pay by hedging in the futures six months before. What we have done is reduced our hedging activities to the simple procedure of exchanging cash, not wheat. The same level of protection is afforded by the futures market because it is not our wheat, or our bread, that we are protecting, but our bank balances. Thus it makes perfect sense to simply hedge the money, not the crop.

The implication here, therefore, is that the 3% to 97% breakdown is not a breakdown of hedging to speculating. It is simply a breakdown of cumbersome commodity exchange to simple cash exchange. So if this is true, then what exactly is the ratio of hedgers to speculators? The answer is, no one knows. One is not obliged to fill out a notice of intent before trading in the futures market.

Do speculators, then, serve any useful purpose? Before we address that chestnut, we must first be introduced to one section of the futures trading community who wear their speculative intentions like a badge—the 'local' member. (No, no, no, nothing to do with politicians). A futures exchange does not only have broking firms as members. Individuals may also become members of the exchange. As individuals, they do not have any clients. In reality they are, themselves, their only client. But, unlike the farmers and bakers of the world, the 'local' is permitted into the trading pit to conduct his (or her) own trading. For this privilege, the local must first buy or lease a membership, deposit money with a 'clearing' broker, pass the same examination to be allowed into the pit, and otherwise be subject to the same margin call limitations. Locals make a living out of speculating on futures markets all day, every day. Usually they will stick to one pit, say wheat, and get to know it. Most locals tend to run *intra-day* positions, rather than overnight positions, so that they are not caught out by new information that reaches the rest of the world while they are asleep. (Some locals I've known are so compulsive, they rarely sleep anyway). The result of this tendency is that, on average, locals account for some 60% of the daily turnover of futures contracts, but only about 2% of the open position (ie futures that have not been 'closed out'). Now, we can say with some certainty that, on average, 60% of daily turnover is speculative. Of the remaining 40%, we assume some is also speculative, but that some is also legitimate hedging. So back to the question: what purpose does speculative trading serve?

These percentages look familiar. Do you remember back in my brief description of the foreign exchange market that I pointed out that something like 90% of all trades on the Aussie dollar each day are by banks having a punt? And that the remaining 10% was legitimate business between exporters and importers, or others with foreign currency exposure? Well, the futures market is very much the same. Like the foreign exchange market, speculation on the futures market is a *zero sum game*. For every speculator who makes $1,000, another must lose $1,000. What all this speculation does provide is *liquidity*. The sheer volume of speculative contracts, constantly exchanged in the pit, ensures that a 'tight' price is always available for the hedger. What this means is that if *one* seller and *one* buyer (like you the farmer and me the baker) had to negotiate a price between themselves, chances are they'd just reach some Mexican stand-off and no trade would occur. With speculators constantly buying and selling, they have the effect of crystalising the sum of all opinions into one selling price and one buying price which are as close as one 'tick' (the minimum increment of price that the exchange allows). Therefore, in the futures market, the buying hedger and the selling hedger achieve virtually the same price without even having to haggle.

Volatility

The argument thus persists, irrespective of one's opinion on the evils of gambling, as to whether speculation *decreases* the volatility of a market or *increases* the volatility of a market. 'Volatility' refers to the tendency for prices to jump around wildly, or to shift violently in one direction. If the only users of the wheat futures market were farmers and bakers, then prices would tend to move around jerkily as infrequent deals were struck between the buyers and sellers. Desperation would play an important role. Moreover, the concentration of sensitive time periods (ie planting time and harvesting time) would most likely lead to a rush to hedge or unwind, all at the same time forcing sudden extensive price swings. The constant, day-to-day activity of the speculators provides a smoothing effect on the inevitable price movements. Jerky movements are largely avoided. Sudden price swings, due to crucial timing, are somewhat dampened. All in all, speculation is beneficial in the reduction of volatility.

That is...sometimes, but not always. The counter argument is that speculation actually exacerbates sudden price movements. Speculators do live and die by their trades after all, so it's no surprise that they will often have a tendency to panic. Imagine passengers rushing, en masse, from side to side of a listing ferry, only to cause the ferry to rock even more violently than it would if they'd all stayed still in the first place. Futures markets can often resemble rocking ferries. Moreover, history is dotted with countless cases of 'speculative bubbles' (eg the stock market crash of '87). These result from the fear of missing out on a 'sure thing'. Buyers are still pushing a market up long after the real value has been surpassed simply because it seems that the price rise will never stop. It's self-fulfilling. It's simply a price rise based on hype. And eventually what goes up must...Another historically well-documented activity is the attempt to 'corner the market'. Do you recall that I mentioned, back in Chapter 1, the Japanese copper trader who tried to corner the copper market as recently as 1996? Well Yasua Hamanaka, of Sumitomo Bank, was not buying physical copper. He was buying copper futures (and options, but that's not important at this point). Like the futures contract on any commodity, copper has the capacity for open positions to far exceed actual copper inventories. Mr Hamanaka pushed the open position to unheard of levels, and consequently the price continued to rise. Many a copper trader was ruined by assuming that the price *must* soon fall. But still Hamanaka bought copper, without authority.

Finally Sumitomo Bank twigged that something was amiss, and Hamanaka was suspended from trading. Suddenly there was no longer anything holding up the copper market, and when the news broke…well, I think you can guess.

Fig. 1—COMEX Copper Futures Price (January–July, 1996)

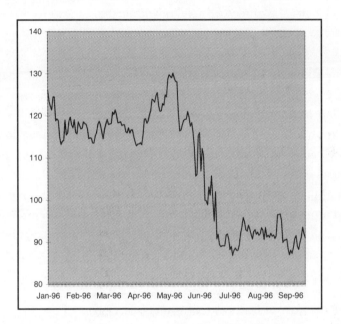

Events such as these lead cynics to maintain that speculation has the effect of increasing volatility, and that futures trading is the cause of all problems. The reality is that they are both right, and both wrong. Sometimes speculation is positive for a market, and sometimes it is negative. The argument will never be resolved. The fact of the matter is that the futures markets are here to stay, and new futures contracts are still opening all the time.

So let's move away for now from the unresolvable argument, and return to consider one point I made a while back. That point is that very few futures contracts ever make it to delivery because it is a lot simpler to exchange cash than it is to muck around exchanging the commodity. Therefore even hedgers close out their futures positions before expiry so that only a cash transaction need take place. This has, however, no effect on their actual hedging needs—the same result is achieved in their bank balance.

As the futures markets have developed over time we have seen the gradual increase of futures contracts that *cannot* be delivered against. These contracts are *cash settlement only*. This cash settlement may be preferred simply because it is less hassle, or it may be that the futures contract is over a commodity that is *intangible* and so cannot be delivered. Whoa, that sounds a bit X-files, doesn't it? The simple point is that there is no end to the types of 'things' that may be able to be traded in futures form. Let's examine some of them.

Futures and Commodities

To date, I have used wheat as my example for the operation of the futures markets. The birth of futures markets is synonymous with agricultural products known as 'soft' commodities. Among the heavily traded contracts in the 'soft' category are soyabeans, corn, wheat, oats, cattle, hogs, pork bellies, sugar, coffee, cocoa, cotton, orange juice, red beans, rubber and canola. And these are just some examples. Many more bizarre commodities are traded around the world in futures form. In nearly all cases, these contracts are deliverable. Below is a small selection of futures contracts, both deliverable and non-deliverable, 'soft' and otherwise, traded in various world exchanges.

A Small Selection of Futures Contracts from Around the World

COUNTRY	CONTRACT	COUNTRY	CONTRACT
Australia	Share Futures	UK	Sterling
	Greasy wool		Aluminium
Austria	Govt bond		Copper
Belgium	Govt bond		Lead
Brazil	Arabica coffee		Nickel
	Live cattle		Zinc
	Sugar crystal		Tin
Canada	Gold		Gas oil
	Canola		Potatoes
	Feed peas	USA	Anhydrous ammonia
	Flaxseed		Corn
China	Copper		Oats
Denmark	Mortgage bonds		Rice
Finland	Govt bond		Silver
France	Mark/Franc		Soyabean oil
	Potatoes		Wheat

Country	Product	Country	Product
France	Rapeseed	USA	Australian dollar
	White sugar		Feeder cattle
Germany	Bund		Fluid milk
	Dax index		Live & lean hogs
Hong Kong	Hang Seng		Live cattle
Hungary	Black seed		Lumber
	Feed barley		Mexican peso
	Milling wheat		Pork bellies
Italy	Notional bond		Gold
Japan	Imported soybeans		Cheddar cheese
	Azuki beans		Cocoa
	Rubber		Not fat dry milk
	Raw silk		Raw milk
	Dried cocoon		Sugar
	Palladium		Western natural gas
Malaysia	Crude palm oil		Black tiger shrimp
Netherlands	Live hogs		Cotton
New Zealand	Bank bills		Orange juice
Norway	Govt bond		Heating oil
Portugal	PSI index		Propane gas
Singapore	Robusta		Crude oil
	Brent crude oil		Palo Verde electricity
	Eurodollar		Platinum
South Africa	Krugerrand		Unleaded gasoline
Spain	Notional bond		Airline index
Sweden	90-day deposit		Forest & paper prod
Switzerland	Market index		Semiconducter
UK	Brent crude oil		Utility index
	Baltic freight		
	Cocoa no.7		
	Coffee robusta		
	EC wheat		
	White sugar		
	Long gilt		

Two of the most heavily traded commodities around the world, as I have stated previously, are metals and oil. Oil is in fact the greatest traded commodity in the world. But again the trade in these commodities through futures contracts outweighs that of the physical commodity.

Gold, which we have conceded is more of a currency than a commodity, is a popular protector against inflation. It is also a damned heavy metal to cart around in its 'bar' form and dangerous to store lest it be stolen.

Although jewellery is a popular form of gold investment one is also paying for craftsmanship when one buys a piece of jewellery, as well as the actual gold content. No problem—the Commodities Exchange in New York offers the world's most popular gold futures contract. Buy the gold but never see it glitter. (All that's gold does not glitter?) You will never have to worry about storing your gold because in reality all you have is an account with a futures broker that holds a position directly linked to the price of gold.

Miners, too, use the futures contract, although in their case it is a legitimate hedge. There is no point in going through the effort, and expense, of finding gold, digging it out of the ground then find that once the gold actually reaches 'bar' form the price has fallen to a point where digging it out of the ground was a waste of money. Miners 'sell' the gold they have not yet dug up through the futures market, and thus ensure a price.

It's no great leap of logic to appreciate that oil futures are also a very handy instrument if you own an oil well. And what's more what industry is not in some way affected by the price of oil? In order to hedge against the oil (or even petrol) expenses of your business it is not convenient to buy tanker loads of the stuff. Just buy futures, and make sure you close out your position before delivery time. The New York Mercantile Exchange offers the most popular oil futures contract based on West Texas Intermediate crude.

Base metals are commodities that are used for all sorts of purposes in vast quantities. If you use a lot of copper it might be a good idea to buy a lot of copper and put it in a warehouse for future use. That way if the price rises dramatically it will not effect your bottom line because you already have all the copper you need. But storing loads of copper costs money. If you're worried about the price going up then just buy futures. That way when you do go to buy more copper at a higher price you will have already covered the added expense in your futures account. The London Metals Exchange has long been synonymous with the trade in base metals. Nowadays it deals exclusively in futures contracts.

It might now be a bit easier to see why the futures equivalent of any widely traded and utilised commodity out-trades the commodity itself. When the price of a commodity is quoted nowadays, perhaps in the media, it is quite likely that that price is, in fact, the price of the nearest futures contract rather than the price of the actual commodity. Commodities futures are the simplest form of futures contract.

But I promised you some more complicated ones.

Futures and the Money Market

In Chapter 1, we addressed the processes by which corporations and financial institutions go about the business of borrowing or lending money. Specifically, I introduced two instruments, outside of cash, that are heavily traded for this purpose—bank bills and government bonds. It will probably come as no great surprise when I tell you that both these instruments are also heavily traded in futures form.

In the case of 90-day bank bills, the role of the *physical* (see box) instrument has changed dramatically over time. Once the dominant money market instrument, the bank bill has been virtually replaced altogether by its futures equivalent for use by professional money market participants. One of the reasons for the extent of this replacement is the flow on to other forms of derivative instruments such as options which are explored later in this book. Bills issued by banks are still, however, used as investment tools.

Let's Get Physical

The expression 'physical' is used in reference to the underlying security of any futures contract upon which that futures price is based. Therefore, in the case of wheat, the price at which one can buy wheat today, as opposed to the price of the six-month future, is the 'physical' price. The implication is that wheat is a physical commodity and the futures price is just, well, an intangible concept.

The expression has gone on to be used, however, to refer to the price of *any* underlying instrument. One cannot really consider a 90-day loan to be a 'physical' concept. But convention has dictated that this is the expression used to distinguish from the 'futures' price.

To make it even more interesting there is another expression often used instead of 'physical', and that is 'cash'. So if one knows the price of a six-month wheat futures, one might inquire, 'What's the cash?' Again, this refers to the price of actual wheat.

The 90-day bank bill contract is available on the SFE in 90-day cycles of March, June, September and December expiries. This cycle then repeats in a second year ('new' March etc) and a third year (called 'red' March etc) right through to a fifth year. The price of a *physical* 90-day bill will change over the period as the time to maturity of the 'loan' reduces each day. In other words, the 90-day instrument eventually becomes a 60-day instrument and then a 30-day through to a week and a day. At these various points, the cost of borrowing or lending money may change depending on the demand for finance over that particular period of time. Therefore, the interest rate reflected in the price of the bill may change with the reducing time period remaining in the bill.

An important point to grasp is that the *futures* price of a 90-day bank bill will *not* change, as the expiry date approaches, as a result of the time to maturity gradually getting closer. Rather, the price of the futures contract reflects the price, ahead in time, of a bank bill that is *always a 90-day maturity*. Confused? Let's look at it this way: If a bank was to issue a 90-day bank bill every day for 90 days, then the first bill issued would be reaching maturity just as the last bill was being issued. Each bill would edge one day closer to maturity each day and their prices will change to reflect the shorter period of borrowing. The new bill issued each day, however, would always be issued at a price that reflects a full 90 days to go. Where the futures contract confuses the issue is that it also trades in the 90-day cycles described above. The price of a bank bill future, expiring in March, is a reflection of what the market believes will be the price of a new 90-day bank bill issued at the expiry date, *not* what the price of a 90-day bank bill issued today will be in March.

Looking at one full year of expiries, ie March, June, September, December, it is easy to make the mistake of thinking that the price of each contract reflects the cost of borrowing money for 90, 180, 270 and 360 days respectively. This is not true. The price of the futures contract of each successive expiry reflects the market anticipation of the price of a 90-day bank bill that will be issued 90, 180, 270 and 360 days ahead. Remember, a futures contract reflects a market anticipation of something that will happen in the future. Whereas you and I were earlier trying to anticipate the price of wheat in six-months time after the harvest, so to are the users of bank bill futures concerned with the price of 90-day finance at a point in the future.

So why, then, are bank bill futures far more popular an instrument than their physical companions? One of the main reasons is that the available market for short-term finance is concentrated into distinct periods of maturity, being overnight and quarterly (or 90 days). Availability of funds for periods greater than 90 days and less than about three or so years, where the bond market takes over, is very thin, and the spread between borrowing and lending rates much wider than those available at the 90-day mark. The beauty of bank bill futures is that the contracts available at each quarter out to five years, allows the market participant to put together a 'strip' of financing protection out to any number of quarters between now and five years, which provides a pre-placed hedge against movements in the cost of 90-day finance from quarter to quarter. This is a strategy known as 'boot-strapping'. A corporation, with financing requirements out to, say, 18 months, will sell (see box) an appropriate amount of bill futures in each contract along the bill 'strip', that is the complete series of expiries through March, June, September and December of each year, up until the fifteenth month. This will protect them against adverse movements in the cost of 90-day finance each time they roll over their 90-day loan. At the fifteenth month, or last quarter, there will only be 90 days to go, and so the last quarter need not be hedged. Just like feeding a boot-lace through each of the eyelets and pulling them tight.

Reverse Pricing

Interest rates, ie the cost of money, are one commodity where it is desirable to lend at the higher rate and borrow at the lower rate. This results in the bid/offer spread of an interest rate being quoted as, for example, 8%-7% which is back-to-front compared to all other commodities where the bid is always lower than the offer.

In order to overcome this confusion in the futures market, both the SFE bill and bond contracts are quoted as 100 minus the rate. So our quote becomes 92-93 which is much easier to handle as it means that the seller of the futures contract is achieving the lower rate, or higher price, and the buyer is achieving the higher rate, or lower price.

Given the natural balance between borrowers and lenders, one might assume that these are the only participants in the bank bill futures market. Not so. Interest rate futures are very popular with our old friends the speculators. In Australia, the bank bill futures contract and the government bond contracts often enjoy the highest turnover of the contracts on the SFE, and often the most number of local traders trying to make a dollar on the short term or long term movement of rates. Speculation of bank bill rates becomes quite obvious at times when it is anticipated that the Reserve Bank may be about to raise or lower interest rates. If the market participants are expecting a 50-point (or 0.5%) drop in rates as orchestrated by the RBA then this drop will be reflected in the price of the next futures contract already trading around 50 points away from present physical rate. This does not mean that the market is always right, often it is not, (and in fact sometimes it's not hard to suspect that the RBA does not always act as expected just to show who's boss) but it is common to hear economic commentators say, before an anticipated rate cut, that 'the futures market has already factored in a cut of half a percent.'

The bank bill futures contract is still a deliverable contract, despite its dominance of turnover over the physical equivalent. Where bills differ from wheat or other physical commodities, however, is that a bank bill can be issued at any time by the appropriate institution (you don't have to sit around hoping that bank bills will grow). Therefore, for the buyer[20] of the bill futures, assuming they are of sufficient credit-worthiness, it is possible simply to issue a bill in order to meet delivery. Alternatively there is a specific range of bills and certificates of deposit that meet the criteria for delivery.

Government bonds, like their short-term bank bill counterparts, are instruments in which the physical activity is now far outweighed by futures activity. The SFE provides two heavily traded maturities, being 3 years and 10 years. These are the two popular periods for which the government, via the RBA, prefers to raise funds from its citizens and from overseas investors. Semi-government and non-government corporations also choose to raise capital through bond issues. Whereas a bank bill is a 'discount' instrument (ie you buy a bill now for less than $1 million and pay back $1 million after 90 days with the extra amount paid being the effective interest rate), a bond is an instrument where the investor lends the full face value and receives an interest payment each year in the form of a 'coupon'. Buyers of physical bonds are investing their money in order to receive this steady coupon stream. The value of a government bond will change over time, due to expectations about the performance of the economy.

As with bill futures, bond futures are available in quarterly contracts. The price of the future in each contract is an expectation of the price of a 3 or 10-year bond at the expiry date. Unlike bill futures, bond futures are traded almost exclusively in the nearest available contract, with activity beginning to spill over into the next available contract as the nearest approaches expiry. As bonds are a long-date investment tool, rather than a

20 *The buyer in this case is the one who has the delivery obligation, not the seller. See the previous box, Reverse Pricing.*

short-date financing tool, there is no impetus to put together a strip of bond futures to hedge ongoing financing needs. Bond futures provide a means of speculating on, or hedging against, changes to the Australian economic situation and the world's perception of that situation.

A notable difference between bill and bond futures is that bond futures are *not* deliverable. Rather they are *cash-settled*. Because the government chooses to issue bonds at various times with different coupon rates, it was initially difficult to decide upon which particular bond would form the benchmark to allow for a permanently fixed set of specifications for the bond futures contract. To overcome this problem, the SFE 'created' a pretend government bond with a face value of $100,000 and a 12% coupon maturing in 3 and 10 years. As this pretend bond cannot be delivered at expiry time, the buyer of the contract settles in cash. The amount of cash required to settle is calculated by the SFE. The SFE will contact the 'official' bond dealers at random times over the last day and ask their price on a basket of government bonds that are similar, but not identical to, the pretend bond. From these quotes, the SFE can then calculate what the price of the pretend bond should be.

Futures and Foreign Exchange

I'm sure you think that I'm about to tell you that futures contracts in foreign currencies have replaced the use of money altogether. Believe it or not, the foreign exchange market does tend to buck the trend and has not gone out of its way to embrace futures to the point where, say, US dollar futures or yen futures are the most heavily traded form of foreign exchange instrument. That is not to say that currency futures do not exist—there is still plenty of activity in various currencies on various exchanges around the world—it's simply that the *spot* and *forward* currency markets, as traded over the phone, or other computerised communication systems, are still the prevailing means of buying and selling foreign currency.

A *spot* trade is simply the exchange of one currency for another at a price today. A *forward* trade is the exchange of one currency for another at some time in the future. This time period may coincide with payments or receipts due in another currency. Forward trades are conducted between two counterparties who then have obligations to, and risks from, themselves alone. You may recall that at the beginning of this chapter, when you were a farmer and I was a baker, we initially agreed to a forward contract based on the price of wheat in six-months time. I then suggested that, for various reasons, it would be more sensible for both of us to conduct our business via the futures exchange. By trading through the exchange, we could overcome any problems of finding the right price, of worrying about the right sort of wheat, and of worrying whether you would actually come up with the wheat and I would actually come up with the money. Why do these reasons not hold up for foreign exchange as well?

The vast majority of foreign exchange transactions are undertaken by banks and major corporations. These institutions have well researched and clearly published credit ratings. They have vast amounts of capital. And unlike wheat, a dollar is a dollar. And furthermore, business dealings requiring foreign exchange transactions are going on around the world all day, every day, not just at a particular time of the year. Speculation, the main source of foreign exchange activity, is a day on day proposition. In short, the foreign exchange market doesn't really *need* futures.

Futures still exist, however, but in most cases the face value of the futures contract is a much smaller amount than the big boys normally play with. This is a deliberate attempt to provide the smaller player—maybe a smaller import or export corporation, or an individual who wants to speculate on exchange rates—with an opportunity to participate in the market. For example, the Australian dollar futures contract, listed on the Chicago Mercantile Exchange, has a face value of $100,000. A standard trade in Aussie dollars by the main players, trading minute on minute, is $10 million.

Futures and the Stock Market

Futures, as we have seen so far, dominate the trading activity in commodities and the money market. Foreign exchange basically sticks to its traditional methods of business. The stock market is unusual because it is a market in which the activity in the physical instruments—in this case shares—and the activity in futures contracts actually exist side by side in roughly equal proportion. The reason for this is that futures in the stock market have not developed as a *substitute* for shares, but rather a *complimentary* tool to be utilised along with share market activity.

How the stock market differs from the other markets is that it is comprised of a number of individual shares of individual companies pursuing individual lines of business. Wheat is basically wheat. An interest rate is an interest rate. The Aussie dollar, although measured against many other currencies, is still just the Aussie dollar. A share, on the other hand, has a distinct life of its own and rises and falls in price alongside hundreds of its fellow shares as are available for public trade on the stock exchange. From the individual's point of view, or even from the point of view of pension funds, insurance companies and the like, shares are simply *investment* tools. A farmer grows wheat because that is his (or her) business. A baker consumes wheat because that is his (or her) business. They will both look at futures as a means to hedge their business activities. Borrowing and lending occurs every day in the line of some specific business. An importer will turn to the foreign exchange market to protect the profits in his (or her) business. When we invest in shares, however, we are investing in *somebody else's business*. Unless we are a Kerry Packer or a Rupert Murdoch, who buy sufficient amounts of a company's shares to then have a say in the running of that company, our investment is in the hands of those people responsible for managing that company.

An investment in shares, therefore, could be considered an exercise in speculation. The buyer is speculating on the success of the company as translated into the share price. Where a futures market comes into its own is in providing a vehicle for both speculation and hedging. If an investor in shares was to hedge that investment by selling futures contracts in those shares, then they are effectively cancelling out that investment. Speculators are basically the opposite of hedgers. All of this adds up to suggest that there is not really a great need for a futures contract on each share that is available on the stock exchange, as there obviously is on wheat. There is no need to provide a speculation vehicle to those who are already speculating.

But what of leverage? Would not a futures contract on a share provide the potential for leveraging one's investment? The answer to this question is yes, indeed it would. Remember that a share purchase must be paid for in full immediately, whereas a futures contract only requires a deposit. But as the share market has, for centuries, been one of the most popular forms of investment, there already exist many other ways of leveraging an investment in shares. Some of these are very old concepts and others are fairly recent. They include such things as margin lending, options and other instruments. We will have a look at a couple of these later on. There do exist, however, futures contracts on individual shares in Australia which are traded on the SFE. At the time of writing, there were 10 share futures available, but trading was thin and intermittent. At the end of the day, the average investor, who is unfamiliar with futures and the like, is comfortable to stick to the tried and true investment formula of simple share purchases. This is true also of the funds, who prefer to stick to solid share investments rather than the supposedly more 'risky' futures counterparts.

Okay, so what are the stock market futures that exist side by side to the stock market in similar proportions that are used as a complimentary tool? Answer: *index futures*. In the previous chapter, I introduced you stock indexes (or stock indices to be correct). In Australia, we have the All Ordinaries index of about 300 stocks. The effect of an index is, in a way, to *commoditise* the stock market, converting it into a single rising and falling price. Individual stocks are affected by individual factors and also *market factors*. There are many market factors that may affect the stock market *as a whole*. Examples are perceptions of a country's economic growth, changes to the tax policy, changes to interest rates (low interest rates make buying stocks generally more attractive than putting your money in a bank or buying bonds etc) and so on. The result is that the movement of the stock market is something that one may wish to speculate on as a whole, rather than simply trying to pick particular stocks that may or may not perform as well as the overall market. Have you ever invested in a stock that just doesn't go up, even when you see every night on the news that the stock market has been performing particularly well? The AOI is a capitalisation-weighted index of about 300 stocks. The difficulty that arises in trying to speculate on the stock market as a whole is that one would need to buy, in the correct proportion, an amount of every one of those 300 stocks. This is unless . . . there were a futures contract.

The Share Price Index futures contract (abbreviated to SPI and commonly referred to as 'the spy') on the SFE is a futures contract over the All Ordinaries index (why they didn't simply call it the AOI contract I have no idea, maybe they thought SPI had a better ring to it). This means that at the end of each contract month, the SPI settles at the closing price of the AOI. The SPI is a cash-settled contract, which is understandable given the difficulty anyone would have in delivering all of the AOI stocks in all the correct ratios come expiry time.

The SPI provides a means for one to speculate on the stock market without ever buying any shares. To this end, many small investors will buy and sell SPI contracts, usually in the popular quarterly contracts of March,

June, September and December. Where the SPI really comes into its own, however, is as a tool for institutional investors, being the large funds managers such as the AMP, National Mutual and so on. It is the institutional investors that provide the bulk of large-volume trades in this particular contract. But the value of this contract to the institutional investors is not as a pure speculation tool (the trustees of many funds would not allow pure speculation in futures using unit-holders' money), nor as a pure hedging tool (again, if you were to buy shares and then sell futures, you are simply cancelling out your potential gains on the speculative shares). Rather the institutions use the SPI to move quickly in the market, allowing positions to be established with expedience before actual shares are purchased. Let me explain this in more detail.

Big Players in the SPI

Most fund managers offer a variety of different funds which invest in shares. At the less risky end of the scale are the 'market tracking' type funds which aim to deliver the same return to investors as the AOI over the period. 'Less risky' does not mean 'no risk' as the AOI will always rise and fall over time. A 'market-tracking' fund simply provides the diversity of investment of all or at least most of the shares comprising the AOI for the investor who has already made the decision to invest in the stock market. Further up the scale of risk/return are the 'blue chip' funds which invest only in the larger companies listed on the stock exchange (typically the top 50 to 100 companies by capitalisation). In these funds, it is the role of the fund manager to determine the 'weighting' or ratio of each of the stocks held in the portfolio. At various times, the fund manager will reassess the portfolio weightings and buy and sell stocks according to their beliefs on the potential performance of specific stocks in the next period. More often than not this is done quarterly. At the high end of risk/reward are the 'stock picking' type funds which may invest in a combination of blue chips and smaller companies, or smaller companies alone, given, again, the funds manager's beliefs in the potential value of those companies. Small company funds have become more popular of late with both the large institutions and the smaller, 'boutique' funds management operations. 'Balanced' funds provide the unit-holder with a mix of investments in, say, cash (probably bonds), property and the stock market. At times the fund manager will adjust the mix of investment, possibly reducing or increasing the stock market component.

In the case of the larger 'market tracking' and blue chip funds and the balanced funds, the institutions will hold large parcels of various companies. When they wish to re-weight these parcels at various times of the year it is not always easy to buy and sell the large parcels of stock quickly, either due to a lack of availability of sellers and buyers at the time or due to the fact that too aggressive an approach may telegraph their intentions to the rest of the market and adversely affect the prices of the stocks at the time. Moreover, decisions to buy and sell stocks, particularly in the case of large institutions, are not made lightly or in haste. What this all means is that the process of accumulating stocks and divesting in stocks is a slow and deliberate one, often occurring over a period of days or weeks.

It does not escape the attention of the fund managers, however, that the market has a tendency to move around all the time and not just when they are making decisions about changing weightings, or even when they may receive fresh parcels of money to invest from new accounts, such as a large company superannuation fund. Consequently, a fund manager may make a correct decision to invest in more stocks, or divest in stocks when the time is right, but in the process of actually implementing the investment or divestment he (or she) may completely miss the boat because he (or she) is simply unable to move fast enough.

Enter index futures.

As the SPI contract is a surrogate for the entire AOI, a funds manager can hit the market quickly by buying or selling futures contracts while allowing the slower process of buying or selling the actual shares to run at its natural pace. As the stock trades fall into place, the funds manager simply reverses the equivalent number of futures contacts. This way the funds manager is not caught out on the timing. A fund manager can also use the futures to take advantage of perceived temporary peaks and troughs in the market without having to upset the entire portfolio of stocks. By using futures, the fund manager is also avoiding the stock market commissions and fees which are levied as a percentage of the full value of the stocks, as opposed to the futures commissions and fees which are at a fixed rate per contract and decidedly less imposing. In short, the SPI becomes a useful complimentary tool for the fund manager.

Stock index futures are a heavily traded commodity around the world. In the US, the most focussed-upon stock index is the Dow Jones Industrial Average of 30 stocks. These 30 stocks, however, are not particularly representative of the greater US stock market. There is another index which many consider to be the more accurate measure of US stock performance, and that is the Standard & Poors 500 index which, as one might guess, is a much broader index of 500 stocks. It is this index upon which one of the world's most heavily traded futures contracts is based. The S&P 500 futures contract is traded on the Chicago Mercantile Exchange. Another heavily traded index future is the Nikkei 225 index of Japanese stocks. Much to the chagrin of the Japanese, who have never been particularly thrilled about the prospect of foreigners tampering with their stock market through futures trading, the Nikkei futures are traded on the Singapore International Monetary Exchange. SIMEX also offers futures on Hong Kong's Hang Seng index, but so does the Hong Kong Futures Exchange, and therefore it is more popularly traded at home. Hong Kong had a bit of a problem with their futures contract after the crash of '87, but more on that later. All around the world the major trading nations, and some not so major, provide a futures contract over an index of the local stocks.

Portfolio Insurance

I have made mention of how fund managers can use index futures to move quickly in the market when they perceive a short-term rise or fall. As fund managers are always 'long' stock, ie an investment in shares means that you only buy them, not sell them, then a short-term purchase of index futures is akin to speculation, on top of the shares held, which is already an exercise in speculation itself. A short-term sale of stock index futures, on the other hand, is akin to hedging, as the fund manager is attempting to offset the short-term loss of value of the share portfolio. When index futures are used in this hedging capacity, it is often referred to as 'portfolio insurance'. If you remember back to the introduction, I highlighted the US response to the crash of '87 and a subsequent witch-hunt for someone or something to blame. One of the culprits, as determined by a government inquiry, was the activity of portfolio insurance. When it became apparent to US fund managers that the stock market had peaked, and was turning around rather fast, many of them realised that selling out of the stocks held in their portfolios would not be possible within the time frame and that rather hefty losses were on the cards. So, in an attempt to offset the potential losses, they sold S&P 500 futures instead. And they sold, and they sold, and they sold. And the more they moved the price of the futures down by their selling, so did this cause the stock market, already being devastated by the selling of stock positions outright, to fall even further. And as the stock market fell further, what did the fund managers need to do? Yep, sell more futures.

Does this mean that the activity of portfolio insurance was the cause of the crash of '87? No. On the basis of the tenet of 'what goes up, must come down', the overheated US stock market was always shaping for a major correction eventually. The frantic sale of futures on the day did, however, serve to exacerbate the situation and probably affected a sharper fall than *may* have been the case if futures did not exist. This is largely because the sale of futures was not restricted to portfolio insurance and straight out selling of existing futures long positions. Selling was also conducted for the purpose of 'program trading' and for the hedging of option positions. I won't go into program trading or options just now as they are dealt with specifically in the following chapters. Suffice to say, at this point, that there were also other activities exacerbating the correction. In Australia, activity in the SPI futures also served to fuel the crash, although, with the Dow Jones index already closed at 500 points down, a similar response was always a likelihood in the local market.

This leads us to an interesting question. Do the stocks lead the futures or do the futures lead the stocks? It's a bit of a 'chicken and egg'. Basically the answer is both occur, but at different times. Sometimes specific activity in stock trading will move the AOI, and the SPI will follow, and sometimes specific activity in index futures trading will move the SPI, and the stock market, or AOI, will follow. I said a couple of paragraphs ago that when futures selling occurred in the US during the crash, the result was to force the stock market lower and this triggered even further futures selling. A snowball effect. If the portfolio insurers are selling futures *instead* of stocks why then must the stocks, follow down the futures? Again the answer to this is program trading—stay tuned for the next chapter—but the reason that program trading occurs is because of the effects of *premiums and discounts*.

Premiums and Discounts

This might be a good point to come back to a comment I made at the very beginning of this book and that was that those unfamiliar with the futures market often assume that futures traders must have some kind of crystal ball. Well, after all, they are *futures*, aren't they. Are those who trade in futures markets attempting to 'predict' the future? And if so do those 'predictions' come true? Having read this far, you can probably have a go at these questions yourself. If we divide a futures market up into the traditional two groups of participants, the hedgers and the speculators, we'd probably arrive at the following conclusions. Hedgers are not attempting to 'predict' the future. They are simply recognising that future prices of a commodity, and let's go back to our friend wheat as the example, are at worst totally unpredictable and at best a bit of a gamble. Anything might happen between planting and harvesting and usually does. By hedging the price of his (or her) wheat crop, by securing a price today for wheat delivered in the future, the farmer has removed the problem of unpredictability. The only thing appearing in a farmer's crystal ball is an unnerving haze. A speculator on the other hand, perhaps the buyer of wheat ahead of harvest time, must, by definition, be doing a bit of crystal-ball gazing. One assumes that the crystal ball is utilised in the sense of a legitimate, considered opinion of possible movements in the wheat price between now and expiry, but any speculator who has ever lost money (ie all of them at some stage) will tell you that even the most carefully thought out opinions have a habit of coming apart at the seams.

Do futures prices, which are representative of a meeting of minds of the hedgers and speculators, succeed in 'predicting' what the price of the underlying commodity will be at expiry time? Clearly not. If this were the case, then the price of futures contracts would not fluctuate during the life of the contract. Futures prices fluctuate just as the underlying price fluctuates. In fact, in the rush to hedge or speculate as every new little snippet of information enters the market (eg overseas crop reports, weather forecasts, insect plague alerts), the exuberance of futures traders will often see the futures price fluctuate far more wildly than the underlying price. Just like the passengers on the listing ferry rushing too quickly from side to side and causing the ferry to rock even more. And yet it is the fluctuations of the underlying price from which many traders of futures are trying to protect themselves from in the first place. The futures price at any given time, therefore, is a combination of an immediate rejigging of predictions and the familiar forces of demand and supply. If there were more hedgers trying to protect themselves than there were speculators wishing to back their predictions on the future price of wheat, then the futures contract price would be forced down artificially. Having been forced down artificially, it would then reach a level where speculators would think, 'Hang on, that wheat futures price seems awfully low. I might buy some of those.' And then the price would swing back the other way…or maybe it wouldn't. Speculation is a dangerous game. But on it would go, backwards and forwards, until the expiry date loomed near. At the approach of the expiry date, the fluctuations would become less and less dramatic as all the traders will agree that the possible movements in the underlying price are less likely to be enormous with only a little time left before the futures price and the underlying price become one and the same. The price of the futures contract at any given time, therefore, is not necessarily an accurate prediction of what the price will be at expiry.

Let's just say that if you concede that futures trading does involve at least some concept of a crystal-ball approach, then you can rest assured that no one has yet produced the perfect crystal ball.

Now, back to those price fluctuations. I think it's safe to divide those factors that will affect a futures price into three categories. (1) Movements in the underlying price: if the underlying price of wheat rises for whatever reason, then the price of wheat futures will rise also. (2) Demand and supply: a large order to hedge a significant amount of wheat will more than likely force the price down in the short term. (3) Information: both the underlying price and the futures price will move on any new information that may affect future wheat prices. In the case of the underlying, a new price is set only when there is an actual sale of wheat. In the case of the futures, new prices are constantly being set without wheat changing hands.

The result of such fluctuations is that, at any time during the life of a futures contract, the price may be higher or lower than the physical price. When the futures price is higher than the physical price, the futures are said to be 'at a premium'. When the futures price is lower than the physical price, the futures are said to be 'at a discount'. Obviously if the price of the, say, June wheat future, is higher than the price of physical wheat, then the market is, as a whole, anticipating higher wheat prices come the end of June. Conversely, if the price of the June wheat future is lower than the price of physical wheat, then the market is anticipating that wheat prices will be lower.

Before there is any new information fed into the market that might have an affect on the wheat futures price, one must consider that the wheat futures price must *always* be higher than the physical price. This has absolutely nothing to do with harvest cycles or past trends or anything else to do with wheat. It's all about 'cash and carry'. No, we are not in the supermarket now. 'Cash and carry' relates to the natural *forward* price of wheat.

Cash and Carry

If you buy wheat today, you will pay for that wheat either out of funds at hand that might have been sitting in a bank account, or by borrowing the money to do so. If you take the money out of a bank account, you are then forgoing the interest that would otherwise have been paid on that money. If you borrow the money to pay for the wheat, then you are being charged an interest rate on that borrowing. If you then sold the wheat one month later, at exactly the same price at which you bought it, have you broken even? (Let's just ignore commissions etc and storage costs for the moment). The answer is no, because you either paid interest for a month, or forwent interest for a month, in order to hold the wheat for a month. In reality, you have lost that amount of interest and, therefore, you have lost on the trade. For you to have broken even, you would have needed to sell the wheat at a price above the price at which you first purchased the wheat. In other words, the break even equation is:

sale price = purchase price + interest.

Let's look at an example. You have money invested at 12% per annum. You decide to buy 100 tonnes of wheat at $172 per tonne. You also decide that you will sell the wheat in one month. It will effectively cost you 1% of the interest you would have otherwise received for the month that the wheat is held. Therefore, when you sell the wheat, you will need to receive both the $17,200 that you spent plus 1% of $17,200 that it cost you before you break even. That is you must receive $17,200 + $172 = $17,372. This price of $17,372 is known as the one month *forward* price. (And when talking about forward prices, it is the convention to refer to the physical price as the *spot* price).

Now not everyone deposits and borrows money at the same rate. So to determine a universal forward price at each date into the future, the convention is to adopt the most popular financing instrument, the bank bill, and take an interest rate from there. So the 90-day forward price of wheat is the physical price plus the 90-day bill rate. What all of this means for futures contracts is that before we start injecting information and views and hedging requirements into the futures price, our starting point will always be the forward price. And, therefore, as I said, the futures price must *always* be higher than the physical price. Well...that is until you do start injecting the hedging requirements and speculative views of the market participants. Then the futures price could end up anywhere, higher or lower than the physical. But if the market is higher, then the 'premium' of the futures price is really a premium to the forward price and not the spot price. And conversely, the 'discount' of the futures price is really a discount to the forward price and not to the spot price. In fact, a futures price may be higher than the physical (spot) price, yet still in a 'discount' to the forward price.

'Cash and carry' is the popular expression to describe the forward price. The physical price is the 'cash' and the interest charge is the 'carry'. Financial market people enjoy coming up with pithy expressions.

Contango

Now, on the subject of jargon, there are two expressions used in the futures markets to describe two particular situations. The first situation is where, despite the traditional fluctuation of futures prices over time, each successive futures month available for trading today is at a higher price than the one before. This is called 'contango'. Using the simple notion of 'cash and carry', ie the cost of interest increases over time, it is not hard to see why futures prices *should* increase with each successive contract month.

In the case of physical commodities, there is also a matter of storage. When the consumer of a commodity, such as wheat or copper, comes to make his (or her) purchases, then a decision has to be made as to just how much they will purchase. Do they purchase just the amount required at the time, or do they purchase in bulk and keep a decent stockpile for future use? Or, as we have discussed, do they buy ahead of time by purchasing futures contracts and taking delivery at a later date? In the first case, there is a risk that a temporary scarcity of the commodity could see them paying an inflated price. The second overcomes the risk of a short-term price squeeze but introduces other risks: the price of the commodity may fall, allowing competitors to buy their raw materials more cheaply while you are still running down your expensive stockpile, and the added cost of storing the commodity somewhere may offset the benefits of having a supply on hand.

This storage cost needs to be built into our 'cash and carry' equation such that more realistically:

forward price = spot price + interest cost + storage cost.

Buying futures now for later delivery would seem to overcome the short-term problems, but again a price decision has to be made. If the futures market is in contango, that is each successive contract month is trading at a higher price than the previous one because of interest and storage costs, then there may not prove to be a great benefit in buying ahead.

Difficult, isn't it? It just goes to reinforce the notion that although hedging removes the uncertainty, it may not produce the best result. But now let's look at storage from the supply side as well. A producer of a commodity also has some element of control over availability (and thus decisions to make as well). Do they produce only enough to meet short-term demand? Do they produce at a steady rate so that in times of low demand they stockpile, and in times of high demand they reduce the stockpile? (This is forced upon agricultural producers who only harvest at certain times of the year. They must stockpile to meet demand at non-seasonal times). Or, do they sell their as yet unavailable product ahead of time through the futures market, thus guaranteeing a price now?

Con-tango

All the producers and consumers will evaluate their own situations and make their decisions. This will then have a collective effect on both the spot price and the futures price of a commodity. It will also ensure that both will tend to move around a lot not only because of simple demand and supply, but also because of inventory situations (To store or not to store, that is the question). A commodity futures market should, one would expect, exhibit a natural contango, where prices increase into the future:

forward price = spot price + interest cost + storage cost.

But often we find that the price of the futures in each successive contract month is less than the one before. This is called 'backwardation'.

OPENING PRICES FOR VARIOUS FUTURES CONTRACTS LISTED ON THE CHICAGO BOARD OF TRADE AND THE NEW YORK MERCANTILE EXCHANGE ON FRIDAY, MAY 30, 1997.

CORN		CRUDE OIL	
July	273	July	20.96
September	260	August	21.05
December	256	September	21.05
		October	20.99

OATS		GOLD	
July	169	June	346.0
September	161	August	349.0
December	160	October	352.5
		December	358.8

WHEAT		COPPER	
July	363	June	1.187
September	370	July	1.197
December	382		

		PLATINUM	
		July	409.6
		October	403.0

Backwardation

Backwardation will occur because (1) there is a spot shortage, or (2) consumers will put off buying for as long as possible, or (3) producers are anxious to sell forward.

In the first case, a spot shortage may occur because neither the producers nor the consumers are holding sufficient inventories to meet the immediate demand. This will push up prices in the near-term, but not in the long-term, because producers will up production if possible to meet the demand and consumers will start hoarding to prevent getting caught out again. Thus the shortage will be temporary and prices into the future will be lower than they are today. A shortage may also occur due to some outside influence such as the weather (drought) or political influences (miners' strike).

The second case is closely related to the first. If a consumer is concerned about the high cost of storage and financing purchases, then he (or she) may only purchase raw materials at the absolute last minute to satisfy orders as they come in. The result of this is that demand is always greatest now rather than sometime in the future. Therefore, the spot price will be pushed higher than the price of the successive futures.

The third case relates specifically to the supply side. If a producer can forward-sell a commodity before it is produced, then the problems of storage costs and inventory management are eliminated. This also serves as a hedge against falling prices, particularly if a fall in price renders the production of that commodity uneconomical. If producers are keen to sell forward all the time, and consumers are more inclined to purchase on demand in the short-term, then successive futures prices will be pushed lower.

Most commodities will fluctuate between contango and backwardation depending on the state, and anticipated state, of inventories. Short-term specific events might serve to cause a blip in the succession of higher or lower prices. Some commodities do *tend* to be one or the other most of the time. Gold is probably the best example. As gold is nearly always stockpiled (eg at Fort Knox), then a contango is nearly always in place. Ensuring this situation is the fact that one can *borrow* gold just like one can borrow money. If you don't need to buy it yourself now, then you are not putting pressure on the spot price. (If you're wondering, reasons for why you may wish to borrow gold will come up later). Base metals, on the other hand, are *usually* in backwardation. This is because users of base metals, eg manufacturers, tend to use the metals all the time and don't feel the need to stockpile them. Grains, such as wheat, will fluctuate from one to the other and also exhibit both contango *and* backwardation at the same time between different futures months. This is because grains are harvested only once a year, unlike metals, which are being pulled out of the ground constantly, and so stockpiles will be greater after a harvest and lesser at planting time.

The previous table shows opening prices on a given day on the US exchanges. Note that wheat is in contango while corn and oats are in backwardation. This would imply a lack of corn and oats being held in silos at the time. Gold is exhibiting its traditional contango, while platinum is in backwardation which is normal for base metals. Copper is bucking the trend however, which is probably a result of the recent collapse in copper prices after the Sumitomo affair which would have caused a reluctance of producers to sell their copper into the depressed market and a preference to stockpile it for another day. Crude oil begins in contango and flattens before entering backwardation. Fluctuations in demand and supply or seasonal effects may be the cause here.

Fair Value

There is one 'commodity' that does not follow any particular trend of futures prices verses physical prices and that is the stock index. A stock index future still has a cash and carry price, because if you invest money in the stock market you are not receiving interest somewhere else, or you are paying interest somewhere else. However, in the case of the stock market there is another important factor. *Stocks pay dividends*, and so by holding stocks the interest cost is actually offset to some extent by the dividends you receive as an investor. The price of a stock index, remembering that a stock index represents an investment in a weighted amount of every stock in that index, will thus be adjusted by the value of all dividends paid on all stocks in the index. If you buy a stock index future, you will *not* receive the dividends, they are paid only to the holders of physical stock, but the value of the stock index will drop when the dividends flow out of the individual stocks in the index. The result is that the true cash and carry price of a stock index is:

spot price + interest cost - dividends paid

To confuse matters further, stock index traders tend to refer to this price as the 'fair value', and not the 'forward price'.

In Australia, dividends are usually paid twice a year at roughly the same time. When you divide the year into quarters, as the stock index futures market does, then we find that in two of the quarters, the ones where dividends are not being paid, the 'fair value' of the futures price will be higher than the physical price as in a normal cash and carry situation. In the two quarters where dividends are paid, the 'fair value' of the futures price will be closer to the physical price and may even be lower than the physical price. In order for the fair value to be *lower*, the value of dividends paid must exceed the interest cost over the period.

Now that we know what the fair value of a stock index future should be, we can pretty much ignore it. Stock index futures will fluctuate wildly, depending on the market's perception of future prices. One cannot 'stockpile' stocks so there are no inventory effects in the stock market. Futures prices are simply a reflection of new information entering the market all day, every day. If this information is perceived as good for the market, then the futures will trade at a premium. If the information is perceived as bad for the market, then the futures will trade at a discount. Most stock index futures will maintain a premium or discount for longish periods of time, but woe betide the trader who thinks this is an entrenched trend, for stock index futures can swing wildly from a premium to a discount in a very short space of time.

There is a mechanism, however, that ensures that premiums and discounts can only reach a certain size before they start to turn back again. This is called 'futures arbitrage', and it is the subject of the next chapter.

3. Arbitrage and Program Trading

Something for Nothing

'There's no such thing as a free lunch', or so the saying goes. Gordon Gekko[21] insisted, however, that 'Lunch is for wimps', but then Gordon Gekko used to like to make money with inside information—a situation where he was pretty much guaranteed a profit. But what if there were the opportunity to make a profit, legally, without any risk? You would surely jump at the chance!

The activity of making riskless profits is called 'arbitrage'. Let's say you knew of a company in Sydney that was desperately in need of widgets. They are prepared to pay up to $10 per widget so that they can meet there customers' demands. While on a trip to Perth you come across a company selling widgets for $7 each. A quick check with a freight company determines that the freight cost to Sydney would be $1 per widget. Immediately you buy up all the widgets on offer in Perth, and ship them to Sydney where you sell them for $10. You've cleared $2 per widget on the deal, risk-free, and you're not even sure what a widget is used for. You have just 'arbitraged' the widget market.

It is possible that you could keep this up for a while, but eventually, one would suspect. The Sydney and Perth companies would eventually become aware of each others' presence, and you would quickly be cut out of the deal. Never mind. You were simply exploiting a 'window of opportunity' that arose, albeit briefly, in the market. That is the nature of arbitrage in the financial markets. Occasionally prices do get out of whack, but usually only for a short time. The astute and fast-moving market player may occasionally have the opportunity to act upon a discrepancy and lock in the riskless trade—something for nothing.

When I was trading on the floor of the stock exchange in 1989, only partial computerisation of the market had occurred and most stocks were traded via the old chalkboards. Bid and offer prices for the various stocks were scribbled on the boards. Overlooking the floor were people with binoculars whose job it was to note the bids and offers and punch them into

---

21 As played by Michael Douglas in the classic exposé film of the eighties, Wall Street.

a computer so that screens in brokers' offices around the country could display the prices in next-to-real time. Sydney and Melbourne were the two major exchanges and the bids and offers of a particular stock, say BHP, were displayed on the screen side-by-side from both centres. *Occasionally* a big order would hit one exchange and not the other. Let's say the offer in BHP in both Sydney and Melbourne was $10. A big buyer comes into Melbourne (the smaller of the two markets) and buys up to $10.04, taking out sellers at $10 on the way, but still is not filled on the order. The screen will show an offer in Sydney at $10 and a bid in Melbourne at $10.04. If you were paying attention at the right time, *and if you were quick enough*, you could buy the offer in Sydney at $10, jump on the phone, and sell the bid in Melbourne at $10.04. If you achieved this successfully, you would have completed an arbitrage. You would have 4c per share for nothing. Mind you, if the bid in Melbourne was filled before your phone call got through, then you would be stuck with only one side of the deal, known in market parlance as having 'a leg in the air'. Needless to say, arbitrage opportunities were infrequent, and there was always the risk of missing out.

Opportunities for arbitrage have become less and less frequent with the advancement of market technology and the speed of information. Nowadays there is only one *Australian* Stock Exchange, traded all around the country on computer. Moreover, 'globalisation' has meant that the same commodity, traded anywhere in the world, is unlikely to trade at a different price to anywhere else in the world. If the price is different, the difference will usually reflect the exchange rate, shipping costs, different tax regimes or any number of other costs associated with buying a commodity in one country and selling it in another. That is, the price may be different , but no arbitrage opportunity exists. Gold is a good example of a commodity that often provided overseas arbitrage opportunities, right up to the early eighties. The Australian gold market would trade in Australia without a lot of thought given to the rest of the world, and the US gold market would also do its own thing. Often the two prices, after costs, would be quite different. A gold trader with access to more expedient information than the newspapers, could buy gold in Sydney hours, *book a trunk call* (would you believe) to the US for later that night, and sell on the open US market before anybody else woke up to the price discrepancies. Suffice to say, modern communication systems and information dissemination systems have nipped this opportunity in the bud.

The opportunity for commodity arbitrage has also been stilted by futures markets. Only producers and manufacturers deal in actual physical gold anymore. 'Paper trading' of gold via the futures market have wiped out most of the costs associated with trading gold and having to move it around. Futures markets, in combination with real-time communication across the globe, have also meant that only one or two centres in the world become the trading place for a commodity. With respect to gold, the major trading centre is the New York Mercantile Exchange.[22] When the focus is on one major centre, there is little opportunity for price discrepancies.

Futures markets may have done much to kill off commodity price arbitrage, but in so doing, they have opened up the opportunity for arbitrage of a different kind. Futures prices, by their nature, are usually different to the price of the underlying, physical commodity. Futures prices can fluctuate wildly, as we have noted. If this is so, then there must be times when the price of the future is quite different to the price of the physical. What possibilities could this present?

Futures Arbitrage

Let's stick to deliverable commodities, such as wheat, for a moment. When futures prices fluctuate away from their cash and carry prices, does this present opportunities for arbitrage? If the futures market is in backwardation, then obviously no opportunity exists to arbitrage the market. You can only buy wheat in physical form—you cannot sell something you don't have. There is no point, then, in buying wheat now and selling wheat futures at a lower price. This would result in you delivering wheat and receiving less than you paid for it. If, however, the futures are in contango, meaning the next futures month is at a higher price than the physical, then you can buy wheat now and sell it simultaneously in the futures market and therefore receive the higher price at delivery time. Of course, we have to take account of the cash and carry. If the amount of price difference between the physical and the future is simply the amount of the carrying costs, then we would not be winning from our buy physical-sell futures strategy. In order for us to arbitrage the market, the price of wheat futures must be higher than the cash and carry price. Does this ever happen?

The answer is yes, it can, but only infrequently, and only for a very short time. Remember that to pull off an arbitrage you must do both trades simultaneously, or as close as possible to simultaneously. Otherwise, as I

22 *NYMEX now incorporates the Commodities Exchange*
   (COMEX) where the gold contract is traded.

used to find with Sydney-Melbourne stock trades, you'll end up with a leg in the air. Remember also the chicken and egg problem. Do the futures follow the physical or the physical follow the futures? The answer was both. In some markets, the futures price will adjust to changes in the physical price. In other markets, particularly where trade in futures dominates trade in the physical commodity, the physical price will adjust to movements in the futures price. In yet other markets, it is often hard to tell who's leading whom, and sometimes one side will move because the other side moved, but they moved because the other side moved in the first place, and so they play leap frog until it dawns that nothing has actually changed. In all instances, the common denominator is that both sides are fully aware of the price of both the physical and future and any given moment.

So let's say you're watching a computer screen displaying the price of physical wheat and June wheat futures. Suddenly, a big buying order comes into the wheat futures and the price on the screen ticks up dramatically. *But the price of the physical wheat hasn't moved!* A quick calculation indicates that the future is now trading higher than the cash and carry price. You jump on the phone and sell wheat futures. Then you jump on the phone and try to buy physical wheat. To your dismay, the price quoted to you for the physical wheat is higher than the price on the screen. You hang up. As you hang up, you notice the physical price tick up on the screen to the price at which you were just offered physical wheat. All that's happened is that the order in the wheat futures has caught the physical price-makers off guard. The guy might have been reading the paper. But he has a screen in front of him as well by which he monitors activity in the futures market so that he's not blindly selling wheat to an arbitrageur such as yourself. It is virtually impossible to trick someone into providing you with an arbitrage. (By the way, better buy back those wheat futures).

Discrepancies in wheat prices will crop up from time to time (*crop up— get it?* Sorry). Maybe a futures buying order will simultaneously coincide with a physical selling order, but don't hold your breath. In fact, in most markets, the activity of inhaling and exhaling normally is recommended. The cash and carry price effectively puts a cap on futures prices. If the futures do exceed this price, then the physical price will rise to compensate. Below the cash and carry level, there are no arbitrage opportunities anyway.

There is one type of futures contract, however, where the difficulty in actually buying the underlying commodity, for the average punter, results in extended periods where the futures price is at a significant premium to the cash and carry price. Unlike most futures contracts, an opportunity for arbitrage clearly exists.

Stock Index Arbitrage

As you recall, a stock index is a number which represents the prices of a number of stocks weighted by their capitalisation (share price x number of shares). A stock index is a means of 'commoditising' the stock market and allowing for a single figure indicator of the movement of the stock market, in general, over whatever period. In Australia, the All Ordinaries index represents around 300 stocks from the biggest at the moment, News Corp, with 8.78% of the index, to the smallest at 0.0-something%. Listed on the Sydney Futures Exchange is the Share Price index future, which is a cash-settled contract over the AOI. The SPI is settled each quarter at the closing value of the AOI.

Like every futures contract, the SPI has a cash and carry price. In this case the 'carry' is the interest cost minus dividends paid on each stock during the period. Unlike most futures contracts, the SPI, and similar overseas stock index futures, often trade for long periods at a premium to the 'fair value' or cash and carry. At other times, they will sustain a hefty discount. If this provides the opportunity for arbitrage then (1) why does this occur, and (2) why aren't we all doing it?

To answer these questions, let's create our own, imaginary stock index.

The Readers' Own index consists of 10 stocks which we'll designate stocks A through J. The capital weighting of these stocks is, remarkably, 10% each. This means that the price of the ROI represents the share price x number of shares of each of A through J in equal weightings. There is also a futures contract over the ROI.

Presently the ROI is at 100. The fair value of the June ROI futures contract is 105 (ie the carry cost is 5 points). The market is positive, and the June ROI is trading at 125. If this were a wheat contact, we would immediately buy physical wheat at 100 and sell June wheat futures at 125, clearing a risk-free 20 points after costs at delivery time. But this is not a wheat contract. To 'buy' the ROI, we must buy 10 stocks in equivalent amounts while simultaneously selling June ROI futures. To lock in the arbitrage, we must sell the equivalent dollar value of futures to the dollar value of stocks we purchase. Well, that doesn't sound too hard, does it?

We decide to throw $100,000 at it. (Does that seem a lot? Well, it is an arbitrage). We ring the stockbroker and place orders to buy $10,000 worth of each of A, B, C etc. As the reportings come back from the broker, we will call a futures broker and sell the equivalent amount of June futures at 125 and eventually lock in the 20 points ($20,000 arbitrage profit).

The broker calls back and reports that we have bought all of our A, B, C, D and E, some of our F, G and H but as yet none of our I and J. We sell some futures. While waiting for further reportings, we notice that the ROI value has slipped to 98 and the futures are now trading at 120. Not only has our arbitrage margin narrowed, but also the bids we put in for our stocks were at a price that reflected an ROI level of 100, not 98. We have to pull back our buying prices! Another call to the stockbroker reveals that the F and G have already been filled so we were too slow to pull back there. The H, I and J, however, we manage to cancel and replace the order at a lower price. We sell more futures. The broker calls again and tells us that the H and I have been filled but there just don't seem to be any sellers in J. We sell some futures at 120 but some of them we have to sell at 118. The ROI slips to 95 and the futures to 110. Not surprisingly, our J order is filled before we can move the price down again. We sell the last futures at 110. Oh well, our arbitrage wasn't perfect, but a final calculation reveals that we did manage to lock in 12 points, so that's a tidy profit of $12,000, less, of course, commissions and fees. It would seem that arbitraging the ROI is a worthwhile exercise.

Okay, back to the real world. Try doing that with 300 stocks! And every single one of them with a different weighting to any other. None of this tidy 10% each business. I think you'd agree, it would be a logistical nightmare. You would just about have to have the stockbroker on the phone permanently, the futures broker on the phone permanently, and a computer to keep track of what you've bought, what you haven't bought, and how many futures you need to sell. What's more, it would take more than a day to get all the fills in all the stocks. It might take a week. And all the time the AOI and the SPI would be moving around, causing you to have to readjust your orders. In fact, the futures price may well return to a level where there is no premium to fair value. And you're only halfway through! What do you do now? Sell everything?

It may have become apparent why a stock index future will trade at a premium despite the 'on paper' opportunity it might suggest for arbitrage.

The premium is created because the stock market is positive and buyers are anticipating higher future prices. The scramble to buy futures will push the futures price well above the physical price. These levels will be sustained because, for the average market participant, the process of arbitraging the market is just too damned hard. Even for most institutional players, with teams of dealers and sophisticated computers, it's still too hard. And although we have given little consideration to commissions and fees, they do cut quite a hole in the profits, which is another reason why institutions usually forsake arbitrage opportunities.

Replication and Risk-Arbitrage

Is there a way around these problems? Yes, there is. But the solutions are usually still outside the realms of the average individual market player or even institution. Firstly, it is almost imperative that you *own* a stock-broking operation and secondly, that you have bucket-loads of capital. Thirdly, you need a pretty sexy computer program.

If you own your own stock-broking operation, you have direct access to the market. Not only are you able to see immediate changes in stock prices via your Australian Stock Exchange-issued market computer (issued *only* to stockbrokers), but you can also place and replace orders immediately and directly. No phone calls. And what's more, no commission costs. Bucket-loads of capital are required because, let's face it, mucking around in hundreds of stocks and running the risk of not being able to buy all that you need in a short space of time, lest you run the risk of the premium disappearing mid-arbitrage, is not a worthwhile exercise with trifling amounts of money.

If you conservatively make the assumption that a premium, on the screen, of 20 points, may only realistically yield 10 when it's all said and done, then you need to throw a decent amount of capital at it to make the exercise worthwhile in the first place. The computer program is needed because, realistically, you *cannot* buy 300 stocks. About half of those stocks are so illiquid, meaning they trade only on occasion and not always in sufficiently large amounts, that buying the right amounts of each in the time available is, in fact, impossible. What a computer program will allow you to do is 'replicate' the All Ordinaries index.

So what does it mean, to 'replicate' the AOI? Well, let's go back to our Reader's Own index again. Originally the ROI consisted of stocks A through to J in equal 10% weightings. Let's assume now, more realistically, that the stocks are not equally weighted. The new weightings are listed in this table.

Weightings of the ROI	
STOCK	% OF ROI
A	25
B	20
C	15
D	12
E	10
F	7
G	5
H	3
I	2
J	1
	100

We know from our previous experience that stocks G, H, I and J are pretty difficult to get immediately and at the right price. They are only small companies and they don't trade very often. A glance at our weightings table reveals that together, G, H, I, and J make up a total of only 11% of the index. This means that if we reduced the number of stocks that we trade for our arbitrage to 6 instead of 10 we would still have covered 89% of the ROI and sped up the process, as we don't have to hang around waiting for sellers in the other 4 stocks. Actually, while we're at it, let's dump F as well. It's only 7%. This leaves us with a tidy 5 stocks which still represent 82% of the index. Statistically, 82% is pretty good. What we have done is taken a 'basket' of 5 stocks to 'replicate' the ROI.

Putting on the arbitrage now is a hell of a lot easier. The top 5 stocks are liquid and easier to buy quickly, which is what we need to be able to exploit our brief window of opportunity. To complete the replication, we need to 're-weight' our basket of 5 stocks to equal 100% again. Multiply each original weighting by 100/82 and we get: A, 30.5%; B, 24.4%; C, 18.3%; D, 14.6% and E, 12.2%. These are the proportions in which we will buy the five stocks.

There has to be a trade-off, however, and in this situation the trade-off is something called 'tracking error'. As we have only covered 82% of the index, there is still 18% of the index which will do its own thing. If we bought all 10 stocks when the index was 100, and sold the right amount of futures at 125, come expiry we will hope to lock in 20 points after costs (not including commissions and fees). If we only buy our basket of 5 stocks when the market is 100, and sell futures at 125, come expiry time our 20 point profit is not assured. We have not held all the stocks that affect a change in the value of the ROI. Nor will we achieve a straightforward 82% of 20 points—16.4 points. It doesn't work that way. If this were the case, then every stock would need to move, up or down, in *exactly the same proportion*. This just doesn't happen. Stocks will move up and down, in any old amount they like. The index simply serves to give an overall average of the amount of price movement of each of the stocks. In fact, a change of price in any one stock will actually cause a total re-weighting of *all of the stocks in the index*. The index, at any point in time, is merely a snapshot.

What this means is that even if we bought all 10 stocks in the ROI for our arbitrage, we could not just set and forget. We would need to constantly buy and sell small amounts of each stock as their weightings changed. We might do this once a week, or daily, or even intra-day if we wished to maintain an exact equivalent of the ROI. But having done this with a reasonable amount of accuracy, our 20 points is still quite obtainable.

But now we're only buying 5 stocks. Although the stocks we left out only represent 18% of the index, that 18% was measured in the snapshot on the day we put on the arbitrage. If those remaining 5 stocks were to move significantly over the period before expiry, their weighting would increase. Any increase in weighting of those 5 stocks would result in an erosion of our possible 20-point profit. In other words, our basket would not correctly 'track' the ROI and we would have 'tracking error'. The activity of replication therefore introduces a new risk into the activity of index arbitrage and thus it is more correctly a 'risk-arbitrage'. (The definition of arbitrage is a 'riskless' trade so 'risk-arbitrage' is strictly a contradiction of terms. But you get the point.)

Back to the real world once more. Risk-arbitrage is an activity conducted by those in the market who have the capacity to pull it off. Usually they are stockbrokers with the backing of a bank or merchant bank. The bank provides the capital and the computer programming ability. A computer program is necessary to run replications and re-weightings—in short, to tell the trader exactly what he (or she) needs to buy or sell and in what amounts. Direct access to the market through the stock-broking operation provides the logistical requirement that arbitrage demands.

Arbitrage in Australia

Arbitrageurs in the Australian market will replicate the AOI with baskets of between about 20 and 120 stocks out of the 300 odd. The cumulative percentage column in the top 100 stocks at the time of writing revealed that the top 20 stocks represent 59% of the AOI, 50 stocks provide 78% and 100 stocks provide 91%. When 'putting on' an arbitrage, the arbitrageur will start with the highest weighted stocks and build his (or her) basket, as the opportunity provides, until he (or she) is satisfied with the number of stocks and the level of replication they provide. If the window of opportunity is brief, ie the futures go into premium only for a short time, maybe a day, then the arbitrageur may have to be satisfied with just

20 to 50 stocks. If the premium is sustained for a longer period, maybe a month, then the arbitrageur can continue to build the basket and improve the replication.

The Hong Kong Experience

In October, 1987, the Hong Kong stock index, the Hang Seng, was surging along with the rest of the world. The futures contract on the index was also surging and maintaining a significant premium. A large proportion of the futures position was held by local Chinese families—the movers and shakers of Hong Kong. The sell-side was largely held by foreign banks who were conducting arbitrage and were holding long stock positions as a result.

The day before the crash, the Hang Seng index closed at 3362.4 and the futures closed at 3695 (a 331.6 point premium to the physical). When the Dow Jones collapsed overnight, the head of the Hong Kong Stock Exchange panicked and closed the doors of the exchange for four days. When it finally reopened, the index finished the day at 2241.7, a fall of 33%. The futures, having spent three days of suspended trading, due to the downside limits that were in place, finally traded again at 2195, a significant discount.

The local families were mortified. The arbitrageurs were ecstatic. But their ecstasy soon turned to horror when the local families, exploiting the fact that there was no legislation in place, refused to pay. This meant that not only had the foreign banks not made the millions they thought they had, they had incurred a serious loss on the stock side with no futures gains to offset. After extreme protest, the families finally agreed to settle halfway—short shrift. Although a Futures Act and a more satisfactory margining system were later put into place, it was years before foreign banks would touch the Hong Kong Futures Exchange again.

Not every arbitrage strategy is held to expiry. If an arbitrage is put on at a premium today, and the futures then fall back to fair value or discount, then the arbitrageur will 'unwind' the position, which simply means selling all the stocks and buying back the futures. This situation is advantageous for the arbitrageur for two reasons: tracking error usually becomes worse over time, so the shorter the time, the less the expected tracking error, and the opportunity to unwind at a discount adds to the profit potential of the arbitrage. At the other end of the scale, arbitrage positions are not necessarily closed out at expiry time. It may be that the next futures contract is also in a premium to its fair value (and in fact it is usually the case that if the near month contract is at a premium, then the next month contract will also be at a premium). If this is so, then the arbitrageur will leave the stock positions in place and simply 'roll' the futures position. To roll the futures position you simultaneously buy back the near month and sell the next month. A disadvantage of doing this is that you are continuing to extend the time in which tracking error may erode your profits. But there is one big advantage of rolling your futures position.

The SPI is *non-deliverable*. At expiry time, the winners will receive cash and the losers will hand over cash. If we were arbitraging the wheat market we would buy physical wheat and sell the futures contract. At expiry we would hand over the physical wheat in exchange for cash. If it is an arbitrage, then the amount of cash we receive will be more than the amount we paid to buy the wheat in the first place. You cannot, however, deliver the stock index. A stock index arbitrage will result in either the futures side making money when the futures price falls, or the stock side making money when the stock market rises. Either way, in a successful arbitrage the amount you win on one side will be more than you lose on the other. That is the nature of arbitrage. The futures side is cash-settled, but in order to cash in the stock side you must first sell all the stock. What this leads to is the possibility that arbitrageurs will decide to dump their entire basket of stocks on the day of expiry. All that stock being sold will usually have quite a negative effect on the market that day. The negative effect will be exacerbated if two or more arbitrageurs are scrambling over each other to get rid of all their stock before the final bell. Not only will the arbitrageurs then stuff up everybody else in the market, but there's a good chance that they will also stuff up each other, as scrambling to sell stocks will only serve to erode the premium they've been looking forward to all that time.

You may have read a stock market report in the newspaper that puts the movement in the market that day down to 'arbitrage activity' or 'unwinding of arbitrage positions' or 'futures-related selling'. Sometimes these reports are accurate and sometimes they're not. If they are inaccurate it is because the reporter was talking to a contact who was not themselves involved in arbitrage, but surmised that it *must* have been arbitrage that moved the market today. In many cases, the reporter doesn't understand what it all means anyway. But suffice to say, arbitrage activity, at its height, has a very significant effect on the stock market. When arbitrageurs are buying stocks, everyone is usually happy. As the stocks are a lot harder to get than the futures, the 'putting on' of arbitrage positions has a tendency to push the market up. You might expect that the subsequent selling of futures would then push that market down, closing the opportunity for arbitrage. This makes perfect sense, but the reality is that when the stock market is rising, people buy futures as well as stock. So usually there are enough futures contracts being sought after to satisfy the arbitrage selling and so maintain the premium. If the futures buyers knew they were probably buying from arbitrageurs, then they may not be very happy. This would imply that the market was being pushed up artificially, and that the strength is unlikely to be maintained. But not everyone is aware when arbitrage activity is occurring.

The fun begins, however, when arbitrageurs are unwinding. This typically has a negative effect on the market and most market participants are not happy when the market is going down. (The more astute players see arbitrage unwinding as an opportunity to pick up stocks quite cheaply, but more astute players are not the majority). The situation gets really bad when arbitrageurs 'put on' a position when the futures are at a discount. Hang on. How can they do that? That would mean *selling* stock and *buying* futures. And you can't sell stock you don't already own. Can you?

Short-Selling and Discount Arbitrage

In actual fact, you *can* sell shares that you don't already own. This is called 'short-selling' and there are various rules that apply before you can dive in and start shorting BHP. For starters, not every stock can be short-sold. The ASX has a list of about 200 stocks which are eligible, and eligibility depends very much on liquidity. For the average punter—the investor-on-the-street—some stockbrokers will allow you to short-sell a stock if you adhere to a margining system similar to that of the futures market. As with the futures market, the broker will need to be happy with your financial credentials before this is allowed. Larger players, specifically banks, are exempted from the margin system provided they are capitalised beyond a certain amount. Another way to avoid margining is to *borrow* the stock you wish to sell. Once you have bought back the stock on the market, you simply return the stock to the lender. All the while the lender of the stock still appears on the register as the *beneficial owner* of the stock. Borrowing is not really open to small punters. Lenders are only willing to part with their stock to someone with sufficient financial backing, and usually significant amounts of collateral are required.

The borrowing and lending of stock, sometimes called 'stock-banking', is big business. Lenders of stock are typically large local or overseas funds that maintain long-term core positions of top Australian stocks in their portfolios. As they have no intention of selling these positions in the short-term, they are happy to lend the stock for short periods and charge a fee for doing so. This fee will then enhance the return of the portfolio over the longer term. So why short-sell stock? Is it simply to take advantage of perceived weakness of a particular share price over a short period? This does happen among professional stock market traders, but it is not the main impetus. The main impetus is for the hedging of option positions and for negative arbitrage. We shall be learning all about options in the next chapter, so for the moment let's just stick to negative arbitrage.

Negative arbitrage will come into play when the stock index futures are at a discount to the physical index. The arbitrageur will sell stock (which has been borrowed for the purpose) and simultaneously buy futures. It is no different to positive arbitrage, just the other way around. At the end of the futures contract, when the price of the futures is the same as the physical, the shorted stock is bought back or the futures are rolled. The borrowed stock is handed back to the lender.

Just as positive arbitrage has a tendency to push the market up, negative arbitrage has a tendency to push the market down. There is a popular saying in financial circles that stock markets 'go up by the stairs and down by the elevator'. This is because when signs are good, the market will push along steadily and will only begin to accelerate as more and more investors feel they are missing out when the market appears to be strong. When signs are bad, however, *everyone* wants out. Panic can set in and this is what leads to stock market crashes. Have you ever heard of a stock market crashing up? If the stock index futures are at a discount to the physical, then there is already a certain amount of uneasiness. The futures market is suggesting that the stock market is going to go lower from here. People are edgy. Then in the middle of a tense situation in come the arbitrageurs. The arbitrageurs will start selling stock across the board and, despite the fact that the arbitrageurs are countering the selling by buying futures, this will cause stock buyers to retreat further. A downward spiral can easily result.

In the late eighties some Australian funds managers tried hard to outlaw arbitrage. At that time, post-crash, the market was weak and the funds managers perceived that arbitrage was simply exacerbating the situation.

What's more, in the fallout from the '87 crash in the US, arbitrage was being blamed as another potential cause. The ASX decided not to outlaw the activity and this proved a sensible move once the Gulf War began and world stock markets started to rally once more. No one complains, as I have said, when arbitrage pushes a market up. But realistically, what does arbitrage provide apart from profits for the few large players that have the capability to engage in it? Some would argue that arbitrage reduces the volatility of stock markets by reigning in the stock index futures when the market is moving rapidly in one direction. In my experience, this is not the case. Arbitrage usually adds to the volatility at the times that positions are being put on and taken off. There is no doubt, however, that arbitrage does serve to add liquidity to the market. Liquidity is important so that legitimate buyers and sellers of stock have a tight market in which they can trade.

There is one problem that occasionally does arise, however, and that is when the humans hand control of arbitraging over to the computers.

Program Trading

In the US, and in other financial centres, stock index arbitrage is known as 'program trading'. The reason it is called program trading is due to the use of computers in the exercise. I have mentioned how computers are required to replicate the AOI and keep track of positions and weightings during arbitrage activity in Australia. In the US, the main stock index used for arbitrage purposes is the S&P 500 which is an index of 500 stocks listed on the New York Stock Exchange. The Chicago Mercantile Exchange provides a futures contract over this index. Given the sheer size of the US stock market, virtually every one of the 500 S&P stocks is liquid enough to include in the basket for arbitrage purposes, thus eliminating the need for replication. So where do the computers come in?

It would still be nigh on impossible to place orders and receive fills for 500 stocks in the space of time that arbitrage opportunities usually allow. This is overcome in the US by allowing computers to generate and place the orders simultaneously. In this way, a lot of the human factor is removed. One simply programs the computer to monitor the premium/discount situation between the futures and the physical. When the gap reaches a particular, pre-determined level, the computer can place all the necessary orders instantaneously and more or less conduct the arbitrage by itself. The computer can be programmed to place a certain size of order at the first gap level and to increase the size of the orders as the gap increases. The computer can also adjust prices as the market moves, which allows it to 'chase' the stock prices if the futures are still moving in the right direction. What a bonus! Just sit back and let the computer do all the work!

However, computers don't usually have the capacity to know when enough is enough and when what they are doing may be potentially damaging. This was the case in the crash of '87. As the market teetered, and turned from its high point, the futures went into a discount. An army of computers flickered into life. The selling would have started slowly but it quickly gained momentum. Remember portfolio insurance? Panicky funds managers by now were desperately selling S&P 500 futures to offset the losses on the falling stock prices. As the discount widened, the computers simply stepped up a gear and sold more and more stock. Stock prices continued to fall, more futures were sold, more stock was sold, stock prices continued to fall, we all know the result. Five hundred plus points on the Dow Jones later, the final bell rang and the carnage was evident.

Program trading thus became another target of those commissioned with the task of finding a reason for the carnage. Computers were the main offender. Again, I will say that the activities of portfolio insurance and program trading merely served to exacerbate the situation on the day—the non-existence of these activities would not have prevented an inevitable serious market correction. How many computers were active in 1929? One result of the witch-hunt was to introduce a 'circuit-breaker' to the futures market. If the futures fall by a certain amount in one day, then all trading is ceased. Without the futures, arbitrage and portfolio insurance is not possible. The circuit-breaker allows everyone to pause and reflect and possibly put a halt to the out-of-control snowball, at least in the short-term. At the end of the day, if a market wants to go down, it will.

Does program trading occur in Australia? Absolutely. It took some time to catch up with the Americans on this score, but the computerisation of the ASX's SEATS system, including more friendly interface with brokers' computers, has meant that swathes of buy and sell orders can be placed in seconds. Should we panic now? No. Program trading is conducted almost continuously now as the SPI futures swings through premium and discount. In most cases it has little noticeable effect on the market and in fact provides much needed liquidity a lot of the time. So we can feel safe that computers *won't* have an overly damaging impact in any further serious downturn? I assure you— history is riddled with examples of people *not* learning from the past.

4. Options Warrant Attention

A Matter of Choice

At this stage of the book, you may choose to keep reading, or you may choose to take a break and watch some television. It's *your* choice. To put it another way, we could say that you have the option to keep reading, or the *option* to take a break. It's your book, you have the *right* to keep reading if you want to, but in no way are you *obliged* to do so. It's your option—the ball is in your court.

So, I see you've exercised your right to keep reading. It's always nice to have a choice, isn't it? You might call it 'keeping your options open'.

The word 'option' is an easy one to bandy about, and one that I'm sure most of us have used many-a-time in our everyday pursuits. 'I have the option to do this or do that.' Or: 'I haven't decided whether to go ahead yet, but I do have the option.' It is also a word used to describe a particular type of financial instrument. We are familiar with the fact that 'having the option' implies having a choice, and the right to decide one way or another what course of action to take, so what exactly is an option that can be traded in the markets, and appears to get quite a fair amount of attention in the newspapers?

Options and Warrants

For the average person, the share market is the most visible form of financial market, and perhaps the only market in which they have some direct contact. For this reason I have chosen to commence my explanation of options using the share market as the example.

There have been options traded on the Australian share market since the 1960s, and they are still big business today. Volumes in exchange-traded options have fallen slightly in recent years, however, and one of the reasons for this drop-off is the rise to prominence of another form of derivative instrument—the share warrant.

For those of you already familiar with share warrants, be assured of one important thing—a warrant is just an option. But for a couple of minor points of detail, they are interchangeable. Therefore, I will ask you to follow the ensuing explanation of the nature of options knowing that exactly the same applies in the case of warrants. Where there are differences, and there are a couple that are significant, I shall point those out as we go along. Those of you familiar with even sexier products, such as endowment warrants, can check such animals out in a later chapter.

So let's talk options.

Something for Nothing?

For the purpose of our discussion, let's create a fictitious stock. We'll call it United Consolidated Inc (or UCI). At the moment, it is possible to buy UCI shares in the market for $15.00.

Assume you've decided that the UCI share price was likely, in your opinion, to go higher in the next three months. The normal course of action would be to call a stockbroker and buy some UCI shares. If your opinion proves to be correct, you will make money. If, on the other hand, you are wrong, you will lose money. That's life in the big city.

But what if I said I would do a deal with you whereby you don't buy the UCI shares in the market now for $15.00, but rather you buy them in three-months time from *me* for $15.00. That way if the share price has risen—let's say to $16.00—then you can sell the shares you brought from me and make a $1.00 profit. Wonderful. Well, yes, but what difference will it make whether you buy the shares in the market or buy them from me? Either way you will make $1.00.

All right, let me then put in a bit of a sweetener. If the price of UCI falls in the three-month period—say to $14.00—then *you don't have to buy them at $15.00*. In fact, you don't have to buy them at all.

That's right. I will sell you the UCI shares, in three-months time, at $15.00, but only if you want to buy them. If you don't want to buy them, well...hey, that's no problem. It's your choice.

On that basis you would probably not hesitate to go ahead with the deal I'm offering. Why wouldn't you? I am providing you with the opportunity to make a profit without the risk of any loss. Just put off the decision for three months and see if your opinion was correct. If it was—make money. If it wasn't—do nothing. Seems like rather a good idea.

What I have offered you is known in the trade as a 'call option'. I have agreed to sell you UCI at $15.00, if you want. In three-months time, you may 'call' in the shares I have offered you, which you would undoubtedly do if the price of UCI was greater than $15.00. If the price of UCI was less than $15.00, then there would be no point in calling in the shares—we assume you don't wish to deliberately make a loss—and I probably wouldn't hear from you. It's *your* option. The standard text-book definition of a call option is that it is an instrument that provides the holder with 'the right but not the obligation' to purchase something at a given price at a given time. In our case you have the *right* to buy UCI at $15.00 in three-months time, but you are not *obliged* to do so.

If you do exercise your right to buy the UCI—maybe the price has risen to $16.00—you will receive UCI shares at $15.00. Thus $15.00 is known as the 'exercise price'. Alternatively, you could say we struck a deal on UCI at $15.00, and therefore $15.00 is known as the 'strike price'. The terms 'exercise price' and 'strike price' mean exactly the same thing, and are totally interchangeable. In any call option, the exercise or strike price is the price at which you will receive that commodity should you decide to 'call' it.

The exercise price must be agreed upon at the beginning of the deal. So too must the 'time to maturity'. In this case, our 'time to maturity' (sometimes also called 'duration', or other words to that effect) is three months. We can also say that the option 'expires' in three months. The exercise price and the time to maturity are two of the most important factors affecting the price of a call option.

Whoa! Did he just say *price* of a call option?

Yes, he did. Come on, you didn't really think you were going to get something for nothing did you? These are the financial markets. The truth of the matter is that a call option provides the holder with the choice of exercising or not exercising the option, that is calling or not calling the stock at the predetermined price, depending on whether a profit will result. This choice comes at a price, and that price is called the option 'premium'.

Weighing up the Option

I will give you the choice of buying UCI in three-months time for $15.00. In return I want you to give me 50c *now*. If you decide not to go ahead and buy the UCI at $15.00, then you will lose the 50c. That is the price to pay for having the choice.

Now you will want to think more carefully about whether buying a call option is really what you want to do. Your view is simple enough—you believe that UCI has a good chance of rising over the next three months. Buying the shares directly gives you a clear-cut result. If you are right you will make a profit, and if you are wrong you will make a loss. If the share price rises from $15.00 to $16.00, you have made $1.00. If the share price falls from $15.00 to $14.00, you have lost $1.00. Of course share markets can sometimes be rather erratic. Maybe there will be a real run on UCI over the period and the price rises to $18.00. Way to go! $3.00 profit! Then again, something that you just didn't expect may surface in the meantime ('*UCI boss sacked over fraud allegations*'. Or: '*Mass walk-out of UCI employees*') and the share price falls to $12.00. A $3.00 loss.

What can a call option do for you? Let's say you decide to pay 50c now to have the option to buy UCI in three-months time at $15.00. If the price in three-months time is $16.00, then you exercise the option, sell the shares for $16.00 and bank $1.00. Your initial outlay was 50c, so your profit is 50c. If the price in three-months time is $14.00, then you will not exercise the option, but your loss is the initial outlay—50c. How does this compare to simply buying the shares?

If our two possible outcomes are a price of either $16.00 or $14.00 in three-months time, then buying the shares gives us the two outcomes of a $1.00 profit or a $1.00 loss. Buying the call option gives us the two outcomes of a 50c profit or a 50c loss. This comparison is hardly likely to have you rushing to buy the call option every time. But now compare the more erratic scenario. If our two possible outcomes are a share price of either $18.00 or $12.00 in three-months time, then buying the shares will provide the two outcomes of a $3.00 profit or a $3.00 loss. Buying the call option, however, will give us the upside result of $3.00 minus the 50c premium for a profit of $2.50, and the downside result of, well, just the premium cost—a 50c loss.

What this means is that the outright purchase of shares will result in an equivalent amount of profit and loss for each dollar the share price moves on the upside or the downside. The purchase of a call option, however, will provide an unbalanced result. On the upside a dollar for dollar increase in profit will result, minus the cost of the premium. On the downside the loss will only ever be the cost of the premium, no matter how far the share price may fall in the period. Bear in mind that the premium is set at the beginning of the deal and can never be altered—it is always a known quantity.

The following table compares our profit and loss result for a share holding or a call option holding given various potential prices for our UCI shares in three-months time. Bear in mind, we have paid 50c for the option.

PRICE OF UCI SHARES	P/L ON SHARES	P/L ON CALL OPTIONS
20.00	5.00	4.50
19.00	4.00	3.50
18.00	3.00	2.50
17.00	2.00	1.50
16.00	1.00	0.50
15.00	0.00	-0.50
14.00	-1.00	-0.50
13.00	-2.00	-0.50
12.00	-3.00	-0.50
11.00	-4.00	-0.50
10.00	-5.00	-0.50

This table provides a comparison of profit and loss for our two investment choices—buying the shares or buying call options. If the share price rises, the results look fairly similar—only the premium cost provides the difference. However, if the share price falls, the results are quite different. When holding a call option, the loss can never increase—it will only ever be the cost of the premium, and we know from the beginning exactly what this cost will be.

The most important benefit of an option lies in the control of *risk*. The financial markets are all about risk. The risk of prices rising and falling. The risk of investing in a company over which you have no control. The risk of devastating influences from overseas markets, from wars and tempest, from government policy changes. The risk of drilling a hole and not finding oil. The risk of digging a hole and not finding gold. The risk of producing a widget that no one will buy or growing a crop that no one will eat. In short, if you invest your money in something—*anything*—there is always a risk you will lose it. Buying an option, on the other hand, provides a means of controlling the risk. In fact risk is reduced simply to the chance that you will lose the premium paid for the option—an amount that is known from the start—rather than the risk that you will lose the shirt off your back. As long as one is comfortable with losing that premium, then one can maintain a peace of mind and, let's face it, sleep at night.

A comparison of the risk of a share purchase versus the risk of a call option purchase is probably best illustrated graphically. Fig. 2 highlights the difference in profit and loss resulting from equivalent movements in the share price of UCI.

Fig. 2—Profit & Loss of Buying Shares vs Buying Calls

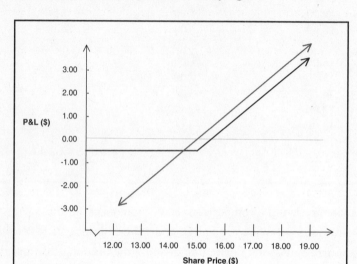

Another Benefit

The ability to control risk is by far the greatest advantage that an option provides. There is, however, another benefit in purchasing an option rather than purchasing a share. You may recall in Chapter 2 we discussed various benefits of buying wheat futures rather than buying wheat, or maybe buying shares in a company that grows wheat. A significant benefit in buying futures is *leverage*. As the purchase of a futures contract requires only the payment of a deposit, and an ongoing margin, rather than a payment of the full value of the futures contract, then the purchase of a futures contract requires a lot less money to be invested for the purpose of making a profit.

An option works the same way. If you decide to buy 1,000 shares in UCI at $15.00 because you believe that the price is going to rise in the next three months, then you will have to pay for them. That is, you will need to put up or borrow $15,000 which will not earn any interest for you once it is replaced by UCI shares. (Unless a dividend is paid during the period.

Dividends and share options have an important relationship that we will address a bit later.) If you buy the option to buy 1,000 shares at $15.00 in three-months time, or, put another way, 1,000 options to buy UCI shares for $15.00, then right now you need only put up the premium cost, in this case 1,000 x 50c or $500.00. Given the nature of an option, $500.00 is what we know is all you can lose. At the end of the three-month period, you will decide whether or not you will exercise the option. If you decide to exercise the option, *then* you will have to come up with the $15,000. A call option is an option to *buy* those shares in three-months time, and thus in exercising it, you are then obliged to buy the shares. This suggests that the leverage inherent in options is only temporary, which is true, but remember that your decision to exercise the option will be based on the fact that it is beneficial to you. If the price of UCI is now $16.00, giving you a profit of 50c, then you may choose to sell the shares immediately after exercising them. That way you will need to put in $15,000, but you will simultaneously receive $16,000. Alternatively, you can put up $15,000 and hang onto the shares for a further ride in the market (but your risk control has now expired).

There is a way to avoid putting up the $15,000 altogether while still benefiting from the rise in the share price to $16.00, and that is to actually *sell* the option rather than exercise it. But now we're getting ahead of ourselves. Bear in mind that options provide leverage, as well as risk control, and let's first have a closer look at that 50c price of the call option.

Insurance

You may well decide at this point that call options are so beneficial, from the point of view of risk reduction, that you'd be mad to ever buy straight shares again. This same principal is one that you have most likely applied to the decision to comprehensively insure your car.

If you're driving around in a $20,000 car and have a decent prang, it might cost you $10,000 to fix it. You might as well pay the $10,000 to fix the car because that's still a lot better than forking out another $20,000 for a new one. You now have a car that's cost you $30,000 but that you wouldn't be able to sell for $20,000. Unlucky. Of course what you could do is pay, say, $800 every year to an insurance company to insure against the cost of having to pay your own repair costs in the event of an accident. The $800 is your insurance *premium*. If you do prang the car, then $800 (plus excess) is what you'll pay instead of $10,000. Seems like a pretty sensible deal. But what if your $20,000 car is in fact a fully restored 1960s British sports car? The insurance company is going to look at the greater risk of having an accident in an old car and the greater cost it would involve to fix it. Consequently, the insurer may expect you to pay not $800 but $2,000 each year as a premium to insure this particular vehicle. Paying $2,000 a year on a $20,000 car? Is it worth it?

This you will have to weigh up. What are your chances of having an accident? Will you just take the risk rather than part with $2,000 every year? The bottom line here is that your decision to insure your car will be dependent on the premium you have to pay to do so, and whether you are happy to take the risk or not. The lower the premium, the more likely you are to insure. The higher the premium, the more likely you are to run the risk. As you may have guessed by now, the same goes for call option premiums.

A 50c premium on a $15.00 stock may seem a reasonable price to pay for protection against the price of the stock falling. Or, if you like, *insurance* against the price of the stock falling. What if the option premium—the cost of the option—were $1.50? Would it still be worth it? This would mean that the price of the shares would have to rise to $16.50 before you were even making money (see Fig 2). At what price does it cease to be worth it? The answer to this question is, I'm sorry to say, that there is no answer. Just as two different people would come up with two different decisions about insuring the same car, so would two different people have a differing view on the value of buying a call option at a certain price. That's why we have a 'market'. When you insure your car you are at the mercy of the insurance companies. You can shop around for the best price but ultimately you will have to pay the price that someone else has set. Likewise, when you buy a call option you will have to pay the price at which someone else is prepared to sell it to you.

What then would affect your decision? Is the price on offer justifiable? It is not difficult to see why an insurance company would expect a higher premium for a rare and mechanically primitive motor car. Within the cost of the premium, the insurer has considered the risk of an accident and the subsequent cost of repairs. When someone offers you a call option at a certain premium, they too have taken certain factors into consideration. Factors that would raise or lower the price at which they're willing to sell. Let's have a look at these factors.

We're in the Money

We have made a decision that we want to buy shares in UCI. At the moment they are offered at $15.00 per share. We could buy the actual shares or we may decide to buy a call option which allows us to buy the shares in three-month's time at $15.00. The $15.00 is the 'exercise' or 'strike' price. Because the exercise price is the same as the price of the shares, then the call option is said to be 'at-the-money'.

Let's say we go ahead and buy the option. The share price is $15.00 and the exercise price is $15.00 so the option is at-the-money. After one month's time, the share price has risen to $16.00—well done. Because the share price is now higher than the exercise price, the option is now said to be 'in-the-money'. The next month—disaster—the share price has fallen to $14.00. Not looking good. The option is now said to be 'out-of-the-money'. We can sum up as such: when the share price is higher than the exercise price, the option is in-the-money, when it's the same as the exercise price, it's at-the-money, and when it's lower than the exercise price, it's out-of-the-money.

So far we have considered the possibility of buying shares at $15.00 or an option with an exercise price of $15.00. Leaving the exercise price at $15.00, let's consider what difference it would make if the shares were at some other price. Let's say that the shares are offered at $15.63. This means that before we even consider buying a $15.00 call option, the shares are already trading 63c above the price that we would have to pay if we exercised the $15.00 call. What might we then pay for the call in order to have the right to exercise the option at $15.00 in three-months time?

One thing's for certain—we would definitely pay at least 63c. With three months to go, however, there is still plenty of risk that the share price will fall below $15.00.

You will still have to pay a premium to remove that risk. Therefore, when the share price is $15.63, a realistic price for the call would be $1.03. What are you getting for your $1.03? Well, you're already ahead by 63c, so in reality the risk premium inherent in the call price of $1.03 is:

$$\$1.03 - 63c = 40c.$$

This means that the cost of your insurance is actually 40c. This compares more realistically to the cost of insurance of 50c when the share price was offered at $15.00.

In buying a $15.00 call, when the share price is $15.63, you are buying what's known as an 'in-the-money call'. The $15.00 call option is already 63c in-the-money. The $15.00 call option is also said to have an intrinsic value of 63c. The difference between the price of the call and the *intrinsic* value is the real risk premium, in this case 40c, but together the option will cost you a 'premium' of $1.03.

An in-the-money option will always be more expensive than an at-the-money option because it will always have some intrinsic value. You have probably noticed, however, that although the price of the call option is greater when the option is in-the-money, the actual value of the risk premium has dropped. At $15.00, the risk premium of the $15.00 call is 50c. At $15.63 the risk premium is 40c. Why is it less?

This is because when the call option is at-the-money, *any fall* in the share price will result in you not exercising that call. In the case of our in-the-money call option, the share price can fall 63c before you decide not to exercise the call. Therefore, the risk is less, so the risk premium is less.

Now let's look at the opposite scenario. The shares are offered at a price of $14.37. What would you pay for a $15.00 call option? You might say, well, why on earth would you consider buying a $15.00 call option if the share price is already lower than the exercise price? Why start from behind?

Although the share price is lower *now*, in three-month's time there is still a chance that the share price will rise above $15.00 and you will ultimately exercise the option for a profit. Remember, it was your view that the share price will rise over the period that prompted you to consider buying the shares in the first place. When the share price is at $14.37, the $15.00 call option is said to be an 'out-of-the-money call'. The reason you may consider buying an out-of-the-money call rather than an at- or in-the-money call is because they will always be cheaper. In this case, a realistic price for the call would be 40c.

An out-of-the-money call has no *intrinsic* value. Rather it has value that needs to be made up before you would consider exercising the call option. It still has a risk premium, given the chance that the share price can still rise above the exercise price in the period. The chance of the $15.00 call being exercised when the starting point is $14.27 is, however, less than the chance of the $15.00 call being exercised when the starting point is $15.00. Therefore, the risk premium is less, ie 40c instead of 50c.

The further out-of-the-money a call option is, the more rapidly the premium will drop off (not quite to nothing, because no one would ever sell something for nothing). The further in-the-money a call option is, the more expensive it will become by virtue of the increasing intrinsic value. However, the portion of the option premium, which represents the risk premium, will also rapidly drop off until the price of a deep in-the-money call is almost the same as its intrinsic value.

The risk premium will almost be at its greatest when the call option is at-the-money. That is simply because it's a fifty-fifty chance. There's no previous intrinsic value nor value to make up. The share price could go either way. This is, of course, a purely mathematical view. Your view is that the share price will rise and so you will weigh up the price of the option with that view in mind.

Often it is possible to have the choice of several exercise prices for call option on the same shares for the same period. This is the case with exchange-traded options and warrants. I will later expand upon the various ways options can be purchased, but for now let's just consider that UCI shares are on offer at $15.00 and we have the choice of buying either the $13.00, $14.00, $15.00, $16.00 or $17.00 call. We'll put all these values into a table.

Three-month call option prices for UCI. Share price = $15.00

CALL OPTION	PRICE	INTRINSIC VALUE	RISK PREMIUM	IN- , AT-, OR OUT-OF-THE-MONEY
$17.00	$0.10	0	$0.10	Out-of-the-money
$16.00	$0.35	0	$0.35	Out-of-the-money
$15.00	$0.50	0	$0.50	At-the-money
$14.00	$1.35	$1.00	$0.35	In-the-money
$13.00	$2.10	$2.00	$0.10	In-the-money

You have a view that the price of UCI shares will rise over the three-month period. Which call option will you buy? There is, unfortunately, not a simple answer.

You would most likely reject the in-the-money options as being too much of an outlay to begin with. In fact most options are traded when they are at- or out-of-the-money for this very reason. Do you then pay the highest risk premium for the at-the-money option, or do you reduce your cost with a lower risk premium by buying the out-of-the-money option and in so doing give up some of the initial rise in the share price? Well, this is all up to you.

Options, as you have probably gathered, are a game of chance. Yes, we're back in the casino again. But if you consider that investing in shares is also a game of chance then options are providing you with a means of controlling at least some of that chance. You believe that UCI is going to rise in the next three months. If you think that it will only rise to $15.80 in that time then you will most likely buy the $15.00 call. There's no point in buying the $16.00 call because you don't believe it will ever get there. If, however, you believe that UCI will rise to $18.50 then maybe the $16.00 or $17.00 calls are for you. Your profit will be less ($18.50 - the exercise price) but your outlay will also be less. Only you can weigh up the circumstances.

A very important factor in the price of a call option is the relationship between the share price and the exercise price. That is to say, the first two variables to consider in the price of an option are the share price and exercise price. Then comes chance. But there are more variables to consider that are very much affected by chance.

Time is of the Essence

It was Albert Einstein who decided that time was the fourth dimension. Great comedy is all in the…timing. We never seem to have enough time, or at least so we believe.

Options, too, are very much beholden to time. This is because options are all about chance, and chance and time are inexorably linked.

What are the chances that you will become rich? (A lot more after reading this book, we hope.) Yeah…maybe? Maybe not? What are the chances that you will be rich by next week? Pretty slim? What are the chances that you will be rich before you die? Not sure, perhaps, but certainly a lot better than the chance that you'll be rich next week.

What are the chances of man walking on Mars? It won't happen before 2000, but only a fool would deny that it is certainly possible one day. Anything is possible, given time.

What are the chances of UCI shares, now trading at $15.00, reaching $20.00? Okay, so you don't know that much about UCI (probably because we made it up). A move to $20.00 represents a 33% increase. What are the chances of it occurring *sometime*? Probably pretty good, I would have thought. In fact, if *sometime* is infinite, then statistically I suppose you'd say that UCI *must* reach $20.00 at some point during infinity. What are the chances of UCI reaching $20.00 by next year? Hmm. A 33% increase in one year? That's probably optimistic. What are the chances of UCI reaching $20.00 by next week? Nup, not a snowflake's.

You have a view that UCI shares *will* rise. Even you're not sure, however, that $20.00 is possible. But you must concede that the longer the time frame, the greater the possibility that UCI will, in fact, achieve this goal. When we contemplated the movement of the UCI share price previously, we were looking at a three-month period. This was a fairly arbitrary choice on my part. Let's say you did decide to buy the at-the-money call because you believed, that given three months, the UCI share price would rise. Now, what if I said that the call option was only good for *one* month. That is, in only one month's time you will have to decide whether or not to exercise the call. You will exercise the call if the price of UCI is greater than $15.00. Will the price rise in one month?

Hmm. You do believe that the price will rise, but in one month? Not all that confident. At least, not confident enough to pay 50c for a $15.00 call. Bear in mind that the share price will have to rise above $15.50 before you are ahead on the deal. You're still happy to buy a call option to protect yourself from being totally wrong, but 50c is looking a bit steep.

Okay, how about I offer you the $15.00 call option for 25c? That sounds a bit better. You will still have the same protection against the share price moving down over the period, but you will start to make money if the share price rises above $15.25. The bottom line is that there is less chance of the UCI share price rising 50c in one month than there is in three months. Consequently you are only prepared to pay 25c for that same $15.00 call.

Conclusion? The greater the amount of time to maturity of an option, the greater will be the price (or premium) of that option.

So it follows that if you wanted to purchase a $15.00 call for a period of six months, you would have to pay more for the option. The share price of UCI has a greater chance of rising higher in six months than it does in a mere three. A realistic price for the six-month call would be $1.00. This means that the UCI share price would have to rise to $16.00 before you break even.

Let's have a look at a table of call option prices. In the following table, the UCI share price is fixed at $15.00 and the exercise price is fixed at $15.00. Only the time to maturity changes.

TIME TO MATURITY	CALL PRICE
1 day	$0.02
1 week	$0.10
1 month	$0.25
3 months	$0.50
6 months	$1.00
1 year	$1.50

As one would expect, the call option prices increase with time. You may have also noticed, however, that the increase in call price is *not linear*. That is, each extra month of time does not result in an equivalent increase in the call price. Rather, the prices jump quickly in the early stages but then the increases start to taper off in the latter stages. Why is this so? We will find out in due course.

For the time being, let's just be happy with the fact that time is another important factor affecting the price of an option. So now we have three factors: share price, exercise price and time to maturity. What's next?

Interest Rates Again

Do you remember back to when we were talking about futures? I introduced the concept of the *forward price* of a commodity. A forward price comes about by virtue of the fact that if we buy wheat futures, we will need to either borrow the money to do so or take the money out of the bank and forgo the interest. Thus if we buy the futures, we expect to at least return the amount of interest we're paying or have given up. The forward price is then the spot price plus the cost of interest.

The same goes for options. The price of a call will take into consideration the cost of interest. Remember that a call option provides you with the right to exercise that option at some time in the future. While you are hoping that the share price will rise over the period, it is costing you money to own the option. This will again affect your bottom-line profit and thus adjust your break-even point. If you buy the $15.00 call for 50c, and in three-months time the share price has risen to $16.00, you will exercise the call and you may sell the shares for a 50c profit. However, if it has cost you 3c to fund the position over the period, then in reality your profit is only 47c.

It thus follows that the cheaper your funding cost (lower interest rate), the more you can afford to pay for the call option because you won't be giving up as much profit in the end. On the other hand, if your funding cost is higher (higher interest rate) then you will not be prepared to pay as much for the call option because of what you will lose in funding by the end. Lower interest rate—higher call price, higher interest rate—lower call price.

Your funding rate will differ in two ways. Firstly, it will possibly be different between two different people. Someone else may have access to cheaper funding than yourself and so be prepared to pay more for a call option than you are. Secondly, it will be different depending on the time to maturity of the option. Different periods of time attract different interest rates.

The interest rate, or funding rate, is the fourth factor affecting the price of an option. We now have the factors of share price, exercise price, time to maturity and interest rate. There is one more.

A Volatile Situation

The four factors affecting the price of an option, which we have considered so far, all have one thing in common—they are *known* values. We know what the share price is at the time, and we know the exercise price. We know how long the option has to run, and we know how much it will cost us in funding. If the price of an option was determined only by known factors, then basically there would be no option market. Everyone would agree that an option was worth a particular value and so the sellers (looking for a margin) would never offer a price that the buyers were prepared to pay. Everyone would go home.

But there is an option market. There is a very big option market. All around the world there are option markets where people are furiously buying and selling options all day. Why are some people prepared to buy options and others prepared to sell? What factor affects these decisions?

To answer this question we must come back to the fundamental concept affecting the price of an option—chance. With every analytical tool at our disposal, we can still only make a prediction about the movement of a share price that might be right or might be wrong. Different people will have differing views on the chance of a share price rising or falling, and thus the chance of an option being exercised or not. They might agree, however, that a particular share may have more chance of rising or falling than another particular share, even if their prices are the same now. How might this be so?

Let's fantasise again. United Consolidated Inc (UCI), with which we have become familiar, is a company that has diverse interests in various businesses including manufacture, transport and import. They have proven a steadily successful, if not overwhelming, performer over the years with varying profit results but an overall trend of expansion and decent returns.

Fingers Crossed Goldmines (FCG) is a wildcat gold exploration company. Over the years they have had some success with their exploration, but often their costly exploration investments have come up with nothing. Some years they make zilch, other years they reap it in. One always feels with FCG, however, that they're just one drill hole away from the mother lode.

The Very Boring Group (VBG) is an investment company that concentrates on conservative, low-risk-low-return investment opportunities. They've been around since Moses had a passbook account, and some of the board members are from the Jurassic era. VBG is not interested in rocketing share prices. They simply want to provide their shareholders with a safe, steady return through their yearly dividend payments.

Now consider that the share price of each of these companies is trading at $15.00. You're looking to invest your money and you decide to diversify and invest in all three. You decide to do this by buying call options. The share prices are the same, so one assumes that the call option prices would be the same. Won't they?

Let's have a quick look and see where the prices of these shares were this time last year. UCI—$13.00, FCG—$18.00, VBG—$14.80. UCI has thus risen steadily, FCG has been disappointing and since fallen when a promising exploration site turned up nothing, and VBG, well, they plodded on. We'll go back another year: UCI—$12.00, FCG—$10.00, VBG—$14.80. Again UCI has been unspectacular but firm. This was the year in which FCG discovered the famous 'Oh my God!' field. VBG was VBG.

You want to invest your money for three months. What chance do you think each stock has of rising or falling? UCI, one would think, must be a chance to post the same sort of steady performance. There's a possibility their shares could rise to about $16.00 or more. One does get the jitters though when a stock has not had a losing year for a while. One may be just around the corner. FCG, well, who knows? In two years, the share price has gone $10.00 to $18.00 and back to $15.00. Depending on what they find or don't find, the share price could either be $5.00 or $25.00 next year. VBG? I think we can safely say that VBG will be hovering somewhere around the $15.00 mark.

You've now weighed up the chances. How much would you pay for the options? You're happy to invest in UCI, but you would like some protection against a possible fall. You feel they still have upside potential, however, so you're happy to pay 50c for the $15.00 call. And you want to be in on FCG in case they really hit the big one. This could see the share price really rocket! But by the same token, it might collapse—you need protection. If FCG has a greater chance of large share price increase, and a greater chance of complete disaster, would you not pay more for the call option? I think you would. The $15.00 calls are offered at $1.00. VBG are not likely to rally much, and they're not likely to drop much. In fact there's very little chance that they'll go anywhere much, barring some shock (*85-year-old chairman caught in nude sex romp!*). Would you pay much for a $15.00 call option? I doubt it. Should you even buy the option at all? Perhaps, in this case, the purchase of shares is more sensible. The VBG $15.00 calls are offered at 12c. Nah, forget it.

Here are three stocks all trading at $15.00. But for a three-month call, you're prepared to pay 50c for the first, $1.00 for the second, and yet baulk at even paying 12c for the third. Why? Because the chances are different for each stock that either good gains or dangerous falls are possible. Basically, some stocks are more *volatile* than others.

Volatility is the fifth and last factor affecting the price of an option. The greater the volatility of a stock, the higher the call option price. People will pay more both to protect themselves from the greater possibility of loss, and to participate in the greater possibility of gain. UCI is a moderately volatile stock. Its movements are steady and not too disturbing. FCG is an extremely volatile stock. Its share price is up and down like a yo-yo. VBG displays very little volatility at all. The stock price does not often vary.

Do we know the volatility of a stock? Can it be measured? The answer is yes it can, *but* only after the event. In other words, we can look at what a share price has done over a given period and thus assign it a measure of volatility. What the share price might do over a future period is anybody's guess. Suggesting that share price volatility can be accurately predicted is the same as saying that the share price itself can be accurately predicted. I will be discussing the concept of volatility in far greater detail later in this book, but for now take it from me—volatility is the unknown quantity.

Being an unknown quantity ensures that different investors will have differing opinions on the potential volatility of a stock and the chances it might have of rallying to a certain level or to collapsing in a heap. And therein lies the market. We can now summarise those factors which affect the price of an option.

Mathematically it would be summarised as such:

$$O = f(S,X,T,i,v)$$

Where: O = option price; S = share price; X = exercise price; T = time to maturity; i = interest rate; v = volatility.

This means that 'the option price is a function of the share price, exercise price, time to maturity, interest rate and volatility'.

And this means, that when one considers the value of a call option as an alternative investment to shares, one must take into consideration five different variables, one of which is unknown.

Good heavens. You'd need a computer to do that, wouldn't you? Well, yes, computers have become very important tools in the option market.

However, options far outdate the computer. For one thing, the stock option market in Australia began in the 1960s while Bill Gates was still in short pants. Moreover, it is recorded that ancient Romans, Greeks and Phoenicians traded options against outgoing cargoes from their local seaports. They wouldn't have got much out of the Microsoft help line in those days.

Without a computer, pricing options is simply a matter of judging the value and applying one's own opinions. Value will vary in respect to each of the five variables. Another table might help here.

Option Price Table

WHEN THIS IS HIGHER...	THE CALL PRICE WILL BE:
Share price	Higher
Exercise price	Lower
Time to maturity	Higher
Interest rate	Lower
Volatility	Higher

We have some idea now of what price we might pay for a call option. Where would we go to buy one?

Over-the-counter and Exchange

Anyone *could* sell you an option. You might have a conversation with Fred next door about your opinion of UCI shares and how you'd like to invest while protecting your downside. And he'll say 'How about I sell you the $15.00 call then?' Possible, but not likely. You could call a bank or broking house that specialises in selling options. Between yourself and themselves, you could organise the exercise price and time period to suit. A price would be agreed and a contract drawn up.

This is called buying an 'over-the-counter' option. Over-the-counter options are, however, really in the realm of the big players. Companies or investment funds might buy options over-the-counter from a bank for various reasons. One reason may be that they don't want anyone else to know. Another reason may be that the particular stock that they are interested in does not have options or warrants listed on an exchange.

Earlier in this book, we compared a *forward* contract with a *futures* contract. The difference is a that forward contract is an agreement between two parties (over-the-counter). A futures contract is traded at the futures exchange. Shares are traded at the stock exchange. In each case, the exchange is a place where people gather to buy and sell the particular commodity. There are standard features of the contracts put in place and there is legislation in place to protect the buyers and sellers from unscrupulous dealings. Stock options are also listed at an exchange.

In Australia there are three different forms of exchange-traded stock options. There are 'company options' listed on the stock exchange. There are 'exchange-traded options' listed on the Australian Options Market. And there are warrants, also listed on the stock exchange.

Confused? Let's have a closer look at each.

Company Options

Some stocks listed on the stock exchange also have options listed on the stock exchange. If you look up a particular share price in the newspaper, say XYZ, you may also find listed underneath a price for XYZO. Or if there are two call options available, they might be XYZOA and XYZOB. These are generally known as 'company options'. This is because a call option has been offered by the company as another means of raising capital. The company has set the exercise price and the time to maturity of these options. An important feature of company options is that when you exercise the options, you will receive stock that *didn't previously exist*. A company will always issue a fixed number of shares in its initial capital raising. If it also offers options (sometimes 'attached' to the shares from the beginning), then it is a way of raising further capital once a certain share price has been reached (the exercise price). The stock that you receive, and pay for at the exercise price, is new stock.

Exchange-Traded Options

There are an abundance of company options listed on the stock exchange. The greater amount of stock options are traded, however, on the Australian Options Market (AOM). These are known as 'exchange-traded options' or 'ETOs'. At the time of writing, there were 54 stocks out of the All Ordinaries index that had listed ETOs. As with the futures exchange, the AOM provides standardised options contracts that can be bought and sold and rebought and resold among the members of the exchange who are representing their clients. Like the futures exchange, an options contract *does not exist* until two parties agree to buy and sell from one another. Unlike the futures exchange, where any number of contracts are allowed to change hands, there is, however, a limit on the number of option contracts that may exist.

The reason for this is straightforward. A company option, listed on the stock exchange, is an option over new stock and is controlled by the company itself. An ETO is an option over *existing* stock. That means that when a call option is exercised, the seller of the option must provide the buyer with stock that is already listed on the stock exchange. The seller cannot just invent new stock. If the buyer of a call option exercises that call option, and the seller does not own any of the particular stock, then he will have to go into the market and buy the stock in order to meet his obligations. The company, over who's stock the option is traded, has no say in the matter. The ETO market runs independently of the companies themselves. There is a limit placed on the number of ETOs that can exist in a particular company so that there is no threat of a clandestine takeover. There are very strict rules about announcing one's intentions if one buys large slabs of stock in another company. One must declare whether one is intending to take over that company or not. Without limits on the number of options available, a potential takeover merchant could buy enough call options to launch a takeover once the options are exercised and thus avoid the usual disclosure procedures.

The AOM offers a selection of maturities for each stock option listed, and a selection of exercise prices. Maturities will typically run in cycles of three months thus providing the buyer with the opportunity to buy a call for three, six or nine months. When one quarter rolls off, another one begins. Therefore, if you come in one month into the cycle, you'll be looking at buying options for two, five or eight months. A spot month is also offered. This means that there is a new one-month option offered each month. New exercise prices will also be added as the stock price moves up and down. This ensures that there are always in-, at- and out-of-the-money options on offer. Confusing? It certainly can be.

Stock options were traded on an open outcry basis, similar to that of the futures exchange, up until October 1997. Now they are traded on a computer system known as CLICKS. This is similar to the computer-based stock market system known as SEATS (Stock Exchange Automated Trading System) with the exception that 'CLICKS' doesn't actually stand for anything. It is merely so-called because using it requires an awful lot of mouse work (click, click, click). As with all exchanges, if you want to buy an option you must ring a broker and have them purchase the options on your behalf. Option premiums are paid up front in full. When exercised, call options require the holder to pay up the exercise price immediately in full. In both cases the broker will take a commission.

Share Warrants

I have said previously that, for all intents and purposes, a share warrant is the same as an option. So why do share warrants exist?

Warrants were introduced into the Australian market in the early 90s having previously proven popular in other locations such as Japan and Hong Kong. One of the original reasons for the issuing of warrants was to provide investors with the opportunity to buy call options with longer maturities than those offered by the Australian Options Market. Typically, at that time, ETOs provided no more than six months duration. The first warrants provided more like eighteen months duration.

The fundamental difference between options and warrants is that warrants are issued by a *third party*. This third party is typically an investment bank. Presently, in Australia, there are a number of investment banks that have listed warrants over a variety of stocks. The stocks over which the warrants are listed are stocks that are themselves listed on the Australian Stock Exchange. The warrants are also listed on the Australian Stock Exchange.

As with a call option, when a warrant is exercised, the holder receives stock at the exercise price. Warrants are similar to ETOs in that the stock delivered on exercise is stock that *already exists*. Therefore, the issuer (seller) of the warrant must, if exercised, buy that amount of stock in the market if they haven't already done so in order that it can be delivered to the warrant holder.

If warrants are almost identical to ETOs, and ETOs have existed for many years, why have warrants recently become so popular?

There are various reasons one could put forward. One reason is that warrants are traded on the stock market, with which many investors are familiar, and not a separate options market. (Note, however, that the AOM is merely a subsidiary of the ASX). They are thus readily visible to stockbrokers all over the country who are linked to the SEATS system.

Another reason is that the issuer of the warrant, the investment bank, usually guarantees a tight buy/sell spread and good liquidity. In this way, the warrant buyer is happy in the knowledge that he (or she) can buy in, and subsequently sell out, at the best available price. Often ETO prices are wide and liquidity poor. Furthermore, as the investment banks are not beholden to the rigid strike and maturity setting formula of the AOM, they are able to be more flexible in the setting of strike prices and maturity dates for their own listed warrants. Nor must an investment bank limit itself to issuing warrants only on those stocks with listed ETOs. Many of the warrants currently listed do not have an ETO alternative.

But all these reasons aside, the main reason warrants have become so popular in recent times is reflected in a resurgence of interest of the 'mums and dads' in direct share market investment. This has largely been a result of the 'bull run' in the market from 1995 to 1998, and the 'floating' of government-owned companies such as the Commonwealth Bank, Telstra and the TAB. As investment banks also act as stockbrokers it was in their interests to tap into the newfound retail boom and offer clients their *own* products, namely listed warrants.

Warrants are also popular on their own because they provide exactly the same risk control capabilities and leveragability as an option. That is because they *are* options. And once again, when we proceed with our discussion, remember: whenever I use the word 'option', the same applies to warrants.

To Exercise or to Sell?

Options, we've decided, can be valued in relation to five factors. There is another option characteristic that we need to consider. In the good old days, most options came with the stipulation that they could only be exercised on the day of maturity. These are known as 'European' options. This meant that the holder of the option had no choice but to wait till the last day of the contract before taking up his (or her) right to exercise. European options are still around, but they are no longer very popular.

These days most options, particularly those traded on an exchange, can be exercised at *any time* after the day of purchase. These are known as 'American' options. In this case, the option holder simply notifies the broker who notifies the exchange and the options are exercised whenever the holder so chooses. Despite their fundamental difference, there are very few cases where the value of a European option and its American equivalent are actually any different. In the case of stock options, a difference will arise due to dividends. Suffice to say, for now, that the two option types result in the same option value.

The reason they are the same value, despite the added benefit of being able to exercise whenever one chooses, is because in nearly all cases, it would be foolish to exercise an option before its maturity date. Right up until the death, an option will still carry some risk premium, that is some value, however small, representing the chance that the option may be exercised. If you exercise the option early, you forgo that added value.[23]

Let's say you had bought the UCI $15.00 three-month call for 50c. There's one more month to go and UCI is now trading at $16.00. You could exercise right now and pick up a dollar, leaving you with an overall profit of 50c. Why wouldn't you? You wouldn't because the $15.00 call is now trading at $1.15. Of that price, $1.00 is intrinsic value and the other 15c is the risk premium remaining. If you exercise the option now, you will forgo that 15c. If you really want to cash in now, you would choose to sell the call option at $1.15.

Exchange-traded options, like futures, can be sold at any time during the life of the contract. And once again, you do not have to sell it back to anyone in particular, but rather to anyone who wants to buy your call option. If you sell your $15.00 call now for $1.15, your profit will be 65c as opposed to the 50c you would have gained had you exercised the option. In almost all cases it is more beneficial to sell the option before maturity than it is to exercise that option before maturity. A further benefit gained from selling the option is that you don't have to come up with the money required to buy the shares on exercise. You don't have to ever cough up $15.00.

The value of the option you have purchased will constantly change over the life of that option as the five variables change. The exercise price is constant, and it's most likely that your funding is fixed for the duration. The share price, however, will be constantly changing. Your time to maturity will tick down day by day. And your volatility factor, well, it is a moveable, intangible beast. Volatility can rise and fall with company announcements, profit results, a war, a regional economic crisis—anything that will have an effect on the share price and an effect on the chances of the share price

---

23 *In the case of very deep in-the-money options, it is sometimes better to exercise early when the cost of funding the position is greater than the remaining risk premium value. This will usually only happen very close to expiry.*

moving up or down in a sudden burst, or staying put for the time being.

Given that the value of an option is constantly changing, we can look at options as a trading instrument in their own right. Instead of trading shares themselves, we can choose to simply buy and sell options. Not only do options provide risk control, but they also provide leverage. For the same amount of money, we can trade a lot more options than we can shares. And our losses are specifically limited. That does not mean, however, that there are *no* risks inherent in trading options.

Risks

Many a call option buyer has been frustrated when a share price has risen, but the call option he (or she) purchased has remained much the same. At other times, call option buyers have found that despite an unexpected plunge in the share price, the call option has retained most of its value. Do options have a mind of their own? Let's focus again on the three changing variables.

Assume for the moment that the level of volatility of a stock is stable and that there is still plenty of time to run on a call option. We bought our UCI $15.00 call for 50c when the share price was $15.00. The share price is now rising. With the share price at $15.00, the call was at-the-money. When a call is at-the-money, its risk premium is at its greatest (See the following table). As the share price rises, the call becomes in-the-money, and begins to gain intrinsic value. Each additional one cent of share price will add one cent in intrinsic value. As the call rises further into the money, however, the risk premium component begins to diminish. Thus, because, as the share price gets higher, there is more and more chance that the call will be exercised, and thus the risk of it not being exercised is getting less and less. Thus we have two competing forces. The risk premium falls as the intrinsic value rises. The rate of fall of the risk premium will be steep at first, but taper off as the share price rises.

Think of a swinging pendulum. When the pendulum reaches dead centre at the bottom of its swing, it is moving at its greatest speed. As it continues to swing higher and higher toward the top of its arc, its speed is gradually being reduced until the point where it finally stops. This is when it has reached its highest point.

Consider that dead centre of the pendulum's swing is at-the-money. As it rises in its arc, it is becoming further in-the-money and thus adding intrinsic value. But at the same time, its speed (risk premium) is reducing from its highest level to its lowest level. The value is rising at a diminishing rate. Let's put this concept into a table.

Call Price Table 1

SHARE PRICE	CALL PRICE	INTRINSIC VALUE	RISK PREMIUM
$15.00	$0.50	0	$0.50
$15.25	$0.62	$0.25	$0.37
$15.50	$0.77	$0.50	$0.27
$15.75	$0.95	$0.75	$0.20
$16.00	$1.15	$1.00	$0.15
$16.25	$1.37	$1.25	$0.12
$16.50	$1.60	$1.50	$0.10

What does this table tell us about trading call options? Notice that the increase in call value is 12c, as the share price moves from $15.00 to $15.25. Now notice that the increase in call value is 22c when the share price moves from $16.00 to $16.25. In the first case, the option price increased only by about 50% of the share price, but in the second case it increased about 90%. Is this call option really worth buying then when, at the beginning, you're only making a gain of 50% of the gain in the share price? And even at $1.25 higher, the option still only provides 90% of the gain? Before we answer this question, let's look at what happens to the value of the $15.00 call if the share price does what you weren't expecting and *falls*.

Call Price Table 2

SHARE PRICE	CALL PRICE	INTRINSIC VALUE	RISK PREMIUM
$15.00	$0.50	0	$0.50
$14.75	$0.37	0	$0.37
$14.50	$0.27	0	$0.27
$14.25	$0.20	0	$0.20
$14.00	$0.15	0	$0.15
$13.75	$0.12	0	$0.12
$13.50	$0.10	0	$0.10

The first thing we notice is that because out-of-the-money options have no intrinsic value, the call price is simply the value of the risk premium. The second thing we notice is that the risk premiums are diminishing at the same rate as they did when the share price was rising. They are symmetrical, just like the swinging pendulum. If we plotted these premiums on a graph, they would form a bell curve. The reduction in call value, when the share price falls from $15.00 to $14.75, is 12c—again about 50%. The reduction in call value, when the share price falls from $14.00 to $13.75, is 3c or about 10%. It is now to our advantage, as the call buyer, that an immediate fall in the share price only results in the call price falling by 50% of the share price. Subsequent falls in the share price result in the call price falling by a lesser and lesser proportion. (These proportions are known in the trade as the 'delta' value of the option. We will discuss delta in more detail later.)

Okay, enough of the maths. What can we conclude from this? A call option provides the buyer with the opportunity to participate in the rise of a share price without risking any more loss on the downside than the premium paid for that option. If the buyer holds the option to maturity and exercises that option, he (or she) will have profited by the amount of share price rise minus the initial premium. If the share price falls and the option buyer does not exercise, then the loss is simply the amount of the premium.

Alternatively, the option buyer need not hold onto the option all the way to maturity. The option will change in value at a proportion to the change in share price. This proportion will vary, depending on the risk still inherent, but what the option holder loses on movements on the upside, he (or she) gains by still having value on the downside. The option holder can sell early and still pick up added value from risk premium when the share price has risen. If the share price has fallen, the option holder can still sell the option and pick up some value to reduce the overall loss.

That was factor one—the movement of the option price with respect to the share price. Now let's consider another factor—time.

Fighting Time

Earlier in the Chapter, I explained how the chance of an option being exercised will be greater over a longer period of time and lesser over a shorter period of time. This results in the risk premium of an option being greater with a greater time to maturity and lesser with a lesser time to maturity. Return now to our $15.00 three-month call. Let's assume now that after you buy the call for 50c, the share price never again moves from $15.00. A bit far fetched, perhaps, but it will illustrate a point. If the share price is still at $15.00 on the day the option expires (reaches maturity), then the option on that day will be worth zero. You have lost your 50c. This implies that as every day goes by, and the share price doesn't move, the value of the call option is ticking down from 50c to 0c. This is called 'time decay'. As time moves on the value of any option will gradually decay. But as the rate of decay is not linear, the value will be lost slowly at first and then gain momentum before rapidly diminishing toward the end as in Fig. 3:

Fig. 3—Time Decay of Option Value

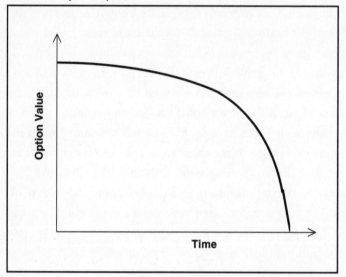

Time decay does not only affect the value of an option when the share price is not moving. I simply used this example to be able to illustrate the effects of decay on a two-dimensional graph. No matter whether the share price is reasonably static, or shooting up or down in a big way, the value of an option will always reduce over time, because the risk reduces over time.

Imagine you are paddling a canoe up a river. When you set out on your journey, the river was wide and slow moving. As you continue, the river becomes gradually narrower and the current becomes stronger. You find that you are paddling at the same rate but covering less and less distance as you continue further up the river. Eventually, you find that your paddling only results in you staying in the one spot. Perhaps it's time to get out.

Now consider that you have bought the $15.00 call. You are looking for a rise in the share price. You do not intend to exercise the option, but rather sell it at some point. As predicted, the share price rises, albeit slowly. The value of your call option rises too. After a couple of months, you notice, that despite a continuing rise in the share price, the value of your option is barely moving. You expect it to move, however, because by now the risk premium is not diminishing as quickly as it did in the beginning. Something's wrong.

What's wrong is that now you are fighting time. Time decay has added a new dimension to the change in value of the risk premium. The reduction in risk premium is now accelerating rather than diminishing. The value of your call option is rapidly heading towards its intrinsic value only.

The effects of time decay are again best illustrated graphically. Taking the previous risk premium tables, and forgetting the intrinsic value for the time being, we can produce the bell curve of which we spoke. See Fig. 4.

Fig. 4—Risk Premium vs Exercise Price

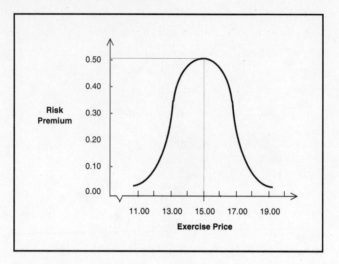

Fig. 4 represents the risk premium values with respect to the share price with three months to run. Now, let's see how that curve looks with different periods of time remaining before the option expires. See Fig. 5.

Fig. 5—Risk Premium vs Exercise Price and Time

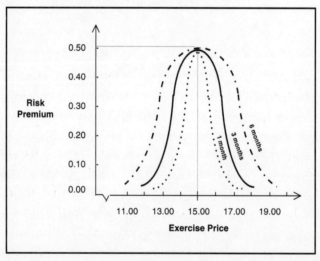

Time is not on our side, is it? What can we do about it? Not much. Time decay is simply an extra consideration when buying and selling options. One little tip might be: an option will provide the best return if sold before time decay starts to speed up. However, if the share price is continuing to rise, then it can still be beneficial to hang on. These are decisions only you can make.

Volatility Rules

The movement of the share price and the effect of time decay provide a multi-dimensional set of values for a call option and possibly a headache for the buyer. But we can draw little graphs and contemplate bell curves and see that everything does actually make sense (I hope). The only problem we now have is that of the effect that a change in the volatility of the share price has on the value of the call option. Throw all your graphs out the window. Volatility does not follow rules.

That's actually not quite true. The higher the (perceived) volatility of a share price, the greater the value of a call option. That's a definite rule. Remember Fingers Crossed Goldmines and the Very Boring Group? As a hit-and-miss gold exploration group, FCG's share price is always very volatile. As a conservative investment company, on the other hand, VBG's share price displays little volatility. Knowing this, the potential investor will always be prepared to pay more for FCG options than they would for VBG options. But now come back to our friend, United Consolidated Inc. As a diversified industrial company UCI shows more share price volatility than VBG, but not as much as FCG. The volatility of FCG will always be high, and the volatility of VBG will always be low, but it's possible that the volatility of UCI will change from time to time.

What does it actually mean that the volatility will change? Before we answer, that let's first introduce an important point. The share price of any company can be affected either by what's happening in that company specifically, or by what's happening in the stock market in general. In times of nationwide or worldwide economic growth, share prices do tend to rise in general. It is most likely that UCI would rise along with them. But what if UCI suddenly came out with an unexpectedly poor profit result? Then UCI would fall while other stocks were rising. This would be seen as a sudden jump in the volatility of the stock. Volatility very much feeds on uncertainty and unexpected outcomes. On the other hand, what if UCI posted a really good profit result on the day after the US stock market suffers a record crash? Any consideration of profit results would be out the door, and UCI would go crashing along with everyone else. This would cause a huge jump in market volatility and consequently the volatility of the UCI share price.

When something unexpected or untoward happens to a stock, be it an individual concern or a market concern, then it's no great surprise that options on that stock suddenly become more popular. Why do they become more popular? Because they offer *protection*. If you were uncertain about what was going to happen next, would you rather own shares or call options? The actual manifestation of an increase in the perceived volatility of a stock is an increase in the value of its options. If the risk is greater, then the risk premiums will be greater. The price of options will be pushed up by that simple old concept of *demand*. At the end of the day, the options market is still just a place where demand and supply fight it out.

So there you are with your $15.00 UCI call options paddling your canoe and swinging your pendulum and thinking that you've just about got this option thing nailed. *Whammo!*—the stock market crashes and UCI shares drop like a stone to under $15.00. As the dust clears, however, you notice something extraordinary. Despite the drop in the UCI share price, the value of your call option has hardly dropped at all! The added volatility in the share price has caused a greater demand for the protection offered by call options, and so the market has pushed the value of your call higher than it otherwise might have been if the share price had simply slipped below $15.00 quietly. Volatility has worked for you. Isn't volatility wonderful?

Not always. Consider another scenario. When you bought the $15.00 call for 50c you, and many others, were expecting the UCI share price to have a nice rally. What if this nice rally doesn't actually happen? What if the share price just inches up slowly and painfully? Well, at least two things will happen. You won't be getting much of an increase in intrinsic value, and time decay will be eating away at your risk premium. But another thing may happen as well. All those people, who thought the $15.00 calls were a good buy, will start to change their tunes. Not only will they stop buying the calls but, they will start selling them out again as well. Demand will drop right off. In short, the volatility will fall. These UCI shares may not be going down, but they're certainly not going up in a hurry either. Your call option value will be getting whacked. Changes in volatility can work in your favour or against you. Relationships with share price movements may be straight-forward and time decay uniform, but changes in volatility are hard to predict.

So ends our discussion on the factors affecting the changing value of an option price. What have we learnt? That share price movements, time decay and changes in perceived volatility all have a constant push–pull effect on the option value. Although we can isolate these factors, and apply some rules to their cause and effect, the combination of all three can lead to very varied results. Does this make options too hard? Of course not. At the end of the day, a call option is still a valuable, risk-controlled and leveraged alternative to buying shares directly. One simply needs to be aware of what's going on.

5. Put in Perspective

The Option to Sell

All through the previous chapter, for reasons which were never quite apparent, you were of the opinion that shares in United Consolidated Inc were going to rise in price in the next three months. This allowed us to have a good look at the prospect of not buying the shares but rather buying call options. What if your opinion was that the price of UCI shares was going fall in the next three months? What could you do about that?

When you have a view that a share price will rise, it's a fairly simple task to call a broker and buy those shares. When you have a view that a share price will fall, you cannot call a broker and sell those shares. You can't sell shares that you don't already own.[24] There is, however, an alternative available to you. You can buy a 'put option'.

A call option provides the holder with the right, but not the obligation, to buy shares at a given price at a given time. A put option provides the holder with the right, but not the obligation, to *sell* shares at a given price at a given time. A put option is the same in all respects to a call option except that it provides the right to *sell* and not to *buy*.

Buying a Put

Your view now is that UCI shares are going to fall in the next three months. You don't own any UCI shares. You might think this is a good thing if the shares are going to fall in price. But you can actually take advantage of the fall in the share price—you can profit from it. Let's assume that UCI shares are trading at $15.00. You decide to buy the $15.00 put option (the at-the-money put). In three-months time, UCI shares have fallen to $14.00. You got the fall you were looking for. You can now exercise your put option.

Now, remember when you exercised a call option, it was then your obligation to buy the shares at $15.00. This meant paying for the shares. You didn't mind paying for the shares as the reason you exercised the call was because the shares were now trading at a higher price. You could buy the shares at $15.00 and immediately sell them for a profit if you so wished.

24 There are instances where certain parties are permitted
    to 'short sell'. These will be discussed later.

When you exercise a put option, it is now your obligation to sell the shares at $15.00. This basically means handing over the shares to someone else (or *putting* the shares). But you don't *own* any UCI shares. What you must do, therefore, is *buy* UCI shares in order to sell them to meet your option obligation. As the shares are now trading at $14.00, this is not a problem. You buy the shares at $14.00 and sell them at $15.00. Thus you have profited from buying a put option.

If it turned out you were wrong about the Price of UCI shares falling over the period, if in fact they rose in price, you would simply not exercise your put option. Again, by buying an option, you are not at risk of losing more and more money if the shares you want to sell keep rising in price. You will only lose the premium you paid to buy the put in the first place. Ah yes, as with a call option it will cost you a premium to remove the risk of the share price rising. Or, if you like, to *insure* against the share price rising. Your profit and loss diagram would look like this. See Fig. 6.

Fig. 6—Profit & Loss of a Put Option

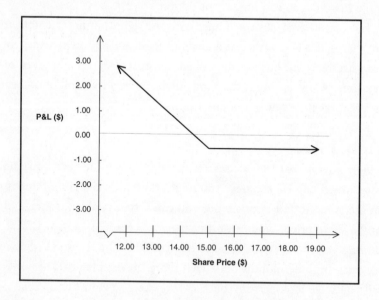

How much would your premium be for a put option? If the circumstances are the same as they were when we were buying a call option—share price $15.00, three-months maturity, interest rate and volatility the same—then the $15.00 put will cost 50c. You got it, the same price as the call. It is the same price because the risk is the same that the share price will move up *or* down. The risk is the same that the option will be exercised or not exercised. Only *you* are holding a particular view—in this case that the shares will fall. The price of the option is based on chance. The chance that the share price will move.

Hang on. Didn't we decide, in the previous chapter, that in reality an option price is only based on demand and supply? We did. But the demand for options is driven not simply by the view that the share price *will* go up or down but by the *chance* that the share price will go up or down. Options provide protection against risk and, despite anyone's view, there is always the same *chance* that a share price can go up or down.

When the exercise price of an option is at-the-money, the price of the call and the put will be the same.[25] As the share price moves up and down, the option becomes in- or out-of-the-money. The value of the put option will be the same as the value of the call option at each equivalent level. The only difference is that a call option becomes in-the-money when the share price rises. A put option becomes in-the-money when the share price falls. Similarly, a call option becomes out-of-the-money when the share price falls and a put option becomes out-of-the-money when the share price rises. Got it?

Okay. To put this all in perspective have another look at Call Price Table 1 in the previous chapter. This shows the value of the three-month $15.00 call as the share price rises. Let's now look at the equivalent $15.00 put and how the put price is affected by a rise in the share price.

Put Price Table 1

SHARE PRICE	PUT PRICE	INTRINSIC VALUE	RISK PREMIUM
$15.00	$0.50	0	$0.50
$15.25	$0.37	0	$0.37
$15.50	$0.27	0	$0.27
$15.75	$0.20	0	$0.20
$16.00	$0.15	0	$0.15
$16.25	$0.12	0	$0.12
$16.50	$0.10	0	$0.10

Keeping this in mind, now turn to the table Call Price Table 2 in the previous chapter. This shows the change in price of the $15.00 call as the share price falls. Let's look at the change in the price of the $15.00 put as the share price falls.

25 *The prices can vary slightly when there is a dividend involved. This will be discussed later.*

Put Price Table 2

SHARE PRICE	PUT PRICE	INTRINSIC VALUE	RISK PREMIUM
$15.00	$0.50	0	$0.50
$14.75	$0.62	$0.25	$0.37
$14.50	$0.77	$0.50	$0.27
$14.25	$0.95	$0.75	$0.20
$14.00	$1.15	$1.00	$0.15
$13.75	$1.37	$1.25	$0.12
$13.50	$1.60	$1.50	$0.10

The only difference between the two sets of tables is that put options gain in value as the share price falls, and call options gain in value as the share price rise and vice versa. The risk premiums in all cases are the same because the risk of the share price moving up or down is equivalent. The relationship between exercise price and share price is simply reversed for the put option. What of the other factors that affect the price of a call option? Are they reversed as well?

No. When considering the effect of time decay, funding cost and volatility on the price of a put option, remember that although a call is an option to buy shares and a put is an option to sell shares, in both cases you are *buying* that option. Because you are buying the put option, you will suffer the same time decay effect. The value of your option will reduce day by day as you approach expiry. Funding the purchase of a put option is exactly the same as funding the purchase of a call option. The higher your funding cost, the less you can afford to pay for your put. And given that the volatility of a share price is its propensity to move up *or* down in either small jumps or huge swings, it stands to reason that the higher the volatility of the share price, the more you would be prepared to pay for a put option.

Taking the five factors affecting an option price into account, and comparing them with the Option Price Table in the previous chapter, we can summarise for the put option.

Put Option Table

WHEN THIS IS HIGHER...	THE PUT PRICE WILL BE:
Share price	Lower
Exercise price	Higher
Time to maturity	Higher
Interest rate	Lower
Volatility	Higher

Selling Calls

A call is the right to buy shares. A put is the right to sell shares. Does that mean that selling a call is the same as buying a put? No, not at all. Before I press on to explain this, however, let's have a look at why you would sell a call in the first place. Throughout this and the previous chapters, we have talked about buying options. In each case, we have simply taken it for granted that there were options available to buy at a certain price. In order for us to be able to buy an option, there must be someone prepared to sell it to us. Who are the sellers?

They can probably be divided into three categories. The first category of sellers would be those who have already bought the option at an earlier time and are now looking, for whatever reason, to sell it out. Selling this option will 'close out' the position. Options positions are created and closed out in a similar fashion to futures positions.

The second category of sellers will be those obliged to 'make a market' in certain options contracts. In the case of the Australian Options Market these people are known as 'registered traders' or 'RTs'. RTs have a very important role in options trading and I will be discussing them in greater detail in a subsequent chapter. For the moment, accept that they are in a position to sell options to you. In the case of share warrants, the 'market-maker' is the issuing investment bank. The third category of sellers we will look at in more detail.

An option contract will not exist until there is an agreement between a buyer and a seller at a certain price. In order to create such contracts, the initial seller will have to sell 'short'. The short seller will now have an exposure to movements in the share price, and the possible exercise of the option, that are the reverse of the buyer. This means that the seller has taken on board the risk that the buyer of the option is looking to offload.

The seller of a call option will be exposed to any upside movement of the share price but on the downside will only ever receive the amount of the premium. In other words his (or her) profit can only ever be the amount of the premium, but the amount of potential loss is unlimited.

Have a look at Fig. 7 over the page.

Fig. 7—Profit & Loss of the Short Call

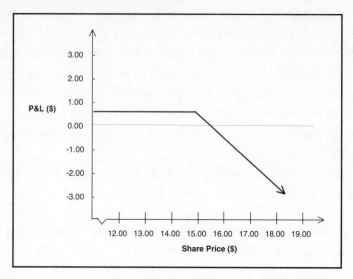

Why would anyone want to be in this dangerously unbalanced situation? To answer this, let's return to our car insurance company. If you insure your car for, say, $800 a year, and then have a prang in the third year that results in $10,000 worth of repairs, the insurance company has only received $2,400 from you and handed out $10,000 in return. The insurance company is hoping that you never have a prang. They will assess the risk that you might, given your age, driving record and the type of car you're insuring and charge you a subsequent insurance premium. If you never have a prang, then they're way ahead. If you do, then they are the loser, but that's the risk they're prepared to take. However, their risk is dissipated by insuring an awful lot of cars.

Anyone who short sells a call option is making a similar assessment. What is the likelihood of this option being exercised? What are the chances of losing money? The short seller of a call will consider the same five factors that influenced the call buyer's decision—share price, exercise price, time, interest rate and volatility. Having made his (or her) own decision of the value of that call option, remembering that the level of volatility is an unknown factor that can only be estimated by either party, the seller will offer the option at that price. On the other hand, he (or she) may simply look at the prices being bid for a particular call option and decide that they're just too high under the circumstances. They will then look to make money from the sale of those calls.

Selling a call is a very different kettle of fish to buying a put. The only similarity is that, in each case, the position requires the share price to fall in order to profit. The risk position of each is, however, quite the opposite. The put holder will make more and more money as the share price falls. As the share price rises, the holder will lose the put premium and only the put premium. No further losses will be experienced. A short call holder will profit as the share price falls, but only ever to the amount of the call premium. No matter how far the share price falls the short call holder will make no more money than the initial premium. If the share price rises, however, the short call holder will lose money and continue to lose more and more money the further the share price rises. There is no limit to the potential loss.

If the seller of a call option does prove to be wrong, and the call option is exercised by the buyer, then the call seller must provide the buyer with the shares at the exercise price. If you buy the UCI $15.00 for 50c, and the share price is trading at $17.00 on the day of expiry, the call buyer will have to give you shares at $15.00. You will have to pay the $15.00. If the call seller does not actually own the shares in the first place, he (or she) will have to buy them from the market at $17.00 and give them to you at $15.00, losing $2.00. From this loss we subtract the initial premium that you paid up front, 50c, and the call seller has a net loss of $1.50.

If you were wrong and the seller was right—let's say that UCI was trading at $13.00 on the day of expiry—then you would do nothing. The seller would also do nothing. The seller's profit will be that amount that you paid up front—50c.

Selling calls is not for the faint-hearted. It requires exposing oneself to risk and being confident that one's assessment of that risk is sufficiently accurate. Some brokers will not allow individuals to short sell options, only buy them. Those who do allow short-selling require some form of collateral up front, be that cash or shares in the company over whom the call is being sold, in order that they are happy with the transaction. This is not required when buying options because the broker knows that the loss can only ever be the amount of the premium. In the case of short options, the broker must themselves make an assessment of the risk of selling the option and consequently an assessment of how much of your money they want to hold in their hands before they will allow you to proceed. Mike Brady once said to his son, Greg, with all the wise sincerity that only Mike could muster,

'Caveat emptor'—buyer beware. In the case of options, it's very much a case of 'seller beware', but I don't know the Latin word for seller.

Selling Puts

As you could probably guess, someone also has to want to sell you a put if you are to buy one. Every assessment is the same as if you were selling a call. The only difference is that the put seller will suffer as a result of a fall in the market rather than a rise. For the same reasons as before, the selling of a put is very different to the buying of a call. The only similarity is that both positions benefit from a rise in the market.

If you buy the UCI $15.00 put for 50c, and the share price is at $13.00 at expiry, then you will exercise your put. The seller of the option will have provided you with a short stock position at $15.00. If he (or she) has not previously short sold shares (Remember: only some people can do this. RTs are one group. More on that later), then he (or she) will have to sell shares at $13.00 and then effectively 'buy' them back from you at $15.00. The seller's loss is $1.50.

If the share price at expiry is $17.00, then you will do nothing. The put seller will do nothing. The put seller's profit is the 50c you paid up front.

Selling Warrants

Despite my constant and tedious reminders that warrants are merely options, there is one rather significant difference between a warrant and its equivalent ETO. One can short sell an ETO. One *cannot* short sell a warrant

In this instance, warrants have a great similarity to shares themselves. If you don't already own them, then you can't sell them. It would be like me ringing you up and saying I just sold your house when you never actually wanted to sell your house. There are, however, some instances where the short selling of shares is allowed. There is *never* any instance where the short selling of warrants is allowed by anyone other than the issuer.

This leads to an important point about warrants. Remember that the short seller of an option is most likely someone who believes that the option is too expensive. The ultimate price of an option, at any given time, will be the price at which the buyer is prepared to pay up to and the seller is prepared to sell down to. But if no one, other than the issuer, is allowed to short sell warrants, then what's to stop the issuer charging a highly inflated price for the warrants?

The answer is well...nothing really. But if a warrant is too expensive, then no one will buy it. An issuer will have to offer a selling price that is attractive to the potential buyers. Furthermore, warrant issuing is a competitive business. If one issuer is offering an overly expensive warrant, then there is every likelihood that there is another, cheaper warrant being offered elsewhere.

A more dangerous proposition for the warrant buyer is if the issuer were to *hold the price* down after you had bought it. If you buy BHP warrants, and the price of BHP shares goes up, then so too will the price of the warrant. But the warrant issuer, now losing money on the short warrants, actually could keep the price at the same level by continually selling warrants at the same price as you bought them in the first place. Left to the mercy of an investment bank! Could this happen?

No. For one thing, the warrant issuer will usually 'hedge' their short warrant position in the stock or option markets (This hedging is the subject of a later chapter). So they may not actually be losing money as the warrant price rises. More importantly, though, a warrant issuer does not have a bottomless bag of warrants to sell. Before being listed on the ASX, the issuer must register the 'size' (number of warrants) of the issue. Although they do not have to sell all the warrants on day one, they do have a limit as to how many they can sell over time. Thus if an issuer were to artificially hold down the price, more and more buyers would come in and 'buy out' the issue. With no more for sale, the price of the warrant would suddenly jump to a realistic level.

Although the issuer of a warrant can control the price to a large extent, warrant investors can rest assured that the effects of competition, exchange controls and simple supply and demand will always ensure a realistic price for that warrant. However, and it is an important 'however', because no one else can short sell a warrant, the price of the warrant will usually be slightly higher than the equivalent ETO. Just bear that one in mind.

Playing the Vol

In each of the cases of selling calls and selling puts, my examples (share price reaching $13.00 or $17.00) have implied that an option seller is usually taking a different view on the *direction* of the share price and the subsequent risk of the share price moving in that direction than the buyer of the option. This will be true in a lot of cases. More often, though, the seller will be betting that the share price will not move very much at all. This means that the seller is looking for less *volatility* of the share price than the buyer is hoping for. Where an option seller is most likely to be an overall money maker is in believing that the volatility expected by buyers (and reflected in the amount of premium paid) will not eventuate.

Let's say you buy the $15.00 put for 50c. At expiry, the UCI share price is $14.90. Because the share price is lower than the exercise price, you will exercise the option. In exercising, however, you will effectively only receive 10c. As the option cost you 50c, you are a net loser of 40c. The seller of the put option will have to sell shares at $14.90 and effectively buy them back from you at $15.00 for a loss of 10c. But because the seller sold you the puts for 50c, his (or her) net profit is 40c.

Although you were right about the direction of the market, you overestimated the extent of the fall. The seller, on the other hand, was convinced that a large fall was unlikely, in other words the share price would not be particularly volatile, and so they profited in the end. The seller is often looking to be right about overestimated volatility rather than be right about the specific direction of the market.

Are selling a call and selling a put as equally dangerous as each other? Mathematically, you would say yes. Remember that an at-the-money put option will be the same price as an at-the-money call option because there is always, mathematically, an equal chance that the share price could go up or down. Therefore, there should be no difference in selling either. Mathematics, however, does not always work in the real world.

When talking about stock markets, there is a popular adage that markets go 'up by the stairs and down by the elevator'. We mentioned this in Chapter 1. This means that share prices tend to graft their way up slowly but surely when everything is positive. Sometimes there are some impressive surges, but these are rarely enormous. On the other hand, when things start to turn bad, share markets rarely react with calm resolve. Markets do not tend to edge down quietly and with dignity, they tend to *collapse*. Often these collapses are overdone and result in stretching the rubber band a bit far and experiencing a rebound the following day or week. Either way, markets crash *down*, they do not crash up. Bad news incites panic and panic incites volatility. And increased volatility is the natural enemy of the option seller. So which would you rather sell—a put or a call?

In stock markets, it is invariably more dangerous, but not to the point of never ever considering such action, to sell a put rather than a call. The selling of calls is quite a popular activity, particularly out-of-the-money calls at exercise prices that some sellers don't think can be reached. The selling of puts is most often left to professional option traders, such as the afore-mentioned RTs, who are actually *obliged* to make a selling price for puts. But even they can get it very, very wrong.

Back to The Crash

Before the stock market crash of 1987, many people, investors and professional traders alike, had sold puts like there was no tomorrow. They were happy to do so because they believed the market was just never going down, it would only continue its upward surge. Others, looking at it from a volatility point of view, believed the risk of the market falling a long way in one day was fairly remote, even if possible. Thus, on reflection, they sold puts at rather cheap levels. No one expected what came next. One day earlier, the Australian stock market fell 100 points—the biggest ever one-day fall. Many investors were burnt, as were many put sellers. Most people thought that was the last of it—the correction that may have been needed had happened. Most people went home scarred but happy. Next day: the market fell 500 points. In order to counter a put seller's haemorrhaging position in a falling market, he (or she) will need to sell shares. They will need to do this to be ready for the time when they will need to hand over their sold shares to the buyer of the put at some exercise price which is now a long way away. Therefore, when the market really started to fall out of bed in 1987, the put sellers were madly trying to sell shares. The more they tried to sell, the more the market fell. And the more the market fell the more they had to sell. In Chapter 3, I described how program trading had an effect on the crash. The selling of shares by short put holders also served to exacerbate the situation.

Barings Bank

When Nick Leeson, 'the man who brought down Barings', was getting into deeper and deeper water with the futures position that was running against him, he came up with an idea. Every day he had to report his position, by now an ever-increasing loss, and request, if necessary, that cash be transferred into the account to pay the required margin calls. But Nick was trying to keep this losing position a secret from his superiors. How could he come up with the cash? Nick's answer was to sell put options on the Nikkei share price index futures. (Yes, there are options on futures too. Stay tuned for Chapter 6.) The premiums that he received from selling the options he used to offset the cash requirements that he would otherwise need from London. The systems checks in London were not sufficient to reveal what was actually going on. As long as the market turned around and started going up instead of down, then Nick would be safe and no one would be the wiser. Then came the Kobe earthquake. The market collapsed further, Nick's put option positions added considerably to the already substantial losses and Barings was gone.

Suffice to say it is considered around stock markets that the selling of puts is more risky than the selling of calls. Many people buy puts, particularly out-of-the-money ones, as protection against the events of October 1987 or October 1989 (a lesser but still significant crash sometimes known as the 'crashette'). What this often means is that there is a bias to puts rather than calls so that out-of-the-money puts are significantly more expensive than the equivalent out-of-the money calls (ie calls that are an equivalent dollar value 'out-of-the-money'). Not surprisingly, this is often the case around…October.

October 1997

When the Asian currency crisis struck in October 1997, the Australian stock market fell about 400 points in four days including 200 points on the last.

The next day it rebounded about 150 points. Such volatility had not been seen for ten years. This huge and sudden jump in volatility was just what the sellers of options did not need. Although many market players still remembered 1987, and therefore the practice of unbridled put selling had been very much nipped in the bud, another problem had arisen. There had been a huge new market come to the fore in the form of share warrants, and these warrants were issued, or 'sold', by many and various investment banks.

When the share market collapsed, and then rebounded, there were a few warrant issuers, both here and overseas, that lost an awful lot of money. Now ...you're going to say, ' How can the seller of a call option lose money if the market falls?' And that's a fair question. In order to fully understand how they lost an awful lot of money, you will need to read a later chapter. In the meantime be assured that anyone who sells an option, and therefore 'sells' volatility, is at considerable risk if volatility increases violently.

Options and Dividends

We are coming to the end, for the time being, of our discussion of options on shares. Before we move on, there is one consideration that needs to be raised. That is the effect of dividends on option prices.

When we consider purchasing a share, there are two factors to look at. In funds management parlance, these are 'capital growth' and 'income'. Capital growth is the growth in the capital of a company over a period of time, and this is reflected in the share price of that company. As a company expands and invests money in new opportunities or in plant and labour, that company is (hopefully) becoming more valuable (as long as they don't over-extend themselves with debt). When you buy shares, you are looking for capital growth and thus a rise in the share price.

The income side of the equation is that proportion of the annual net profit of the company which management decides to distribute to share-holders in the form of dividends. This is your cut of the year's success. If you buy shares, you may or may not receive dividends, depending on the company's performance or dividend policy, yearly or twice yearly. You may decide that the safest way to invest in a company is not to buy shares, but rather to buy call options over those shares. By doing this, you have controlled your risk. As a call option holder you will not, however, receive the dividend paid by the company to shareholders. This may or may not put a new twist on your decision whether or not to buy call options. But if you are wavering now, because you won't be participating in the income distribution, there is one thing to bear in mind. On the day dividends are paid the share price will automatically fall, all other things being equal, by the amount of the dividend (actually a bit more than that, depending on the level of franking attached to that particular dividend). If the share price falls for whatever reason, the value of call options would also fall. This is not, however, the case when dividends are the reason for the fall. If the call price fell each time a dividend was paid, then it wouldn't be too hard to sell the calls the day before and then buy them back for an almost guaranteed profit. This is not on. What does happen is that prior to the payment of a dividend, the price of a call is adjusted to reflect a dividend payment on the underlying share at a date before the date of expiry. Come the payment date, the share price will fall, due to the dividend being paid, but the call price will remain the same.

The amount of a dividend to be paid is always announced about a month or so ahead of the actual payment date. At this stage, the dividend adjustment is a known thing. But call options are bought and sold often well before the announcement of a dividend. If the dividend is not known, then how can the call price adjust for it? The answer to this is that the dividend will need to be estimated. Estimation of dividends is not quite as scary as it sounds and often companies will maintain a consistent distribution policy. An important role of stock analysts is to estimate the amount (and sometimes even the timing) of a dividend. Your stockbroker will provide you with this information.

Put options, similarly, are not affected when the dividend is paid. By holding a put option, you will not be advantaged when the share price falls on the day that the dividend is paid.

Coming back to the difference between American and European-style options—ie, European options can only be exercised on the day of expiry, but American options can be exercised any time before expiry—a situation can arise where it is better value to exercise a call option early. This happens when the value of the dividend you receive, if you exercise your calls before the 'ex-date' (payment date), is greater than the amount of risk premium left in the option. This will often be so for deep in-the-money calls nearing expiry. If you have a good broker, they should inform you of this opportunity.

And here we leave stock options. I chose stock options as the example to introduce options in general because the stock market is one market that people can relate to without much difficulty. Options, however, exist on a multitude of different market instruments. It's time to look at a few of those.

6. Plenty of Options, Swaps and More

Money Market Derivatives

Back in Chapter 2, we learnt that the money market in Australia and around the world is now pretty much dominated by interest rate futures. Trading in futures contracts has all but replaced trading in the underlying borrowing/lending instruments such as bank bills and government bonds. Such contracts can be reasonably substituted for any specific period of financing and used to hedge future borrowing or lending requirements. Futures do not, however, provide all the answers to the problems that arise in the world of finance. There are some other extremely popular derivative instruments that are based on the physical instrument.

FRAs

One such instrument is the *forward-rate* agreement or FRA.[26] Do you recall that when we first started talking about futures you and I agreed to do a deal whereby I bought your wheat in six months time for a predetermined price? It was simply a deal between you and I—there was no Exchange involved—and so it was not strictly a futures contract, but a *forward* contract. Forward contracts were really the predecessor to futures contracts and, as such, futures have, to a great extent, replaced forwards. Forward contracts do, however, have one advantage over futures. That is, that the contract can be *specifically tailored* to the needs of the individual party in terms of maturity, amount, settlement procedure etc. Forwards are an 'over-the-counter' instrument between two parties. The two parties are usually brought together by a broker or some other intermediary. The other side of the tailored forward is often agreed to by a proprietary trading house such as an investment bank.

An FRA is an agreement to borrow money for a predetermined period at a predetermined interest rate. The commencement of the loan is at a predetermined time in the future. Let's say a company knows that it will need to borrow money in five months time for a three-month period. They know what sort of interest rate they would be paying *now* if they borrowed

---

26 *This is pronounced either as an acronym (ie F-R-A) or as a word (that sounds like* frar*).*

money for three months, but they don't know what the three-month interest rate will be in five months time. An FRA allows the company to *fix, today,* the interest rate at which they will borrow money in five months time. This way the company is fully hedged against an adverse movement in interest rates, ie an increase in cost to the company. Whatever they have agreed to do in five-months time, ie whatever they are going to borrow the money for, may not prove profitable if interest costs are higher than expected.

An important feature of the FRA is that although one party agrees to 'borrow' money from another at a certain rate, there is never any principal involved. This means that, in five months time, the lending party does not actually lend to the borrowing party, but rather an adjustment is made with regards to the bank bill rate. If it turns out that, in five months time, the bank bill rate is higher than the rate agreed in the FRA, then the provider of the contract pays the borrower the difference in value between the agreed rate and the bank bill rate. The borrower goes ahead and borrows at the bank bill rate, but the adjustment provided by the FRA means the effective rate is the (lower) FRA rate. If the bank bill rate is lower than the rate agreed, then the borrower pays the provider the difference in value. The borrower goes ahead and borrows at the bank bill rate, but the adjustment required by the FRA means the effective rate is the (higher) FRA rate. The advantage of hedging future borrowings or loans with FRA, rather than futures, is not only the ability to tailor the specific details but also the fact that no deposits or margins are required.

Swaps

Outside of futures and options, one of the most popular forms of derivative instrument is the *swap*. The greatest volume of transactions in the swap market involve interest rate swaps. Currency swaps come in second, and then we drop down to the smaller but rapidly growing areas of equity swaps, commodity swaps and just-about-anything-you-can-think-of swaps. The nature of, and the reason for, the swap vary slightly in different markets.

The most actively traded form of swap occurs in the domestic interest rate markets. For whatever reason, it will often occur that one organisation has access to a cheaper floating rate (or variable) funding, that is to say they can borrow at a lower rate, than another organisation. In the meantime, another organisation will have access to cheaper fixed-rate funding. If, however, the organisation with better access to variable funding would like a fixed loan, and the organisation with better access to fixed funding would like a floating loan, both can take advantage of this anomaly by agreeing to 'swap' their loans once the borrowings have occurred.

Now introduce a global marketplace, and often you will have an Australian company with access to Aussie-dollar denominated funding, but needing to borrow money in the US, and a US company with access to US-dollar funding, but needing to borrow money in Australia. One solution is to take the risk on a foreign exchange transaction. The other solution is to simply 'swap' loans.

Swaps really are as simple as they sound. If you imagine two next-door neighbours, both with daughters who play netball on Saturday and sons who play soccer. The netball courts are in one suburb and the soccer field in another. Both families could attempt to spend each Saturday darting around town trying to accommodate both children. It would, however, be quite sensible to enter into a 'swap' with the neighbours—we'll take Sally and Brooke to netball this week, and you take Jack and Kevin to soccer, and next week we'll take Jack and Kevin, and you can take Sally and Brooke. Brilliant!

What if you were an investor with large positions in government bonds who decided that, at least for the short term, the stock market was likely to be a better performer? You could sell out all of your bonds and buy 100 different stocks and then, after the short term, sell out all those stocks and buy back all your bonds. (And pay serious amounts of brokerage). Or perhaps there is someone out there who may have the opposite view. Someone who is long term in the stock market, but preferring to retreat into government bonds, just for the short term. You've got it! Why not simply 'swap' the return on government bonds for the return on the stock market over the given period. Then you would still have the positions you started with, you would have made the short-term investment you wanted, and you would have saved an awful lot of hassle.

Swaps, therefore, are an extremely simple, useful, flexible and popular form of 'derivative'. A swap can be conjured up for anything where two opposite requirements exist—interest rates, currencies, the stock market, the copper price, the oil price, the soybean price. The list is endless.

Taking swaps one little step further, we can take our first look at a 'derivative on a derivative'. If there is a sufficient level of uncertainty in the market, and hence your decision to swap, why not simply buy the option to swap? Yes, they certainly do exist. And naturally they're called 'swaptions'.

Caps, Collars and Floors

The interest rate market loves jargon. The interest rate market also loves options. There is just as much activity going on in interest rate options as there is in stock options. The ability to have the right, but not the obligation, to borrow funds at a specific rate, at a specific time, provides a whole new world of flexibility for the borrower.

Let's say you know you are going to have to borrow money in six-months time for a particular project, maybe...to fund the purchase of a container load of furniture for your furniture store. At the moment, you can borrow money at 7.5%. As long as you can borrow money at 7.5%, the purchase of the furniture, and its subsequent sale, would prove profitable. Your profitability will be eroded, however, if rates were to climb higher than 7.5% in the ensuing six-month period. You run a tight margin, and if you have to pass on too much of a funding cost to the ultimate buyers of the furniture, then in most likelihood they will choose to shop elsewhere. You'll not only be stuck with the furniture, but also stuck with the loan.

You figure that a borrowing rate higher than 8.5% in six-months time could prove ruinous. Do you take the risk?

What you could do is buy an interest rate 'cap'. You buy the right to borrow at 8.5% in six-months time. If, at that time, interest rates are still 7.5%, then you do not exercise your option to borrow. If interest rates are 9%, then you do exercise your option to borrow. Even if interest rates have jumped to 17.5%, you have still purchased the right to borrow at 8.5% and therefore, you are protected from such a disastrous situation. You have 'capped' your potential borrowing cost.

However, as with any option, you had to pay a premium up-front in order to secure your interest rate cap.

A 'floor' is basically just the opposite. A floor is useful from a lender's point of view. If you are going to be providing funding in six-months time, but the profit to you of providing that funding is dependent upon the rate being above 6.5%, then you can buy the option to lend at 6.5%. If rates remain higher, you do not exercise the option. If rates are lower, say 6%, then you can exercise your option and so guarantee a lending rate of 6.5%. You have therefore placed a 'floor' on your potential lending rate.

Who can guess what a 'collar' is? If your business requires you to be constantly borrowing and lending, then you may which to buy an option, which is essentially two options, to cap your borrowing rate at 8.5% and floor your lending rate at 6.5%. You have now 'collared' the interest market. This premium cost will be the greatest, as one would expect, being effectively the addition of two premiums for both the cap and floor.

Caps, collars and floors are offered by money market dealers on an over-the-counter basis. However, far and away the most interest rate option activity occurs in the futures market. This brings us to the most common 'derivative on a derivative' of all—the futures option.

But just before we move on to this extensive area of derivatives, let me discuss one more subject.

Housing Loans

Did you pick it?

If you go to your bank tomorrow and apply for a mortgage, the loans manager will most likely give you choice of a variable loan (say 6%), a loan fixed for three years (say at 7%), or a loan capped for three years (say at 7.5%). If you decide to go with the cheapest loan—6%—you have thrown yourself upon the mercy of the market. Rates may fall, and therefore mortgage repayments become lower, or rates may rise, and mortgage repayments become higher. How high can rates go before you can't afford to meet the repayments?

If you were to fix your loan for three years at 7%, you would have higher initial mortgage repayments than the person who took the variable rate at 6%. Not only that, if rates were to fall over the three-year period, your friend with the variable loan would enjoy even lower repayments, while yours would stay the same. Bummer. But if rates were to *rise* within the next three years, then your repayments would have remained the same—fixed—while your mate's were steadily climbing past yours.

Certainly something to consider. Incidentally, at the end of three years, a fixed loan will turn into a variable loan (unless you renegotiate at that time). You will be 'swapped'.

Had you gone the really expensive route—7.5% capped—what would your repayment schedule look like? For now you would be paying the variable rate at 6.5%. You'd be better off than the person with the fixed rate. If ever interest rates fell within that three-year period, so would your repayments. Your loan is acting exactly the same as a variable loan.

If rates rose within that three-year period, however, your mortgage rate would also rise. Mr 7% fixed would wave as you passed him by on route to

7.5%. If rates reached 7.5%, both you and Mr variable would have higher repayments than Mr fixed. But your loan was capped at 7.5%. If rates went to 8%, so would Mr variable's. You, on the other hand, had your loan capped at 7.5%. Your mortgage repayments could go no higher, at least for three years.

What you have done, in 'capping' your housing loan, is purchased an option. The option to borrow at 7.5%. And you will exercise that option (actually, the bank will automatically exercise it for you) if rates rise above your capped level. There are also other variations on the theme in the form of different styles of housing loan provided by the lender. The sexier ones will undoubtedly involve some form of derivative.

Options on Futures

In Chapter 2, we learnt what a futures contract was. We examined the different players in the futures market and their reason for trading futures. You, as a wheat farmer, and me, as a baker, were involved in wheat futures for the purpose of hedging against a loss of revenue due to a particular movement in the price of wheat. When we came together at the futures exchange, we also encountered those people who provide a bulk of the liquidity in futures—the speculators. These people were simply trying to profit from playing the price of wheat, despite the fact they'd perhaps never set foot on a wheat farm.

In Chapter 4, we learnt what an option was. We saw how, for a given up-front cost, we could control the amount of potential loss involved in trading the stock market. Knowing the limit of our potential loss allowed us to sleep at night.

What happens if we combine the two?

A futures market provides us with a readily accessible, largely cash settled and practical means of trading in—be it for the purpose of hedging or speculating—an almost endless array of financial instruments and commodities. Furthermore, futures contracts provide leverage, as only an initial deposit need be put up and margin calls maintained. This allows us to either create an exposure to a market for a lot less initial cost, or to increase our exposure to the market to a level that would not have otherwise been possible if trading the physical instrument.

Options provide us with a means of investing in a wide variety of instruments while maintaining a specific, limited downside exposure.

Options also provide a form of leverage in that only the initial premium need be put up. If options are sold before exercise, the investor can forever avoid paying the full price for the instrument itself, and so the investor has the opportunity to greatly increase his or her exposure to that particular market.

It will probably come as no great surprise that nearly all futures markets provide options over those futures contracts. In many cases, the turnover of futures options is as great as the turnover of the futures themselves.

Thinking back to our wheat situation, you the farmer were concerned that you may not get the price for wheat, after the harvest, that you need to stay in business. Thus you sold your wheat six months ahead by selling wheat futures. Once you sold those futures, you had effectively locked in your price. If the actual price of wheat did turn out to be lower, come harvest, then you have hedged well. If the actual price of wheat is, in fact, higher, then you have forsaken the opportunity to participate in the higher price. This is frustrating, but at least you *were* hedged. You knew you would not lose the farm.

The ideal situation would be to be able to decide *after harvest* whether you want to sell at the price as it was six months ago, or take the better price now on offer. In other words, it would be nice to be wise before the event. Have you guessed what strategy you could consider taking? You could buy the *option* to sell your wheat in six-months time. If the wheat price is lower in six-months time, then you will exercise the option to sell at the higher price. If the wheat price is higher in six-months time, then you would forget about your option and simply sell your wheat at today's higher price.

You have bought a put option on the wheat future. A derivative of a derivative. When you put it like that, it sounds rather scary, doesn't it? But clearly this is a very sensible approach to consider. Remember that you will have to pay a premium to have the option, whether or not to sell your wheat. Therefore, the option to sell at $172 may cost say, $10. If wheat is trading at $150 after harvest then you will exercise your option and sell at the exercise price ($172), but your effective price will be net of the premium paid—$162. If the wheat price is $200 after harvest, you will not exercise your option, but your effective selling price will again be net of the premium—$190.

Having said all that, I must admit at this point that the wheat contract trading on the Sydney Futures Exchange is one of the few futures contracts that does *not* have options. That sort of stuffs my example, but it does serve to illustrate the point. There are plenty of wheat futures options available in the US market.

Options on futures are very powerful tools. Bearing in mind that a futures contract requires only a deposit to be placed, consider that when buying a futures option one usually has the choice of either paying the premium up-front or putting up a deposit for the premium and being margined accordingly. Leverage on leverage.

This means that the hedger can greatly reduce his or her risk at a fractional cost. It also means, however, that the speculator can lever him or herself into even greater positions with very little capital placed up front. It is not hard to see how the speculator can quickly get his or her self into big trouble. This is particularly so if the speculator is a *seller* of options. But more on that later.

Interest Rate Options

In Chapter 2, we learnt that the bulk of money market activity in Australia, the business of borrowing and lending at the big end of town, is conducted in the interest rate futures markets. The three main contracts are the 90-day bank bill, the three-year government bond and the ten-year government bond.

On each of these contracts there is also a wide array of options available. Options activity in these contracts is extensive enough to warrant separate pits on the Sydney Futures Exchange. (At least while the open-outcry system remains). I introduced you earlier to caps, collars and floors—three of the most popular derivative transactions. Although such deals *are* conducted on an over-the-counter basis, the great bulk of such hedging occurs via the use of futures options.

Although the interest rate futures options market is one where there are a variety of natural buyers and sellers of puts and calls many exchange members, particularly the investment banks, provide options 'market-makers'. These are people who are always prepared to make you a buy or sell price, even though they themselves have no specific borrowing or lending requirement. The activity of trading the interest rate options backwards and forwards fits in naturally with the other money market activities of the investment bank. The benefit of this to the market user is that there is always a price available to be considered for hedging or speculating purposes.

'Market-makers' exist in almost every conceivable options contract be it over-the-counter, exchange-traded or futures exchange-traded. The role of the market-maker is a very important one, and a very risky one. I will be examining this role in greater detail later, when I cite the example of the stock options market-maker. For now, bear in mind that in any options contract, and I shall briefly touch on a couple more examples before we move on, the buyers and sellers do not necessarily have to find each other. Rather, there is usually a market-maker, who is there to provide a buy and sell price.

Gold Options

In 1997, the Reserve Bank of Australia decided to sell out of a lot of its gold bullion. They had decided that value of gold had fallen to the point where the country would be best served if the gold was sold and the proceeds used to fund other investments with a better potential for return. An awful lot of gold hit the market, and so the already soggy gold price was sent into a bit of a tail spin.

Australia is one of the biggest gold producers in the world. The effect of the RBA dumping out gold meant that the share prices of Australian gold mining companies were hit for six. In many cases there were claims that the gold price had fallen to a level where it was no longer economically viable to pull it out of the ground. The situation seemed quite bleak for the miners.

As soon as the panic set in, however, some gold producers were quick to point out that they had already 'forward sold' gold that was still in the ground. Therefore, they claimed, the current fall in the gold price should be of no concern to investors. What did they mean?

There are actually several ways to 'forward sell' gold. If you, the wheat farmer, had sold me, the baker, your unharvested wheat directly, instead of using the futures market, we would have entered into a 'forward' contract. Similarly, there is a market for gold producers to 'forward sell' their as yet unmined gold to the consumers of gold—jewellery makers etc—at a predetermined price. Alternatively, the producers of gold can sell futures contracts to ensure that a certain price is maintained for the gold they are about to spend money on digging for. The most actively traded gold future is COMEX gold traded in New York. In each case the gold miners who claimed there was no cause to panic were absolutely right if they had already sold their gold.

Gold miners are also big users of options. They can choose to hedge their exposure to a fall in the gold price by contacting a gold option broker and organising an over-the-counter option or series of options specifically tailored to the needs of the miner. A popular trade in the gold market is often called a 'floor price agreement'. Here the miner will buy a put on the price of gold thus ensuring protection against a gold price fall. The cost of the premium is then covered by *selling* a call on the price of gold at a higher strike price. Let me explain this a bit further.

Let's say gold is trading at US $300. A gold miner is quite happy to carry on mining gold if it can be sold at this price. If, however, the price were to fall to $250, then the cost of recovering the gold will be greater than the revenue derived from selling it. If the price were to rise to $350, the profitability of the mining company would be greatly enhanced. A floor price agreement would provide the miner with effectively costless hedging. The miner can buy the $250 put for $10. He is then protected from a fall below $250 and therefore his operation remains viable. (By buying a put, he has also 'forward sold' his gold). However, having spent $10, he is now only effectively selling his gold at $290 when the price is $300. Given that he will make extraordinary profits were the gold price to rise then he can afford to sell a call at a level above the present price. He needs to sell the call that will provide the receipt of $10 in premium. This turns out to be the $350 call.

So, where are we left? The gold price is presently $300. Our miner has paid $10 in premium and received $10 in premium. His cost is nothing, thus he can still sell gold at $300. If the gold price falls to $220, the miner is not concerned because he can exercise his put and sell the gold at $250. If the gold price rises to $370, the *buyer* of the $350 call will exercise, and the miner will be obliged to sell his gold at $350. The sacrifice of any further upward gains is the real cost of the floor price agreement. But this cost is offset by the protection provided by the put. If this were on a graph, it would look like Fig. 8.

Fig. 8—Gold Floor Price Agreement

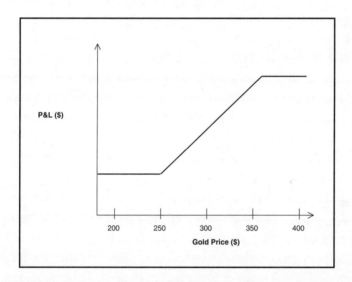

The miner need not have to deal in over-the-counter options. He can achieve the same result by utilising the highly liquid COMEX gold futures options. COMEX provides a multitude of strikes and maturities for put and call.

Oil Options

Oil is the world's most actively traded commodity. Like gold, oil has to come out of the ground. It then has to be piped or shipped on ocean-going tankers to its ultimate destination. Refineries then turn crude oil into its many products, such as jet fuel, heating oil and petrol. Consumers of the products purchase from a refinery by way of, say, a petrol bowser.

Many industries are highly dependent on oil. The price of oil, therefore, is a very important part of their expenses, and therefore their profitability. Countries are also highly affected by the price of oil, particularly those with very little other industry. Australia is one of many oil exporters.

Not surprisingly, there is an enormous world market in oil derivatives— options, futures, futures options, swaps etc. Hedging, forward selling, forward buying and so on occurs both 'upstream' at the crude production level and 'downstream' at the refinery and consumer level. The New York Mercantile Exchange is the largest centre of 'energy' futures trading. Contracts available at NYMEX include Gulf Coast unleaded gasoline, heating oil, light, sweet crude oil, New York Harbor unleaded gasoline, propane and sour crude oil. There are also various natural gas and electricity contracts. The exchange also provides options on most contracts.

Stock Index Options

Options on stock index futures are another product which attracts a high level of activity all around the world. In Australia, many funds managers, amongst others, are regular users of the SPI options. As fund managers are natural buyers of the stock market, they will often buy some downside protection in the form of out-of-the-money put options on the SPI. As with our gold 'floor price agreement', a fund manager will often sell an out-of-the-money call to fund the cost of the put premium. In this market, the trade is known as a 'collar'. This is because it is basically the same deal as the interest rate 'collar'.

The need for market-makers to cover the sale of puts when the market is falling dramatically, will often exacerbate the fall itself. More about that when we talk about market-makers.

Options on Foreign Exchange

I have previously mentioned that the foreign exchange market tends to trade on an over-the-counter basis. Futures exist, but they are not as hugely popular as futures on other instruments. Those futures also have options, but again activity is small by comparison. Over-the-counter options are, however, big business in foreign exchange.

Many companies hedge their foreign exchange risk using some form of derivative product. Some don't, and often you will see a headline in the business section suggesting that XYZ's profits were down this year due to 'foreign exchange losses'. The company makes this statement as if it were assumed that foreign exchange losses are simply unavoidable and awfully bad luck. This, of course, is rubbish.

Those companies who do choose to hedge will often structure intricate protection measures to specifically offset the risk of known cash flows. Many will set up hedging positions out to several years. The foreign exchange market is the greatest innovator of what are loosely described as 'exotic' options. These are more complex derivatives with lots of bells and whistles. I will introduce some of those in a later chapter.

That about brings us to the end of our look at where options are used in various different markets. It was not exhaustive—there are still many instruments and commodities that I haven't mentioned that have options, but to go through them all would be a tad dull. We have, however, hopefully reached a better understanding of the use of derivatives around the world.

The next two chapters deal more specifically with the pricing of options. Volatility is the most important factor in options pricing and we will look at this concept in greater depth. Hedging of option positions is also an important area, particularly from the point of view of options market-makers, and so we will explore the concepts of delta hedging, along with theta, gamma and other 'Greek letters'.

As these areas are of less interest to the layperson, the reader can choose to skip the next two chapters and move on to learn more about other derivative instruments.

7. Volatility—the Magic Number

Optionality

Optionality. *Isn't that a sexy word?* Don't bother trying to look it up in the dictionary though, because it doesn't exist. A bit like 'incentivation'. Yet 'optionality ' is a word often bandied about in derivative circles. Why so?

A derivative instrument is simply an instrument whose movement in value is linked to some other underlying instrument. The reason derivative instruments exist at all is because of their ability to provide leverage and the capacity for risk control. The specific form of derivative, which is best at delivering both these qualities, is the *option*. So far I have described various types of options in various different markets. Starting with the straight-forward stock option. we have moved on into futures options, caps and collars, and other such derivatives or 'derivatives on derivatives'. In subsequent chapters, I will briefly explore other slightly more complex derivatives such as convertible bonds.

What makes a convertible bond a popular trading instrument is that it displays a certain amount of 'optionality'. If an instrument displays optionality that simply means that it exhibits the characteristics of an option. As long as there is some sort of choice involved—a right, but not an obligation—the value of the instrument will greatly depend on how one values that underlying option. Okay. Where is all this leading?

The point is that the great majority of 'derivatives' are in option form, or display optionality. By having a good appreciation of the nature of an option, then one is well on the way to appreciating a great many forms of derivatives. In order to fully understand an option, one must have a good understanding of how an option is priced, or why an option is trading at a particular price. This leads us back to those variables which are the determinants of an option price.

The Five Variables

To date we have discussed at length the fact that the price of an option is the function of five different variables. Those variables are the underlying price, the exercise price, the time to maturity, the funding cost and volatility.

Let's go back to our old friend, United Consolidated Inc. We previously considered that we had the view that the share price of UCI was going to rise, at least in the short term. With the current price at $15.00, we could either buy the shares outright or take the less risky route of buying the right to buy the shares at a later date—a call option. We elected to buy the three-month $15.00 call for 50c.

To arrive at this decision, we had to consider that the premium we were paying up front for the option—50c—was a price we considered to be reasonable under the circumstances. To know whether or not the price was reasonable, we had to consider what factors affected that price. These are the five variables. We know the value of four of the variables. The underlying price of UCI shares is $15.00 today. The exercise price (or strike price) of our call option is $15.00. The time to maturity is three months. Our cost of funding is the rate we are forgoing by taking the money out of the bank in order to buy the call option. Let's say this is 5% per annum. The last variable, however, is unknown. We do not actually *know* the volatility of the share price. We are only guessing as to whether the share price of UCI has the capacity to move significantly within three months.

Given that we know, and thus everybody else knows, the first four variables, it follows that the value of volatility is that factor which *really* determines the price at which an option will actually trade—will actually change hands in the marketplace. Because that value is a matter of opinion, there will be a meeting of demand and supply. Those who are willing to pay up for an option, because they feel the share has the potential to be volatile, and therefore there are risks involved, will meet those who believe the opposite and are willing to wager that they will be keeping the risk premium they are receiving from the buyer of the option.

It would all be a lot easier if we could measure the level of volatility, wouldn't it? That way there would be *five* known variables and we would always know what the correct price for an option should be. But then, if everybody knew what the correct price should be, would options ever trade? The idea in financial markets is to 'buy cheap and sell dear'. That's how an investor makes money. If everyone knows the correct price for an option then no one will sell below that price and no one will buy above it. Result: stand-off. Options would cease to exist.

But options do exist—in a big way. Therefore, it must follow that one *cannot* measure volatility. Is this so?

What Was, What Is, and What Will Be

Come back to the share price itself for just a moment.

UCI is trading at $15.00. Why is it trading at $15.00? Is that the correct price for the stock? Being 'correct' is not really a factor. All that matters is that $15.00 is the price at which the buyers have met the sellers—at least for today. Yesterday the stock was trading at $14.95. The fact that today the price has risen 5c simply indicates that there are more people in the market looking to buy the stock than are looking to sell it. What will the price be tomorrow? Can *you* know for sure?

We know every price that UCI has traded at since the day the company first listed. In other words, we know all its 'historical' prices. These are well documented, analysed, charted and generally dissected. We have no trouble in ascertaining the 'what was' of stock prices.

Nor do we have any trouble ascertaining the 'what is'. That's $15.00. We know that's where the stock is trading right now.

Can we, however, determine the 'what will be' of a stock price? Can we *know* where a stock price is going? Some people actually believe that the answer to this question lies in the historical performance of the stock price. They will pore over charts and apply all manner of theories involving lines and waves and magic numbers and determine with great confidence that there is a high probability that the stock price will be . . . here. I've never met a rich chartist.

The reality is that knowing the historical prices of a stock, or the price at which it is trading now, provides absolutely *no guarantee* of then determining where the price of the stock will be tomorrow, next week or in six-months time. No guarantee at all.

But what we're really here to look at is volatility. We can cover a lot of the uncertainty of buying shares by buying options instead. But...*can we measure the volatility?*

Historical Volatility

The answer is yes—quite easily.

But didn't I just say that if volatility was known, there'd be no option market? Ah yes—but which volatility? The volatility up to now, the volatility right now, or the volatility to come?

Knowing the historical prices of a particular stock, we can clearly see, perhaps by looking at a chart, just how volatile the stock price has been. If there have been steady flows up and down and up, we may conclude that the stock has not been particularly volatile. If there have been wild rallies and crashes in a short period, we would determine that the stock has been very volatile. But looking at the chart is one thing. What we can also do is assign a measurement to the level of volatility for the purpose of comparison. Such a measurement is known as the 'historical volatility'.

A quick lesson in statistics. Let's look at every closing price of UCI shares on every day for twelve months prior to today. Having noted these prices, we can determine the average price for the stock over one year. Once this average price is known, we can then look at every day's closing price in turn and note how far away, in dollar terms, it was from the average price. If we add up each of these differences and again find the average, we have arrived at what is known in the world of statistics as 'standard deviation'.

Now take the standard deviation and divide it by the average price of the stock. Voila! That is the measure of historical volatility. It is a measure of the propensity for a stock price to deviate from its mean (average) over a given period of time. This number is conventionally represented as a percentage. It is not, however, necessary to measure the historical volatility only over one year. Volatility can be measured over any given period—a month, a week, a day. Measurements over different time periods may or may not be consistent—if a stock has been boring all year but in one month leapt up unexpectedly due to, say, a takeover bid, then the historical volatility for that month will be exceedingly higher than the month before, and somewhat higher than the one-year measure.

So. We *can* measure the historical volatility. Does this actually help us? Come back to the UCI share price again. If we know what the historical prices were for a year will we thus know, with certainty, what the UCI share price will be tomorrow? Or next week? Or next month? Of course not. If we know what the volatility of the UCI share price has been over the year, will that tell us what the volatility is going to be from here on in? Nup. Knowing the historical volatility is about as helpful as knowing what the last few numbers on the roulette wheel were.

Mr Black and Mr Scholes

Nevertheless, it's *about the best we've got*. And armed with our volatility measurement, spurious as it may be, we should now have five known variables and thus all the ingredients to determine the right price for an option. Okay, we now know all the numbers, but what do we do with them? *Plug them into an equation, of course.*

A bloke named Charles Castelli once wrote a book titled *The Theory of Options in Stocks and Shares*. Not so surprising in itself, except that the book was written in 1877. In the ensuing years, many others had a go at unravelling the mysteries of options, but it wasn't until 1973 that two guys hit on something that really made the world sit up and take notice. They were Fischer Black and Myron Scholes and they introduced an option-pricing model. For the first time, we had an equation that allowed you to plug in the known variables and come up with the 'right' option price.

Now I'm going to show you the model. It looks pretty formidable . . . but don't worry. I simply want you to appreciate the extent of complex mathematics that has been applied to the area of derivatives. I'll run through each bit once you've had a look.

The Black-Scholes Option Pricing Model

$$C = SN(d_1) - Ke^{(-rt)}N(d_2)$$

C = theoretical call premium
e = exponential function (2.7183)
S = current stock price

$$d_1 = \frac{\ln(S / K) + (r + \sigma^2/2)}{\sigma\sqrt{t}}$$

t = time to maturity
K = exercise price
r = risk-free interest rate
N = cumulative standard normal distribution

$$d_2 + d_1 - \sigma\sqrt{t}$$
= standard deviation of stock returns
ln = natural logarithm

We can recognise our variables within the equation. The 'standard deviation of stock returns' is simply the volatility measurement. The 'risk-free interest rate' is a theoretical concept. It implies that there is a place you can put your money and be *guaranteed* a return. In the real world this equates to our funding rate. The 'cumulative standard normal distribution' sounds impressive but it simply means a bell curve, that being the distribution of probabilities of an option being exercised. 'ln' and 'e' are mathematical concepts.

I said that the 'risk-free interest rate' is a theoretical concept. In actual fact the whole model is based on a range of non-real-world assumptions. It assumes that there are no dividends and no brokerage or other transaction costs. It assumes that markets never close at night and that there is never any gap from one share price trade to another. It assumes that every single person has the same information, so that every next share price move is totally a fifty-fifty chance. (This is known as an 'efficient' market). There are also some other more mathematical assumptions that I won't bore you with, but suffice to say this model only *really* works on a computer, and not in the actual market.

So why is it far and away the most oft-used model in the derivative world? It is a reasonable estimate for one, but more importantly it has become a market benchmark model, and your average market participant feels more secure using the same model as everybody else.

Nevertheless, if our model is designed to *predict* option prices it obviously still has one major flaw. It uses the historical volatility in its calculation and, as we well know, our knowledge of past volatility is no sure indicator of volatility to come. So what, if any, benefits does this model provide us with?

Implied Volatility

The share price of UCI is valued at $15.00 right now. The reason it is valued at $15.00 is because that's the price at which the buyers have met the sellers. Does this make $15.00 the 'right' price for UCI? Whether or not *you* believe that the price should be higher or lower, it is the price at which the *market* in general has valued UCI stock.

We also know that the six-month $15.00 call option is trading at 50c. This is the price at which the buyers of the call option have met the sellers of the call option. Whether or not you believe this price to be cheap or dear, it is the price at which the market, in general, has valued that option.

So, knowing what price the option is trading at, now we can actually use our Black-Scholes model in reverse. If we plug the four known variables and the current option price into the equation, and solve it, we will have solved for our unknown quantity—a measurement of the volatility. That is the measurement of volatility *now*.

This is known as the 'implied volatility'. If the historical volatility tells us the 'what was', then the implied volatility tells us the 'what is'. If I plug our numbers into the equation, I will imply a volatility for the UCI $15.00 calls of 13.5%.

What have we actually gained by knowing the implied volatility? One thing we can do is compare the implied volatility to the historical volatility. If the historical volatility of the UCI share price over the past three months has been 15%, and the volatility implied by an option price of 50c for the next three months is 13.5%, then you would have to assume that right at the moment that particular call is cheap. So, if we buy the call when it's 'cheap', are we then guaranteed of making money? Not at all. If we are buying a call option, we are hoping that the stock price will rise. Whether or not we buy a 'cheap' or 'expensive' call in volatility terms, there is still every possibility that the stock price will fall and we will lose our premium. Moreover, just because our historical measurement is 15% now, it is not a measurement that is set in concrete. If the stock price hardly moves for three months, then the historical volatility will fall. It may prove that 13.5% wasn't cheap after all.

If the price of the $15.00 call is not 50c, but $1.00, implying a volatility of 30%, would we buy that call? Certainly this seems expensive if the historical volatility up to now is 15%. But we have to consider *why* the option is now trading at an implied volatility of 30%. Has there suddenly been a leap in the uncertainty of the stock price, or the market, or the world? Are there takeover rumours? Are there rumours of an extraordinary loss? Why are people suddenly paying a lot more premium for their options?

If there is no obvious reason, then maybe the option is expensive. Maybe we should be looking to sell it rather than buy it. We would have to be wary, however, as something must be pushing that price up. All this leads to a very important point, and that is that, although the historical and implied volatilities of a stock will tend to be similar a lot of the time, it does not follow that they will be similar all of the time.

Consider this scenario. It is rumoured that the Reserve Bank will cut interest rates by 0.5% tomorrow. This belief has been factored into the bank bill futures market so that the futures price is already reflecting a 0.5% lower rate. Despite the price, there are still some in the market that believe there will *not* be a rate cut, and even if there is, it will only be 0.25%. Therefore, there is a level of uncertainty.

The futures market has responded by going very quiet today as everyone waits with baited breath for tomorrow's result. The bank bill price is hardly moving. This will have the effect of lowering the historical volatility. In fact, if you were measuring the one-day historical volatility, it would be close to zero. What is busy, however, is the option market. Given the uncertainty of the rate cut, many market players have chosen to protect themselves against the wrong result by buying options—puts or calls—and therefore options are in big demand. If there is big demand, then the prices will be forced higher, and if option prices are forced higher, so too will be the implied volatility. So here we have a situation where the historical is falling while the implied is rising.

Tomorrow comes—no rate cut. The bank bill futures are in turmoil. They are racing up to recover the 0.5% the market had factored in. Historical volatility has leapt enormously. But over in the options pit, those players who protected themselves from a bad result, no longer need their protection. Either they are profiting from the lack of rate cut, or they have accepted that they have lost their premium (but at least they were hedged had it been the opposite). Options are now being sold out. And, not surprisingly, the selling pressure is forcing prices down, and therefore the implied volatility is falling. Once again, the two volatility measurements are moving against each other.

Future Volatility

Historical volatility can provide us with the 'what was'. Implied volatility can provide us with the 'what is'. But if we are really going to make any money then we need to know the 'what will be' of volatility levels. A and B are not giving us an answer to C. Is there any way to predict future volatility?

No. We can draw upon experience, we can consider past performances, we can even put together a 'history' of implied volatility levels, thus providing us with something called the 'historical implied volatility' measurement, but we can never know for sure what will happen next.

If we knew what was going to happen next, then we would also know where the UCI share price was going next. And if we knew where the UCI share price was going next, we wouldn't need to buy an option.

Are Models Useful?

All of this must lead to one obvious question. If the model cannot provide us with a price for an option that is going to be the 'right' price, and if past and present volatility measurements are no guaranteed indicator of future volatility, what use is the model at all?

When Joe or Josephine Average Investor is contemplating buying an option or a warrant, it is unlikely that they will be plugging variables into an option pricing model in order to help with their decision. This doesn't mean they can't, however, as the average investor armed with a home computer has ready access to affordable option-pricing software. It is more likely, one assumes, that Joe or Josephine will simply make an anecdotal assessment of the value of buying an option, perhaps with assistance from their broker.

When the decision is made, it is quite likely that the option or warrant will be purchased from someone whose job it is to make bids and offers in options and warrants—the previously mentioned market-maker. Because all of the first four variables are known by the option market-maker, he or she is only really interested in the level of volatility at which he or she is prepared to buy or sell the particular option or warrant. In fact, when options market-makers are talking to each other, and perhaps trading with each other, they often talk not in terms of price but simply in terms of volatility. For example, rather than saying, 'My price in UCI $15.00 six-month calls is 55c-65c,' they may simply say, 'My volatility is 10%-12%.' Because the volatility level is the only unknown quantity, it is the specific factor affecting the price at which a market-maker is prepared to buy or sell.

Each market-maker will be armed with a model, usually the same model, which, once the volatility level has been entered, will spit out a price for the option. One option or warrant market-maker may well be responsible for making markets in several stocks, each with several different times to maturity and several different strike prices. This translates into a hell of a lot of option prices, certainly more than one person can keep in their head, and so it is handy for the market-maker to concentrate only on the volatility level of the stock, or their estimation of it, and then have the computer provide the actual prices via the model.

It can be really confusing being a market-maker. The bottom line is that no matter how sexy one's computer, the model is only ever as good as the human who's punching in the numbers. You may have heard an expression in computer circles: 'garbage in, garbage out'. A market-maker is not going to profit from having the best computer and the best model if their estimation of the direction of volatility ultimately proves to be wrong.

The Black-Scholes model is not the only option-pricing model in existence. There have been many supposed improvements to the original model, some attempting to address many of the non-real world assumptions, and other completely different models using more and more complex mathematics. Despite this, the simple Black-Scholes model is still a benchmark and is still preferred by options traders all over the world, particularly in futures options. There does exist, however, another more simplistic model that is often used in options trading, particularly for stock options. The reason for this is that it is better able to cope with the payment of dividends than the B-S. It is worth us having a look at.

The Binomial Model

Do you remember probability trees from school? If you toss a coin, there are two possible outcomes—heads or tails. Toss the coin again, and again, there are two possible outcomes—heads or tails. It follows that after two tosses of a coin, there are four possible results—HH, HT, TH and TT. Toss the coin twenty times and there is a whole matrix of possible head/tail combinations. The results displayed in a diagram resemble an ever-expanding tree.

The binomial model is able to estimate options prices by adopting a probability tree approach. Assuming that a stock price has a 50% chance of going up, and a 50% chance of going down at any point in time, one can draw a similar tree of possible outcomes over a period of time. As with the

Black-Scholes model, the binomial model assumes a natural distribution. Without going into great mathematical detail, let me just say that it is possible to work back from a particular stock price result to ascertain the possibility of that stock price being reached. From this we can estimate an option price.

The binomial model becomes more and more accurate with more and more 'steps' in the tree. It can also accommodate gaps in share price movements. You will recall that the B-S assumes there are never any gaps in share price movements. When a stock goes 'ex-dividend', there will be a gap in the share price, and so the binomial model is often preferred for the purpose of calculating stock option prices. Instruments without such gaps, such as futures or currencies, are most often calculated using the Black-Scholes.

When an options trader uses a computer to assist in price calculation, he or she is also able to derive a lot of other information to assist in the process of trying to make money out of trading options. Let's have a look at some of that information.

8. Learning Greek for Fun and Profit

Greek?

'When you trade in equity options,' asked my friend Franky, 'do you hedge your gamma and theta, or just your delta? And if you don't hedge your gamma and theta, why not?

The equity options specialist nodded for about ten seconds. He obviously had no clue what was meant by the Greek... 'You know,' he said, 'I don't know the answer. That's probably why I don't have trouble trading. I'll find out and come back tomorrow. I'm not really up on options theory'.[27]

So related Michael Lewis from his experiences of the Salomon Bros training program during the eighties. In Lewis' anecdote, it is the young trainee, fresh out of uni, catching out the older 'options specialist' with his use of the Greek. The 'specialist', in actual fact, assuming he had had some years of experience in trading options, probably knew *exactly* what Franky was talking about. The difference is that he had never applied specific labels to his hedging activities, and certainly not a confusing series of Greek letters.

So what is Franky talking about? To understand that, we must first take a closer look at the activities of the options market-maker.

The Market-Maker

If you go to the races and want to place a bet, you have two choices. Either you can go to the TAB, which will pay you out at odds determined by the volume of money wagered on that particular horse in all of the state, or you can go to a bookmaker. The bookmaker will determine the odds at which you will be paid out in the event of your horse winning. He will determine a set of odds for every horse in the race, and those odds will reflect a combination of the bookmaker's opinion of the horse's chances of winning, and the weight of money he is holding on each horse.

The bookmaker is so called because he is 'making a book'. You could also say he was 'making a market'. The bookmaker is happy to be engaged in this activity because he assumes that, more often than not, he will pay out

27 From Liar's Poker by Michael Lewis, Hodder and
   Stoughton Ltd, 1989.

a smaller amount than he has taken in. This is not always the case. Bookmakers can lose substantial amounts of money.

We have already been introduced to the options market-maker. This is a person, employed most often by an investment bank or broker, whose role it is to make a bid and offer, that is a buying price and a selling price, in a particular options market. If you go and buy calls in UCI at 50c, you will either be buying from another participant who is looking to sell them, or you will be buying from a market-maker who is obliged, either by the rules of an exchange, or by his or her employer guaranteeing that particular service to the market, to make a price at which he or she will sell that particular option.

If you are buying the UCI call because you think the market is going up does that mean that the market-maker who is selling you the call *must* have the view that the market is going down? If the market-maker is obliged to make a price, does that mean that sometimes he will win and sometimes he will lose, but really he doesn't have much control over the result?

No. It may be that the market-maker *does* have the view that UCI is going to fall, but this may actually be irrelevant to his decision to sell the call at the price. It is more likely that the market-maker is happy to sell the call at the particular level of volatility implied by the call price. But volatility in itself does not determine the direction of a stock price, only its propensity to move around a lot. This means that although the stock may ultimately display a low level of volatility, it can still do this by moving up slowly, resulting in the call being exercised.

How can the market-maker then capture the lower level of volatility without the stock price ultimately causing his or her demise? The answer to this is to hedge.

Hedging Options

Although an options market-maker is similar in a lot of ways to a bookmaker, there is one fundamental difference. Whereas a market-maker offers the option trader both a sell and a buy price, the bookmaker offers only a sell price. This means the average punter can't go up to the bookmaker and 'lay' a horse with him. Consequently, the bookmaker can offer any odds he likes on a horse, but competition will serve to bring that price closer to what the punter might be prepared to take.

In any horse race there are always a couple of rank outsiders. These are the horses with odds of anything between 50 and 1000-1. A bookmaker will usually ignore the odd one dollar bet at 1000-1 on some donkey, but if he were to take in, say, a $100 bet, he might get a bit concerned. In the absolutely remote but still not-beyond-the-realms-of-possibility event that this horse got up, he would be buried to the tune of $100,000. Time to hedge the bets.

A bookmaker 'hedges' by 'laying off' the bet, in part or full, to another bookmaker. By backing the 1000-1 donkey himself, he has negated the effect of the horse actually winning. Furthermore, the bookmaker may choose to lay off on shorter-priced horses if he is concerned that he is holding too much money. If he laid off at higher odds, he would actually lock in a profit, were the horse to win. If he laid off at lower odds, he would have similarly locked in a loss, but he would have prevented a greater loss.

In reality then, although the bookmaker only offers one side of the price to the punter, he may well be constantly 'buying and selling' the horses in the race. Similarly, an options market-maker is continually buying and selling options. Ideally, he or she would like to sell calls, at the offer price to those who wished to buy, and, as close to simultaneously as possible, buy calls at the bid price from those who wished to sell. As there is a 'spread' between the bid and offer price, the market-maker would subsequently 'lock in' a profit. This would probably work wonderfully if the underlying stock price never moved.

But the stock price is always moving. A market-maker may find that he or she is only selling calls while the stock price rises. No one seems to be selling to the market-maker. Subsequently, the market-maker would be building an exposure to the stock price and therefore taking a risk. One way to overcome this problem would be to buy the underlying stock when selling the call. If the call is exercised, the market-maker has lost, but the stock he or she has bought has risen in value to offset the loss on the option—the market-maker comes out square.

This type of hedge would, in fact, work perfectly except for one small problem—the market-maker could never actually make any money. And although there are obligations attached to the role of market-maker, they are still only in the game to make money. What a market-maker needs to do is to *strip out* the directional risk of the underlying stock and go back to that element I have constantly referred to as the real traded variable in options—the volatility. To do this, the market-maker has to consider the option's *delta*.

Delta

If we buy the UCI $15.00 call for 50c when the UCI share price is trading at $15.00, we have bought the at-the-money option. What are the chances of this option being exercised? We have a view. We think the price of UCI is going to rise. But this is just a matter of opinion. Mathematically, the price of UCI has an equal chance of going up or down. Therefore, the chance of an at-the-money option being exercised is 50-50.

Let's say we had decided to play it safe and consequently we had bought the $14.00 call instead of the $15.00. This call is already $1.00 in the money and has cost us $1.35 in premium. What is the chance that this option will be exercised? Clearly the chance is better than the 50% chance of the at-the-money option being exercised. In fact, the chance is more like 60%.

What if we go the other way and decide that we don't want to pay too much in premium? We buy the $16.00 call which is already $1.00 out-of-the-money. It only costs 35c but the stock has to first rally $1.00 before we can begin to make money. What is the chance that this option will be exercised? Clearly the chance is less than that of the at-the-money option. In fact, the chance is more like 40%.

For each exercise price we consider, even from $5.00 to $25.00, there will be a differing chance of that option being exercised at maturity. The more in-the-money the option, the greater the chance will be. The more out-of-the-money the option, the lesser the chance will be. It is all a matter of probability. And those of you who can still recall any study of probability at school will recognise that if we graphed those chances, we would form a bell curve. Actually it doesn't look like a bell curve at all. But if you look closely at Fig. 9, you will see that if you split the graph at the 50% mark the left side is an upside down half of a bell curve and the right hand side is a right-way-up half of a bell curve.

Fig. 9—Delta vs Exercise Price (Stock Price Fixed)

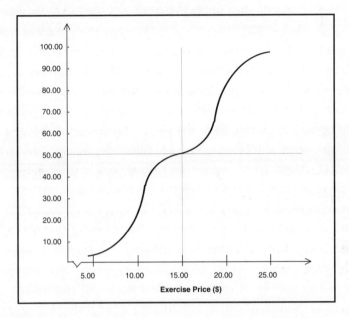

The chance of an option being exercised is a very important consideration for the market-maker. Important enough that option traders like to give it its own special name—'delta'. Why a Greek letter? Because mathematicians gave delta its name, and mathematicians love using Greek letters in their equations.

Delta Hedging

So why is the delta of an option so important to the market-maker?

Let's return to our notion that a market-maker needs to 'strip out' the directional risk of his or her option trades. If we buy the $15.00 call from the market-maker, and the market-maker does not wish to have the risk of the stock price rising and the call being exercised, then he or she could buy the underlying stock and offset that risk. But, as we said, this would result in the market-maker never making money because they would constantly be fully hedged and every gain would be cancelled out by an equivalent loss.

If there is only a 50% chance of the option being exercised, then why hedge 100%? Hedging 50% of the position would, in effect, hedge that 'chance' or risk of losing money. And that, my friends, is 'delta hedging'.

If we buy the $15.00 call over 10,000 shares of UCI, and UCI is trading at $15.00, then the market-maker from whom we bought the call will simultaneously buy 5,000 shares in UCI. He or she will be delta-hedged. If we buy the $14.00 call, that with a delta of 60%, the market-maker will simultaneously buy 6,000 shares in UCI. If we buy the $16.00 call, that with a delta of 40%, the market-maker will buy 4,000 shares of UCI. In each case, the market-maker is hedging out the risk of the option being exercised.

Market-makers also buy options. When buying a call, the delta hedging process simply becomes the reverse of that of selling a call. If the market-maker buys the $15.00 call, he or she will simultaneously *sell* 5,000 shares in UCI. Again, they will be delta hedged. Therefore, we can summarise delta hedging for call options by saying: Buy call, sell stock; sell call, buy stock.

Let's not forget about puts. Market-makers also make markets in puts. As a put is the right to sell, as opposed to the call, which is the right to buy, then again delta hedging for puts is simply the reverse of that for calls. Therefore, if we were to buy the $15.00 *put* in UCI from the market–maker, he or she would simultaneously delta hedge by *selling* 5,000 shares in UCI. Our little adage then becomes: Buy put, buy stock; sell put, sell stock.

If a market-maker sells stock for the purpose of delta hedging, must they have previously have owned that stock? No. The Australian Stock Exchange grants exemption to market-makers in exchange-traded options and warrants allowing them to sell stock 'short'. Having sold the stock, the market-maker must then 'borrow' stock to cover the short. This borrowing comes at a cost, and this cost will be factored into the market-maker's price through an adjustment to their funding cost.

If a market-maker has delta hedged all their trades for the day, does that mean they have now locked in a profit on their trading? This is a popular misconception. Delta hedging is not, as some unfortunately tend to believe, a form of arbitrage. It is anything but. In delta hedging, the market-maker has *not* hedged out the risk through to expiry. Before we consider why this is the case, let's first look at delta more closely. Are deltas always the same?

The Moveable Feast

Fig. 9 has provided us with a distribution of delta amounts across a range of exercise prices. For the purpose of this graph, the stock price is fixed at $15.00. We know, however, that stock prices are never 'fixed'. They move around all the time. We also appreciate that as the stock price rises and falls, so will the chance of a call being exercised rise and fall. The higher the stock price, the more chance a call will ultimately be exercised. The lower the stock price, the less chance a call will ultimately be exercised.

It follows that the higher the stock price, the higher the delta. The lower the stock price, the lower the delta. (Applying to calls. Puts are simply vice versa).

While the stock was trading at $15.00, the $15.00 call had a delta of 50%. If the stock price rises to, say, $15.25 in the next couple of days, it now has a greater chance of being exercised, and the delta of the option will have risen to 52%. If the stock price falls to, say, $14.75, it has a lesser chance of being exercised and the delta will have fallen to 48%. In Fig. 10, we have fixed the exercise price of our call option and graphed the delta of that option against the stock price of UCI. This shows the delta changing as the call option moves from being at-the-money to being either in-the-money or out-of-the-money. Looks pretty much the same, doesn't it?

Fig. 10—Delta vs Stock Price (Exercise Price Fixed)

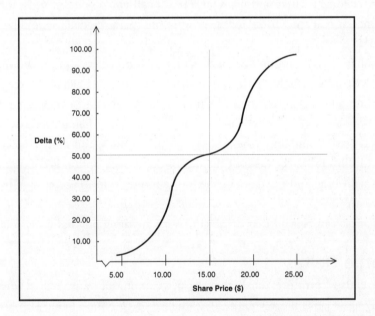

It might also be a good time to note that if we refer back to our Call Price Table way back in Chapter 4, which illustrates the risk premiums associated with the price of the call option at different levels of the stock price, I mentioned that the distribution was in the nature of a bell curve. Given that the risk premium and our measure of risk—delta—are inexorably linked, it should come as no surprise that a graph of their distribution is identical in form.

Time For More Deltas

The value of delta will change for each exercise price of an option series, and the delta of that specific exercise price option will change in relation to a change in the price of the underlying stock. Thus delta is never fixed, but moves around continuously. A moveable feast.

We also know that the chance of an option being exercised will increase the greater the time to maturity of that option. If the chance of an option being exercised increases then, it will follow, so will the option's delta.

The at-the-money option, however, will *always* have a delta of 50%. No matter what the circumstances, and what time there is left in an option, if the stock is trading at the exercise price, there is never more than a 50-50 chance that it will move in either direction. In- or out-of-the-money options will have a greater value if there is a longer time for the option to run because the longer the time, the greater the chance of exercise. It follows that deltas are higher for longer-dated options. Our $16.00 call had a delta of 40% for the three-month maturity. If the maturity were one year, the delta would be more like 45%.

Similarly, as an option approaches maturity, it becomes more and more predictable as to whether that option would be exercised. That is, except for the option which is currently at-the-money. It will always be a 50% chance. An out-of-the-money option has less and less chance of being exercised as each day passes, and an in-the-money option has more and more chance. Thus it follows that the delta of the out-of-the-money option is continually falling with time and the delta of the in-the-money option is continually rising with time.

Again it can be said that delta values are anything but static.

Volatile Deltas

We have also learnt previously that the price of an option is greater when the underlying stock is more volatile. The chance of an option being exercised will improve if the stock has a tendency to move dramatically. It follows that the more volatile the stock, the higher the delta values of options on that stock. Increased volatility will increase the deltas of in- and out-of-the-money options alike (but not the at-the-money, it is always 50%).

Because the volatility of a stock is itself constantly changing, due to market occurrences and factors directly affecting the individual stock, then the delta values of that stock's options will also be constantly changing.

For example, a once out-of-the-money call that looked unlikely to be exercised, and therefore had a delta of 10%, may suddenly look quite a chance after an unexpected profit announcement sends the stock price soaring. The delta could immediately jump up to, say, 40% in a blink.

The conclusion to all of this? Delta, representing the chance of an option being exercised, is pretty much a point in time and space. It is affected simultaneously by the relationship between the exercise price and the underlying stock price, by time, and by the volatility of the underlying stock. Its value merely provides a 'snapshot' of chance, and therefore of risk.

With all of these factors in conspiracy, and deltas moving around like moths in a bottle, how does one actually determine, other than by guessing, the delta of an option?

Back to the Model

Delta, which, when it's not being called 'delta,' is often referred to as the 'hedge ratio', is another value that can be contrived from an options pricing model such as the Black-Scholes.

Many a text book on options will tell you that the delta value can be used to 'predict' the value of an option at a different price in the stock. For example, if an option has a delta of 50% and the stock price rallies $1.00, then the option value should increase by 50c. This is a lot of rubbish. Delta is not fixed, it is constantly changing, and can thus in no way be used to 'predict' anything. What the option buyer can assume, however, is that if a stock has a low delta right now, then a movement in the stock price is not going to have very much affect on the price of the option. On the other hand, an option with a high delta will have a greater change in price for any move in the stock price. Only an option with a delta of close to 100% (ie so far in-the-money that there's very little chance the option won't be exercised) will change in price on a one for one basis with the stock price.

Nevertheless, an option-pricing model can be used to determine an option's delta at any particular point. To do that, we have to plug in the stock price, exercise price, time, funding rate and volatility. Aha! We can never really be sure what the volatility measure should be, can we? So our delta calculation will only ever be as reliable as our volatility estimation. And this is a very important point.

By 'delta hedging', the options market-maker is stripping out the directional risk of the underlying stock. To determine what delta value to use, he or she will derive the delta from the model after assessing the level of volatility. This is how the market-maker comes to be 'trading' the volatility of the option. Their bid and offer is really a bid and offer in volatility. The actual bid and offer price is simply that which the model subsequently calculates.

Rehedging

And delta is constantly changing. What this means is that having delta hedged the option on the initial sale or purchase, the market-maker cannot simply walk away. As delta is reflecting the chance of an option being exercised, the market-maker will need to constantly add or subtract from his or her delta hedge position right up to expiry of the option.

If the market-maker sold us the $15.00 call, and the stock has rallied to $16.00 he or she will have to add to the 5,000 shares initially purchased as a delta hedge. If the delta is now 60%, the market-maker will need to buy another 1,000 shares. If the stock has fallen to $14.00, and the delta to 40%, the market-maker no longer needs all of the original hedge. Subsequently, he or she will *sell* 1,000 shares. The market-maker will buy and sell, buy and sell constantly throughout the life of the option.

The market-maker is forever buying and selling calls and puts at different exercise prices and different maturities. Each of these transactions requires a delta hedge. Each of these delta hedges requires adjustment as the stock price moves. Rather than treat them individually, the market-maker will aggregate all the delta hedge requirements at any given price in the underlying stock. Therefore, he or she will have the need to either buy or sell one aggregated lump of delta hedge whenever the stock price moves.

If the market-maker has bought more options than he or she has sold, then he or she is deemed to be 'long' options or, more specifically, 'long volatility'. If the market-maker has sold more options than he or she has bought, then he or she is deemed to be 'short volatility'. And this is where the fun begins.

In order to rehedge, the market-maker who is 'long volatility' will always be selling stock as the market rises and buying stock as the market falls. This is wonderful! He or she is always selling high and buying low. He or she must *always* make money as the stock price moves. In order to rehedge, the market-maker who is 'short volatility' will always be buying stock as the market rises and selling stock as the market falls. He or she is always buying high and selling low. This is terrible! He or she is always *losing* money as the stock price moves. Why on earth would any market-maker want to get into a position where they are short volatility?

The answer to this question lies in time.

Vol

In the relentless quest for jargon and abbreviations, the market-maker will usually make reference to his or her book in terms of 'vol'. Thus the market-maker, who is long volatility, is subsequently deemed to be 'long vol', and the market-maker, who is short volatility, is subsequently deemed to be 'short vol'.

Spending Time with Theta

You will recall our canoeist paddling upstream against the ever-increasing current. The ever-increasing current in the case of options is the time decay. Every day an option will lose some of its value as the chance of it being exercised becomes either greater or lesser with time. The more obvious it is that an option will/won't be exercised, the less risk that option has and so the less value. Time decay eats away at option values.

Back to our market-makers. The guy who is long volatility basically owns more options than he has sold. He makes money every time the market moves. But he loses money every day in time decay. This time decay is known as an option's 'theta' value. The long volatility trader has a 'negative theta'. In order to ultimately profit from the position he has built he must make more in his rehedging each day than he loses in his time decay. Or at least he must ultimately make more money, over the life of the options he is holding, than the amount he will ultimately lose from his negative theta.

The lady who is short volatility basically has sold more options than she has bought. She loses money every time the market moves. But she *gains* money every day in time decay. She is winning as the options she has sold lose value. The short volatility trader has a 'positive theta'. In order to ultimately profit over the life of her positions, she must lose less in rehedging than she picks up in positive theta.

Theta is calculated as the amount of risk premium lost in an option's value each day. Recalling Chapter 4, we know that the option with the greatest risk premium is the at-the-money (50-delta) option. It follows that the 50-delta option has the greatest theta. An option that is in- or out-of-the-money has a lesser risk premium and, therefore, a lesser theta. The value of theta will not be the same each day. Time decay is not linear.

So it follows that making money out of options market making is a day-to-day battle of delta and theta. The long volatility player is hoping that his deltas change a lot as he will make money from good stock movement. The more the stock moves, the more likely he is to exceed his theta and thus profit. The short volatility player will hope the deltas hardly change at all. A lack of movement in the stock will reduce her need to be rehedging at a loss. If this loss does not exceed the theta she is gaining, then she will be a winner.

Rehedging and Crashing

It first came to light to the markets in general during the crash of '87. It showed up again in the crashette of '89, the crash and bounce of '97 and the roller-coaster of '98.

If a market-maker is short volatility, and the market falls, the market-maker must sell to maintain a sufficient delta hedge. The more the market falls, the more the market-maker must sell. If the market 'gaps' down overnight, meaning that the opening prices on the next day are substantially lower than the closing prices of the previous day, then the market-maker will need to suddenly sell a lot more than they might otherwise have anticipated.

In a crash situation there is an awful lot of selling that needs to be done. This need to sell only serves to put further pressure on an already falling and panicking market. The market-makers sell more, the market falls more, and so the market-makers have to sell more again. It can be self-destructive.

This is why options (a form of derivative) have often been singled out as instruments that are a cause of, or at the very least an additional cause of, market crashes and any other periods of extreme volatility.

To sum up, you could say that the long volatility player is looking for a higher volatility and the short volatility player is looking for a lower volatility. *That is why options market-makers are actually volatility traders.* If a market-maker has become long volatility, it is most likely because he bid a higher price for his options (bid a higher volatility). If a market-maker has become short volatility, it is most likely because she offered a lower price for her options (offered a lower volatility).

Simple, isn't it? Well, just before you go and run off to be an options market-maker let me complicate things a bit further.

Gamma

Delta can be defined as 'the rate of change of an option price with respect to a change in the stock price'. In other words, delta provides an indication of how much an option will change in value as the stock price moves. But we know that this concept has limited use because the delta itself is constantly changing.

Gamma, our next Greek friend, is defined as the 'rate of change of delta'. In mathematical parlance, it is the 'second derivative' of the change in the stock price. As delta is constantly changing, it becomes vitally important to the options market-maker to know just how much a delta value may change. Battling between delta and theta is , after all, the market-maker's game. A 'long vol' player wants delta to change as quickly as possible because he will make more money with each change. The 'short vol' player wants delta to change as slowly as possible because she will lose money with each change.

Gamma is a measurement of how much delta will change from one stock price to the next. It is another number which can be pulled out of the options pricing model. Personally, I never found the absolute measurement of gamma to be particularly useful. I preferred to treat it as a *comparative* measure.

The option with the highest gamma is always the at-the-money option— the 50-delta option. This is the option with the highest risk. Delta changes more quickly around the 50-delta option than any other delta option.

We know that the longer the time to maturity, the higher the deltas on the in- and out-of the money options. As these values are higher, the longer-dated deltas will change more slowly than the shorter-dated deltas. The result is that the short date at-the-money option will have a higher gamma than the long date at-the-money option. But just to make it even more confusing, longer-dated in- or out-of-the-money options will have a higher gamma than their shorter-dated counterparts. Now that's really getting a bit much, and the truth of the matter is that I don't wish to dwell on this because it really is the realm of the options market-maker and not a lot of help to Joe and Josephine Average Investor. So I'll just make a couple of quick points.

My '87 Experience

In reference to the previous box on rehedging and crashes, I would like to relate my experience during the crash of '87.

I was part of a team responsible for one of the largest SPI futures options books in the market. This means I was a market-maker who needed to constantly rehedge my book. In the period leading up to October, there were some astute investors who had anticipated a market correction and had bought hundreds of options. All of these options were sold by myself and other market-makers.

On the Monday evening, the SPI future closed at 2006. It had fallen around 100 points on the day. We had sold futures all day and had come out with only a small loss. We were pretty pleased with ourselves. On the Tuesday morning, after Wall Street had imploded, the first trade was 1600.

It then quickly traded down to 1400. Before this day, we would have considered ourselves legends if we had made $1 million for the year. With the market at 1400 we were effectively down by $12 million on the day. Fortunately, the market rallied temporarily and, with a bit of fancy footwork, we managed to finish the day down only $5 million. It was the scariest day of my life.

A market-maker hedges delta by buying or selling stock. The market-maker can also hedge gamma by buying and selling options. I said earlier that if a market-maker has bought more options than he has sold, he is 'long volatility'. This is not quite true. The market-maker will be long vol if the options he has bought have a greater gamma than the options he has sold. In other words, he could actually sell more options than he has bought, but still be long vol because of the gamma of those options. More realistically, he is said to be 'long gamma'. It will also often occur that due to the movement in stock price and time, the long gamma book will turn into a short gamma book without any further options being bought or sold. Yikes.

The short vol player, who is really 'short gamma', would prefer the deltas not to change too quickly. In this sense, she would prefer to be short low gamma options—except for one thing. The option with the highest gamma also has the highest theta and provides the greatest amount of time decay. So in reality, both players want good gamma, be they short or long.

Gamma is therefore, in essence, the most important of the Greek letters as far as a market-maker is concerned. It is possibly also, as you may have gathered, the most confusing. Anyone who thought market-making was a licence to print money may now being starting to have doubts.

The Minor Greeks

Delta, theta and gamma are the big three in the world of options trading. Hence they were the subject of Franky's cheeky question at the beginning of this chapter. It should be pointed out that (a) many an options trader makes a successful living without ever consulting Greek letters (the variables themselves, and the hedging thereof, can be understood intuitively once one gets the hang of options altogether), and (b) you need a computer to actually pull out these numbers and people were trading options long before computers were invented. The bottom line is that they are a way of making things are bit clearer. (As mud, some would say). So here are a couple more.

Vega is the change in an option price with respect to a change in volatility. Although it is important to both the long vol and short vol player it is not something that you hedge because, let's face it, you are *wanting* volatility to change. The long vol player is hoping the market will move around more (exhibit greater volatility) than the volatility level implied by his buying price. The short vol player is hoping the market will move around less (exhibit lower volatility) than the volatility level implied by her selling price.

The more astute among you will have picked up on the fact that 'vega' is not, in fact, a Greek letter. Where the hell it came from I have no idea. Consequently, although 'vega' is the name most often given to this variable, some options theorists and traders ascribe a different letter. Rho is one that is sometimes used.

The effect of a change in interest rate on the value of an option is something that the option trader will keep a wary eye on and therefore, although it is not quite as important as delta-gamma-theta, it is often ascribed a letter of its own. Lamda is one often used. And there are other less dissected variables which some people like to give names to, and still others use different names than the ones I have just mentioned. It is not important. What is important is that the layman realises that the constant reference to Greek is not a conspiracy or form of secret code. It is simply a means of dissecting options and identifying their specific features with a view to the better understanding of an options' position and the potential for any profit or loss.

This brings us to the end of the complicated section. I hope it has been of some use or interest to those of you who have just pressed through the last two chapters. From here on, I intend to simply describe a few more derivative instruments that many people will have come across and not really understood. It's pretty much down hill from here.

9. Strategies and Strange Instruments

More uses for Options

To date I have introduced options and discussed them in the context of something you might simply buy or, if you're game, sell. As the cliche says, there's more than one way to skin a cat. Options can be used in combinations with each other, or with the underlying instrument, to create different strategies that are specifically designed to take advantage of different circumstances.

There have been a multitude of books written on 'how to trade options'. I do not intend to bore you with graphs and tables and pay-off diagrams of twenty-seven different strategies that are in each way slightly different. If you decide you'd like to go out and get serious about options yourself, then you may wish to purchase a more specific book. In the meantime, I'll just provide a quick run down on some of the more popular option trades.

The Buy-and-Write

This is a very popular form of trade in the stock market. In order to take advantage of a view you may have, that a stock is going to rally, you may consider either (a) buying the stock outright, which exposes you to the risk of the stock falling in value, or (b) buying a call option or warrant, which provides you with a specific, limited loss potential. Another alternative is to buy the stock and simultaneously *sell* a call option that is presently out-of-the-money. *Selling* the option? Is this not risky?

Let's say you buy UCI shares at $15.00 and sell the UCI $16.00 call for 35c. If this call is exercised at expiry, ie the stock price rallies to above $16.00, then you will simply deliver the stock you bought at $15.00 to the call buyer. You are out for $1.00 profit, and you've picked up a further 35c in premium. It doesn't matter how far the stock rallies, any loss in selling the call is covered by the purchased stock.

If the stock falls from $15.00, then you will be a loser. However, you have picked up 35c premium, so in effect you're not losing money until the stock falls below $14.65. If the stock finishes somewhere in between, say $15.50, then you have collected your premium *and* made 50c on the stock.

The buy-write (selling an option is also known as *writing* an option) is a way of enhancing your equity position by taking in option premium. As you are long the stock (ie you have bought the stock), there is no risk of loss in selling the call. All you do risk is the added profit were the stock to rally substantially through the exercise price. Writing call options is also often adopted to enhance existing portfolios. If you are already long the stock, and you feel there is good value in selling the out-of-the-money option premium (maybe volatility is particularly high at the moment), or if you simply believe that the out-of-the-money exercise level is unattainable, then this is a way to improve your profit potential with out adding extra risk.

Fire Insurance

Most home owners have fire insurance. This is a premium paid every year to the insurance company that every home owner hopes they will never have to use. In the infrequent, but nevertheless possible, event that a house burns down, the home owner can breathe a sigh of relief for having paid the premiums religiously every year.

Out-of-the-money puts are fire insurance. Most people investing in the stock market, or indeed in other markets, are hoping that the market will rise over time. What they desperately do not want to see is a crash. A crash could really wipe them out. One way to 'insure' against crash losses is to buy out-of-the-money puts.

The further out-of-the-money, the cheaper the puts will be. There is always a distant exercise price at which puts can be purchased for two or three cents. This will seem cheap in price but will usually represent a very high level of volatility. The further out-of-the-money an exercise price, the greater the volatility required by the seller, mainly because no one is prepared to sell anything at half a cent or less—it's just not worth it.

By spending a small amount on buying these cheap puts, the investor has put a floor on losses resulting from a crash. There will still be losses, representing the distance between at-the-money and the exercise price chosen for protection. But losses will be limited, and the investor can choose an exercise price appropriate for their desired level of protection.

Spreads, Straddles and Strangles

An option *spread* is similar to a buy-and-write. If we wish to purchase the at-the-money call, instead of buying the stock, we can choose to also sell an out-of-the-money call simultaneously. This is known as a 'call spread'. This has the effect of reducing the initial amount of premium paid as premium is also received. If the investor is happy to be exercised at the higher level (meaning the upward view on the stock was correct), then the ultimate profit is enhanced. Again there is only a risk of potential profit lost if the stock rallies very strongly.

The reverse of the call spread is the 'put spread'. Everything is the same except we are pursuing a view on the downside.

A 'straddle' is an interesting concept because it involves the simultaneous purchase of both the at-the-money call and the at-the-money put. Now why on earth would you do that? Surely one cancels out the other? Not so.

A straddle is essentially a volatility play. You believe the stock has the potential to be volatile, but you do not necessarily have a view as to which direction it might move. This may occur, for example, before a profit announcement or an election of a new CEO. The stock might jump dramatically on the news, or might fall dramatically. If you're right, and the stock does jump dramatically, then the profit on the call position will be greater than the premium paid for the put and call together. So too if the stock falls. As long as it falls far enough, your profit is greater than the premium paid. If you're wrong, and stock doesn't move much at all, then you will lose your combined premium and your straddle strategy will have proven to be incorrect.

A straddle can be quite an expensive strategy. At-the-money premium can often be quite costly. To beat this, you may consider buying a 'strangle' instead. A strangle is the same as a straddle except that you purchase a combination of the out-of-the-money call and the out-of-the-money put. The out-of-the-money options are always cheaper. But it now means that not only does the stock have to move, it has to move at least to your exercise price in either direction, and then beyond, before you will be making money.

You may have the opposite view. You think the stock is not going to move at all. You can then *sell* the straddle. This will bring you in a nice lump of premium, but you will be totally exposed to any significant movement in the stock. If you think a stock may only move within a certain band then you might sell the strangle. If you are right, you will keep your premium, if you're wrong you could lose a lot.

So ends our brief look at option strategies. I now want to move on to something more exciting.

Strange Equity Instruments

Convertible bonds, converting preference shares, converting notes, instalment receipts—these are just a handful of equity products that you may have come across. They are all means of raising capital from investors and they are all exceedingly more complicated than the straight out issuing of shares or corporate bonds. Many of these instruments display 'optionality'. This means they are a form of derivative that exhibits similar traits to that of the humble option. Therefore, they will attract not only an investor, but also options traders.

I could go on for hours about a whole range of these instruments, but I won't. A quick look at a few of them will give you the general idea.

Convertible Bonds

A convertible bond is best described as a 'hybrid' of debt and equity. A straight out corporate bond is a means of raising debt capital. This simply implies that the company 'borrows' money from the investor for a period of time and then ultimately gives it back. In the meantime, the company will pay the lender (the buyer of the bond) an interest rate known as a 'coupon'. Coupon amounts are fixed at the beginning and, provided the company doesn't go bust, the investor will receive an interest payment maybe annually or semi-annually and will also receive his or her money back at the end.

When investors buy equity in a company, there is no guarantee that they will get their money back. They are, however, hoping that they can ultimately sell out the shares at a better price in the future. Shares will also, more often than not, pay a dividend. Although a dividend is similar in a sense to a coupon payment, it is not fixed in amount, and may vary substantially over the life of the share.

As the investor, which instrument would you rather use to invest in a company? Debt, which pays a fixed return but does not provide capital growth, or equity, which provides the potential for capital growth and the possibility of a regular payment? If you are undecided, then you may wish to consider the convertible bond.

Back once again to our old friend, UCI. The UCI stock price is at $15.00 and the company is issuing a convertible bond. One bond will cost $100. It will mature in five years and pay a coupon annually of 10%. At any time, the bondholder can 'convert' the bond into ordinary shares which they will receive at a price of $16.00. For one bond they will receive 6.25 shares.

What does all this mean? Firstly, let's break up the convertible bond into its two parts. As a bond, it will cost you $100 and pay you 10% per annum for five years. At the end of the five years, the bond is 'redeemable for cash', meaning they give you back your $100. If you choose to hold the convertible as a bond, you will be indifferent as to what happens to the UCI share price. That is, unless it goes to zero, which implies that the company's gone bust and you won't be getting your 10%, *or* your money back.

But you have the choice to convert the bond into shares at $16.00. What if, after two years, the share price has risen to $17.00? You could convert the bond and you would be $1.00 in front. Once converted, you would no longer receive the 10% coupon or the $100 back, but you will receive whatever dividend UCI is currently paying, and there is still the potential for the stock price to rise. What should you do?

To be honest, I don't care. This is something only *you* can decide, dependent upon your own views and financial situation. What I would like to focus on, however, is this: because you can choose to convert the bond into equity at any time, you might say this provided you with an *option*.

The 'value' of a convertible bond is a combination of its bond value and the value of its 'optionality'. A normal corporate bond issued for $100 will trade maybe slightly higher or slightly lower than $100 depending on whether 10% is a good return, as compared to current interest rates, or not. It may also trade a lot lower if there appears a risk that the company is in financial difficulty and may not be able to pay the 10%. A convertible, on the other hand, has the capacity to trade much higher than $100 if the price of the stock has rallied. This is because you have the option to convert into stock.

If the stock price were to fall well below the $15.00 mark, not because the company looks like going broke, but because markets in general are weak at the moment, then the convertible will act like a bond and not fall as much. This is because, despite the lower stock price, you are still content that you will get your $100 back. If the stock were to rally strongly, then the convertible would act more like an equity and rally along with it. This is because you can choose to convert into stock at $16.00. A rough graph of the value of the convertible would look like Fig. 11.

Fig. 11—Value of a Convertible Bond with respect to Stock Price

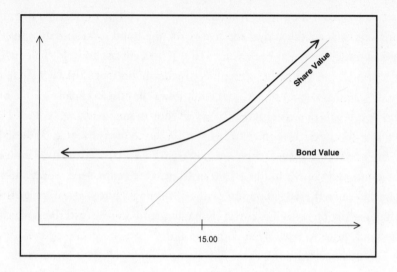

The option component of the convertible can be valued in the same way as a straight call option, using the five variables, but with a lot of other complicated factors that I won't trouble you with here. Suffice to say, just as you would not immediately exercise a call option that's in-the-money with time left to run, you would not necessarily convert the bond either. There is still value in the 'optionality'.

Preference Shares

A standard preference share is similar to an ordinary share except that it pays a 'preference' dividend, which is a fixed percentage of the prevailing stock price and must be paid to preference shareholders as long as there are sufficient profits or retained profits with which to do so. In the case of ordinary shares, the company can choose whether or not it even wants to pay a dividend, and then it can choose how much. The value of the preference share will be greater or less than the equivalent ordinary share, depending on whether the fixed dividend proves to be more or less than the dividend attainable from the ordinary share.

To complicate matters, a company may also choose to issue a 'converting preference share'. As is the case with a convertible bond, the preference share holder may choose to convert into ordinary shares at a specific exercise price if he or she deems this to be the better alternative at the time. However, whereas at the maturity of the instrument the bond will be redeemed for cash, the converting preference share will be redeemed for an amount of ordinary shares. The ordinary shares received on redemption may be received at a discount, or may be received as a cash value divided by the ordinary share price.

Because a convertible preference share exhibits 'optionality', it can be valued and traded in a similar fashion to a convertible bond.

Another important feature of preference shares, and indeed all 'hybrid' instruments, is where the instruments rank in the event of the wind-up of the company. If the company were to go broke, then there is still a possibility of some distribution to holders of capital through a fire sale of assets. Debt will usually rank first, meaning the debt holders will get the first distribution of any crumbs. Ordinary shares will rank last. Preference shares will rank ahead of ordinaries and other forms of hybrids will, on a predetermined basis, fit somewhere in between.

Convertible and Converting Notes

It's getting weird now. You may have noticed that I have so far used the expressions 'convertible' and 'converting'. Bonds are usually 'convertible'. Preference shares are usually 'converting'. The difference between the two, other than the semantics, is illustrated through the instrument known as a 'note'. Incidentally, I'm sure that issuers of capital are hell bent on trying to confuse everyone, the tax man included (and I'll get to that in a moment), with these slight variations on labels.

'Convertible' implies that the hybrid instrument will convert into either one ordinary share or an amount of cash. 'Converting' implies that the hybrid instrument will convert into either one ordinary share or a number of shares based upon a dollar value. In other words, in the latter case, a dollar amount will be divided by the current ordinary share price to provide the ultimate number of shares received. Because the latter case provides the opportunity for an almost infinite number of shares to be issued (ie in the case where the share price has fallen almost to zero), there will be a maximum number of shares permissible on conversion.

A bond will invariably be 'convertible'. A preference share will invariably be 'converting'. A note can be either. If a note is 'convertible', then it is effectively the same as a convertible bond, as on redemption the note holder will receive cash. If the note is 'converting ', then it is similar to a converting preference share because on redemption the note holder will receive an amount of shares determined by dividing an amount of cash by the ordinary share price.

And so you ask why on earth are there such things as notes? The answer really lies in the effects of such instruments on the balance sheet, and on the taxation implications.

Balance Sheets and Tax

I am not going to bore you with this, but it might lend some understanding to why companies go to the trouble of issuing weird and wonderful hybrid instruments in the first place.

If a company exhibits a large amount of equity on its balance sheet, it is deemed to be in a healthier position than a company that exhibits a large amount debt on its balance sheet. This is because shareholders cannot complain if their investment is lost, and they have no control over whether or not the company chooses to pay a dividend, while debt holders have been given an obligation that the debt will be repaid and that their interest payments will always be maintained (come hell or high water).

With that in mind, consider that ordinary shares, preference shares, converting preference shares and converting notes are considered as equity on the balance sheet, and that bonds, convertible bonds and convertible notes are considered as debt on the balance sheet.

From the company's perspective, all distributions are either tax deductible or not. Dividends *are not* tax deductible (but may be 'franked', but that's another story which we won't enter into here). Interest payments, on the other hand, *are* tax deductible. Coming back to our hybrids, it follows that preference dividends, and dividends paid on converting preference shares are not tax deductible, whereas coupons paid on convertible bonds and convertible and converting notes are. Take all of that and then work out exactly what sort of capital a company should issue. And good luck. Suffice to say, the above considerations, and others, determine exactly which form of capital is best issued by a company at the time. And what's more, there are still other variations of the themes of convertibility, redemption and so on. But this is enough for now.

One other quick consideration, however, is that of dilution. If either bonds, notes or preference shares are converted into ordinary shares, then there is no further injection of capital into the company. This means that the value of the existing shares must suddenly reduce due to there suddenly being that many more ordinary shares on issue. This is also something to consider in the case of 'rights'.

Rights

Another way that a company can raise more capital is to issue 'rights'. A 'right' is the right given to existing shareholders to buy more shares in the company at a discount on the current share price. To some extent the company is thus thanking its shareholders by offering this discounted entry into new stock but really, let's face it, it's a sneaky way of raising more capital.

The existing shareholders do not, however, have to 'take up' their rights. In this way a right is thus exhibiting optionality. The right holder has the right, but not the obligation, to pay up to buy more stock. The right holder also has the option to sell those rights to someone else through a secondary market listed on the exchange. In this way, being given a right is the same as being given a call option.

Once a company announces the issue of rights then, again, a dilution factor must come into play. If a number of new shares is issued at a discount, then this will render the existing shares lesser in value. Once the rights are listed on the exchange, however, this dilution factor has been taken into account and the rights will trade at a value that represents the value of an equivalent call option.

Instalment Receipts

Instalment receipts have become a popular form of 'derivative' in Australia in recent years. The partial privatisation of Telstra, and the subsequent issue of shares to the public, is a good example. An instalment receipt is simply a means, from the issuer's point of view, of issuing stock at a price that is affordable to Joe and Josephine Average. Instead of paying the full price up front, the receipt buyer simply puts up a part payment now.

Once the part payment has been made, the stock begins to trade on the exchange at its 'partial' value. This partial value can still rise or fall just like any ordinary share. But ultimately a date has been pre-set where the holders of instalment receipts must choose whether or not they wish to pay up the remaining amount to hold fully paid ordinary shares. At this date, or before, the holder has the option to sell the instalment receipt and avoid the next payment. If the holder decides to sell the instalment receipt, they will no longer hold any interest in, or have an option to hold any interest in, that stock.

An instalment receipt is, therefore, similar in some ways to a right. The holder has the option to pay extra. In the case of a right, the holder already holds stock and is simply deciding whether they wish to pay more to hold more stock. Either way they will still get to hold their existing stock. In the case of an instalment receipt, however, the holder has the right to pay more to continue to hold an interest in that stock. If they sell the receipt, they will no longer hold any interest in that stock.

An instalment receipt is different to a 'partly paid share'. Although both only require part payment upon issue, the holder of a partly paid share is *obliged* to make the extra payment when asked. The partly-paid share offers no option.

Leveraged Equity Instruments

Many investment banks offer the opportunity to invest in the stock market without actually putting up any money. The investor purchases an instrument which may be variously called a 'leveraged equity instrument' or a 'geared equity instrument' or some similar expression. The crux of these instruments is that the bank 'lends' the money to the investor and then buys a stock or stocks on his or her behalf. The investor pays an amount of interest up front, but receives any increase in the value of the shares and all dividends in the period. If the value of the shares falls, then the investor can simply give the shares back.

In paying the interest on the 'loan' up-front, the investor has created a tax advantage which can be offset against any tax payable on dividends or on capital gain. The level of interest paid is usually much higher than the prevailing interest rate. This is because the bank has provided the investor with a put option, the cost of which is incorporated into the interest payment. That's why you can give the stock back if it fails to perform. You are effectively holding an at-the-money put.

Endowment Warrants

An endowment warrant is a long-term investment instrument targeted at those putting their money away for a rainy day, or perhaps for their children or grandchildren to benefit from. It is an instrument whose appeal is based on the fact that, in the long term, stock markets tend to rise in value.

An endowment warrant is given the label of 'warrant' because it also contains an element of optionality. The optionality in this case is similar to that of an instalment receipt.

The basis of the endowment warrant is that you pay a partial amount now to own a stock. Over a period of time, usually ten years, the dividends paid by the company go not to you directly, but towards the gradual repayment of the balance of the original cost of that stock. At the end of ten years, the stock will quite likely be worth more in value than the combination of your partial payment and the dividends paid over the period. Thus you have entered into a long-term capital investment at a proportion of the cost.

It is still possible, however, that at the expiry of the warrant the value accrued through the payment of dividends still falls short of reaching the value of the stock at its current share price. This is where the option comes in. You can choose to either pay up the remaining difference and thus become a holder of ordinary shares or you may choose to sell the warrant into the secondary listed market at the current value.

Exotic Options

We're pretty much approaching the end of my introduction to you of various derivative instruments. Mind you, my intention was never that my list would be exhaustive, but simply that I would touch on, and hopefully familiarise you with, the more popular derivatives. Certainly those which you may have heard mentioned before.

Derivatives which come under the loose heading of 'exotic options' tend to be an ever-growing collection of more and more complex interpretations of the option concept. You may or may not have heard of some of them. You may have heard of others which I haven't mentioned, but either I think they're getting just too obscure or, goddamn, maybe *I've* never heard of them. Anything that comes under the banner of 'exotic' tends to imply that if you haven't got a decent computer and some geek with coke-bottle glasses and pen-holder standing by to program in the maths, then you've probably got buckley's of ever pricing one.

Nevertheless, you may not need to be able to price one properly in order to take advantage of the hedging or leverage aspects the exotic provides. To that end, I'm going to quickly run through a few, and without maths.

Options on options:

If you can have the option to buy a stock, or a currency, or a bond, or whatever at a certain price, why not also have an option to buy the option to buy the stock or currency at a certain price?

Volatility options:

Similar to the above. One doesn't bother mucking around with all the other variables involved in a particular option, but goes straight to the important variable—the volatility. Exercise this option if the volatility of a particular instrument reaches a predetermined level.

Basket options:

You can buy one option over your choice of a collection, or 'basket', of stocks rather than a collection of options over each stock. In a sense, this becomes an option over a mini 'index' of stocks. Basket warrants are also popular.

Knock-in options:

This is one of two forms of 'barrier' option. The holder buys the right to buy an option only if the underlying instrument trades at a particular level.

For example, one might decide a stock is potentially subject to takeover. If, however, it is not taken over, the stock price will go nowhere. Instead of wasting money on buying a straight out call option, one can buy a call option which only 'knocks in', that is comes into being, if the stock trades at a level above where it is currently trading (implying that the takeover offer has been made). The buyer of the knock-in call sets this level. The knock-in call is ultimately cheaper than its straight call counterpart.

Another example. 'Fire insurance' out-of-the-money puts can be cheaper if the put only knocks-in when the market has already fallen to a particular level. You may have already decided that if the market reaches this particular level, it could well fall a lot further. Rather than buy a put now, buy a put that only comes into being when this level is reached.

Knock-out options:

Obviously the opposite of the knock-in. One purchases a call or put for whatever reason. If that reason does not come to being, and the stock moves in the opposite direction, then at a predetermined level the option will knock-out and cease to exist. Again a less costly form of hedge.

Contingent options:

You can buy an option but pay nothing up front. If the option is exercised, then pay up the premium. In this form of option the premium ultimately paid will be more than the premium paid if it were paid up front. But if you don't exercise the option, you don't ever have to pay a cent.

Average rate options:

Also known as 'Asian' options. You can buy an option over a particular instrument for a given period. At the end of the period, the option can be exercised at the *average price* of the instrument over that period, as opposed to the predetermined exercise price of a standard option.

Look-back options:

You can buy an option at a certain exercise price for a certain period. At the end of the period, you can exercise the option (if desired) at the *best price achieved* over that period.

Out-performance options:

These are similar in some ways to a 'swaption'. The buyer is looking to take advantage of the fact that he or she believes, for example, that the equity market will out-perform the bond market over a period of time. He or she buys an option on the actual return of one market over the other. This is instead of actually 'swapping' the return of each market.

Quanto:

I've never figured out why these were so-named. The buyer buys an option over, for example, the stock index but, on exercise, receives the pay-out in a different currency. This allows the buyer to hedge out the currency risk of buying options over a foreign index.

And so on and so on and so on...

10. Hedging and Hedge Funds

What a piece of work is man. (William Shakespeare)

When the stock market crashed in 1987 the world woke up to the effects of a 'new' form of financial instrument—the 'derivative'. The use of futures and options and arbitrage was targeted as being a fundamental cause of the market's spectacular demise. Computers became a defenceless scapegoat in the ensuing witch-hunt for reasons why a stock market should crash, other than the unlikely reason that it was significantly overvalued and running up on hypnotic euphoria. Calls were made for regulation. Apart from a few 'circuit breaker' measures in futures markets, where trading is halted temporarily in the event of a specific down move, little was actually done.

Again in the mid-nineties more 'derivative disasters' were coming to light. People were being sued. A US House of Representatives inquiry called upon the world's most renowned derivatives trader, George Soros, for advice on how this shady, undisclosed market could and should be regulated. George had earlier been held responsible for bringing the European Monetary System to its knees through speculating on European currencies.

George suggested at the time that regulation was probably difficult, but monitoring of outstanding positions was definitely a sensible idea. Again, little was done. In 1995, a futures broker brought down Barings Bank. In 1997, Dr Mahathir, Prime Minister of Malaysia, accused George Soros of bringing Asia to the brink of bankruptcy through his currency speculation.

In 1998, a 'hedge fund' by the name of Long-Term Capital Management found itself unable to fund financial market exposures in the vicinity of US $200 billion. The biggest problem, as it turned out, was that LTCM was leveraged to something like fifty times or more by a collection of some of the world's biggest and most respected investment banks. The Federal Reserve was forced to organise a rescue package for LTCM. Not doing so may have brought down the whole world financial system. Once again, derivatives were held responsible. Once again, there were immediate calls for regulation.

Will they actually do something this time? This remains to be seen, but one thing's for sure—derivatives are the root of all evil.

Two points arise here. *Are* derivatives the root of all evil and, whether or not they are, *can* they be regulated?

Our farmer was not a speculator looking to make fast bucks out of a financial market. He had a legitimate reason to attempt to protect his income, and thus his livelihood, from the uncertainties of the business of growing wheat. By utilising a derivative market in the form of wheat futures, he was able to alleviate that uncertainty. The baker, too, had his reasons for entering the market. The uncertainty surrounding the production and price of wheat affected his business in the same way it affected the farmer's. The only difference is that the farmer was a seller of wheat and the baker was a buyer.

The futures market allowed the farmer and the baker to come together and provide each other with a hedge against uncertainty. By using this derivative as a hedge, both parties were reducing risk, not increasing it. Effectively, both parties came out as winners. The question must then be asked that, if it is possible for both parties to come out as winners in a derivative transaction, then why do there seem to be so many disastrous incidents of financial loss through derivative trading?

The answer lies not in the derivative instrument itself, but in the intentions of the buyer or seller of that derivative in the first place. The existence of tools for the reduction of risk is not a guarantee that that risk can be made to disappear altogether. The fact that our farmer and baker were able to nullify each other's risk is a very rare example of where two parties met with diametrically opposing requirements. It is never quite as simple as that in the universe of millions of daily financial transactions.

A speculator is looking to *take* a risk. A speculator will have a particular view on the direction of the market. The existence of derivative markets offers the speculator a vehicle for potential profit. The hedger does not necessarily have a firm view on the direction of the market. He or she is merely looking to protect themselves against a costly adverse move, should it occur. So the hedger is prepared to pay the speculator the price that the speculator requires. The speculator will take on the risk because his or her view is that the adverse movement will not occur.

Does this mean that someone must always win and someone must always lose? Largely yes. In all financial markets, the end result is always a transfer of wealth. The hedger, however, has already factored in the cost of hedging. If the adverse move does not occur then the hedger merely sees it as the cost of insurance, a necessary expense. The speculator on the other hand has placed his or herself in a position of outright loss. That is the risk of financial markets. The win/lose situation may not, however, be a direct outcome between two trading parties. Wins and losses will often be dissipated through the market.

For example. You buy a call option on a stock from a market-maker. The market-maker then delta hedges his short call by buying a proportion of stock. The person who sold the stock to the market-maker had previously bought the stock at a lower price. The stock price rises. You make a profit on your long call. The market-maker had sold the option at a good volatility level and also profited from buying back the call at a lower volatility level. The person who sold the stock to the market-maker had already closed out for a profit. So who has lost?

Somewhere down the chain of transactions someone will have lost, but it is not readily obvious exactly who that loser is. In all the financial transactions conducted in the world in one day, there will be flows backward and forward and there will ultimately be winners and losers. One thing that is certain is that the hedger will only ever have a limited loss. It is also certain that one who exploits the limited-loss feature of some derivatives, such as through the purchase of options, will also have a limited loss.

Derivative markets came into being to satisfy the market's needs. Speculators provide the liquidity of particular instruments to allow those with legitimate requirements to find a reasonable price for their transactions. Since time immemorial markets have risen and markets have fallen and some have profited and some have not. Without speculation, markets would never exist.

Speculators, too, can hedge. To speculate on a market does not mean simply taking a wild risk and hoping for the best. A speculator can, through the use of derivative instruments, take a position in a particular market and then limit the loss potential of that position. And this brings us to the concept of the 'hedge fund'. In late 1998, the expression 'hedge fund' became a dirty word. Major volatility in financial markets was largely attributed to the activities of these seemingly shady operations. So what exactly is a hedge fund?

A very good question indeed. In simple terms, the average funds manager, such as the person who might be entrusted with the job of investing and managing your superannuation, will make tried and true investments in such things as government bonds, the stock market and the property market. Bonds are safe, and it is proven that over a sufficient period of time stock markets tend to rise and property markets tend to rise. The funds manager is aware that you are relying on your superannuation to ultimately see you through your retirement, and therefore he or she will not undertake overly risky investments lest the value of the nest egg is eroded. If this were to happen, the funds manager would have a bad name and investors would look elsewhere.

Not everybody has to rely on their superannuation to see them through their retirement. Those individuals and companies with sufficient existing wealth are always looking for ways to make their money work harder and thus ultimately make more money. Bring on the hedge fund. A hedge fund is basically an investment vehicle that offers the opportunity for extraordinary returns. The way that a hedge fund can make extraordinary returns depends on various elements.

Firstly, the manager of a hedge fund will most often have had a good deal of experience in trading a particular market or markets over a period of time. Therefore they are offering expertise. Secondly, the manager of a hedge fund will have a good knowledge of derivative instruments, and how these instruments can be used to provide a better return over the same period as the underlying instrument itself. Thirdly, and most importantly, a hedge fund will exploit the first two elements and seek to obtain leverage for the initial investments. Leverage will be provided by an investment bank.

How does this leverage work? The hedge fund starts with an initial amount of money and a reputation. The investment bank then takes this money as a deposit and lends a multiple of that amount back to the hedge fund for the purpose of investing in and trading in financial markets. In order for the investment bank to be happy to lend the hedge fund this multiple, they must be happy that the positions are in fact 'hedged'. Therefore the name 'hedge fund'. The more limited the potential loss of the hedge funds positions, the more the investment bank is willing to lend. Given that derivative instruments provide the means for hedging, it follows that hedge funds are big players in the derivative markets. If the hedge fund's positions prove to be profitable (and hedge funds are a vehicle for providing good returns over a short period of time, not a life time) then the multiplying effect of the leverage will flow through to a multiplying effect on the profits.

In theory then, although a hedge fund is looking to exploit the financial markets for extraordinary profit, this should not actually prove dangerous to the markets in general because the hedge fund is supposed to be hedged. But if hedge funds are supposed to be hedged, how come they suddenly lost billions of dollars?

Another good question. The realities of losses in hedge funds in 1998 may never really come out. One can only theorise that the age-old human failing of greed was instrumental. A fund is successful—it grows in value. With more money at its disposal, it can put on bigger and bigger positions. When things just seem to be going right all the time, then perhaps the need for hedging is not quite so important. The provider of the leverage should be wary of dodgy hedging, but hey—the fund keeps making money. If anything, we should be giving them more.

When Long-Term Capital Management was bailed out, everybody was aghast at the amount of leverage they were operating with. Nevertheless, a significant multiple of leverage is not unusual in financial markets. The investment banks themselves are levered in similar multiples. This extent of leverage should not have been a problem if the positions being held were sufficiently hedged. Were they? Obviously not. Long-Term managed to rack up significant losses by, for one thing, buying Russian bonds and selling US bonds. Although they *were* buying one thing and selling another, this was in no way a hedge. They were wrong. They blew the lot. And in so doing, they almost took their lenders down with them.

Were derivatives to blame? Of course not. Was greed to blame? I believe this was the defining criterion. Yet again there are calls for the regulation of the derivative markets. Regulation of the derivative markets may be beneficial in order to protect those who are simply inexperienced and naive in the vagaries and risks of derivatives from those who are happy to exploit the weak for profit. This is usually the case with most forms of regulation. But derivative markets were born as an alternative to the already regulated underlying markets. No matter how much regulation you attempt to apply, there will always be another instrument or market that will crop up in order to find a way around the regulations. Just ask the tax office.

Greed will always drive a market and, let's face it, we can all admit to possessing some level of greed. Markets were trading and people were making and losing money a long time before derivatives became an issue. If the market exists, then people will trade it. If they feel they can make a lot of money by destroying that market, and the market is there to be destroyed, then they will. Dr Mahathir was happy to prove to the world that Malaysia could be just as successful and prosperous an economy as the rest of the world. To finance this expansion, Malaysia borrowed heavily from offshore. Private investment followed suit and pretty soon a rapidly growing economy was churning along based largely on debt. When Malaysia decided it was time to get serious and float the ringgit against the currencies of its trading partners, there were many who saw, George Soros amongst them, that the currency was significantly overvalued. They sold it. And they sold it and sold it. They sold it because they could.

Malaysia was not the only Asian country to suffer such a fate. Thailand had set things going, South Korea is in turmoil and Indonesia, well, Indonesia is currently a scary place. Dr Mahathir, however, was the one who was quick to point the finger of blame. A Jewish conspiracy to destroy his currency, he said. The reality, of course, is that Dr Mahathir failed to realise that he could not have his cake and eat it too.

When Nick Leeson brought down Barings Bank, he did so through unauthorised trading in derivatives. Prior to this disaster, Barings Bank's Singapore operation had been making fabulous amounts of money. Barings put so little effort into monitoring the activities of its successful operation that Nick was able to lose the Bank from under them. Was it Nick's fault? Certainly he was criminally responsible, but who was really responsible? The management team back in London were quick to point out that it wasn't their fault. This 'rogue' was purely to blame. The management team had been blissfully unaware of what was going on. The management team were forced to take a good hard look at themselves.

Crashes, bankruptcies, currency collapses—all have occurred over and over again throughout time. The most recent ones have usually found a scapegoat villain in the form of derivatives. Derivatives are only as powerful as the people who use them. So what do we conclude about derivatives? Useful investment and risk management product, or evil instrument of greed? Or both? I'll leave it to you to decide.

Glossary of Terms

All Ordinaries index: A capital-weighted index of the top stocks on the Australian Stock Exchange.

American option: An option exercisable at any time during its life.

arbitrage: The exploitation of a price discrepancy between two similar instruments.

at-the-money: When the exercise price of an option is the same as the underlying price.

backwardation: When each maturity of a futures contract is successively less in value.

bank bill: A discounted bill of exchange issued by a bank for the purpose of 90-day financing.

base metal: A metal used in industry such as lead, tin etc, but not gold or silver.

basket: A collection of financial instruments such as stocks.

bid: The price at which one will buy.

bill strip: Successive maturities of bank bill futures.

bimetallic monetary system: A currency system based on the face value of gold and silver.

binomial model: An options pricing model utilising a natural distribution probability tree.

Black-Scholes model: A mathematical options pricing model developed by Black and Scholes.

boot-strapping: The process of buying or selling the bill strip.

Broker: One who is authorised to transact business in financial markets on behalf of clients.

brokerage: The commission charged by a broker to transact business.

buy-and-write: The strategy of buying stock and writing the same number of call options against it.

call option: An instrument providing the right. but not the obligation to buy an underlying instrument.

cap: A purchased option limiting exposure to a rise in the market, or a sold option limiting profit.

capital-weighted: An index of stocks weighted by capitalisation.

capital markets: A combination of the short-term money market and fixed interest market.

capitalisation: The number of issued shares of a stock multiplied by the share price.

cash and carry: The value of an instrument inclusive of both its physical value and funding cost.

cash management trust: A fund investing in money market instruments.

cash settlement: Settlement of a futures contract by cash and not physical delivery.

clearing house: An organisation responsible for the pooling of buy and sell transactions on a financial exchange.

CLICKS: The automated trading system of the Australian Options Market (not an acronym).

collar: The combination of a cap and a floor.

commodity: Anything of a non-financial nature traded in world markets.

commodity money: A monetary system based on bank notes backed by gold or silver.

contango: When each maturity of a futures contract is successively greater in value.

convertible bond: A corporate bond convertible into ordinary shares and redeemable for cash.

converting note: A corporate bond convertible into ordinary shares and redeemable for a number of ordinary shares.

converting preference share: A preference share convertible into ordinary shares.

coupon: A regular fixed-interest payment from a bond.

debt: Capital raised through borrowing.

delta: A hedge ratio representing the probability of an option being exercised.

delta hedge: The purchase or sale of the underlying instrument to the delta amount.

derivative: An instrument whose value is connected to the value of an underlying instrument.

dilution: The effect of the reduction in value of existing shares when new shares are issued.

discount (1): The amount at which a debt instrument is issued or trading at below its par value.

discount (2): When the value of a futures contract is less than the value of the physical.

discount arbitrage: Selling stock and buying futures when the futures are at a discount.

dividend: The income distribution made to shareholders.

Dow Jones Industrial Average: The index of the top 30 stocks traded on the New York Stock Exchange.

endowment warrant: A long-term stock warrant featuring part-payment in return for forgoing dividends.

equity: Capital raised through a share issue.

European option: An option exercisable only at maturity.

exchange-traded: Of an instrument traded on a financial exchange.

exercise price: The price received when an option is exercised.

exotic option: Any option-like instrument that is not a straightforward put or call.

expiry date: The date at which an option expires.

fair value: In relation to stock futures, the physical price plus the funding cost, less the dividends payable.

fiat money: Bank notes backed only by a government guarantee.

fixed interest: Interest payable in amounts fixed to maturity.

floating rate: An interest rate which changes with prevailing interest rates.

floor: A purchased option limiting exposure to a fall in the market, or a sold option limiting profit.

floor price agreement: The same as a collar, as used in the gold market.

foreign exchange: The business of buying and selling different currencies.

forward contract: An agreement between two parties to fix the price of a particular commodity at a date in the future.

forward rate agreement: An agreement to borrow money in a predetermined period for a predetermined rate.

futures contract: An exchange-traded contract fixing a price for a particular commodity at a date in the future.

futures exchange: An official establishment for the purpose of trading futures contracts.

gamma: The rate of change of delta with respect to the change in the underlying price.

government bond: A coupon paying instrument offered to the public in order that the government may borrow from them.

hedge: To limit exposure to an adverse move in the market.

historical volatility: A measurement of the volatility of an instrument based on the history of price movements.

implied volatility: A measurement of the volatility of an instrument based on the current trading price of an option.

in-the-money: When the exercise price of a call option is below the underlying price, or the exercise price of a put option is above the underlying price.

instalment receipt: A derivative of a share allowing the buyer to make an initial part payment followed by full payment at a later date.

interest rate: The cost of borrowing money quoted as a percentage of face value.

intrinsic value: The amount of which an option is in- the-money.

leverage: The ability to deal in a large amount of money while only putting up a small amount of money.

liquidity: A consideration of the amount and frequency of turnover of a traded instrument.

local member: An independent, individual member of a futures exchange.

long volatility: To be in a position to profit from an increase in the volatility of an instrument.

margin: An incremental amount payable each day on top of a deposit in order to cover the exposure of a futures position.

margin call: A request for a margin to be paid.

market-maker: A person either obliged to or prepared to make a bid and offer in a financial instrument.

market-tracking: Of a portfolio of stocks designed to provide an equivalent return to the market index.

maturity date: The date at which a financial instrument expires.

money market: The market for short- and long-term borrowing and lending.

offer: The price at which one will sell.

open market operations: Intervention in the money and foreign exchange markets by the Reserve Bank.

open outcry: A method of trading financial instruments on an exchange in a face- to-face environment.

open position: The amount of outstanding futures contracts in a particular series.

option premium: The price paid for an option.

optionality: The capacity for an instrument to exhibit the characteristics of an option.

out-of-the-money: When the exercise price of a call option is above the underlying price, or when the exercise price of a put option is below the underlying price.

over-the-counter: When instruments are traded between two parties and not on an exchange.

physical: An underlying instrument.

portfolio: A collection of financial investments.

portfolio insurance: The sale of stock index futures in order to protect a reduction in value of a portfolio of stocks.

precious metal: Gold and silver.

preference share: A share paying a predetermined dividend.

premium (1): See 'option premium'.

premium (2): When the value of a futures contract is greater than the value of the physical.

program trading: The use of computer-generated orders in stock-futures arbitrage.

publicly listed company: A company listed on an exchange in which the public may invest.

put option: The right, but not the obligation, to sell an underlying instrument.

registered trader: A market-maker in the Australian Options Market.

replication: The process of choosing a basket of stocks to represent an index of stocks.

risk premium: The value of an option above and beyond any intrinsic value.

SEATS: (Australian) Stock Exchange Automated Trading System.

secondary market: The market in which an instrument can be bought and sold subsequent to its issue.

Share Price index: The futures contract over the All Ordinaries index.

shares: Specific units of equity in a company.

short sell: To sell an instrument without having previously owned it.

short volatility: To be in a position to profit from the reduction of volatility of an instrument.

soft commodities: Those commodities that are not metals, energy, stock or financial commodities eg agriculturals.

speculation: Taking a view on the direction of a market with the sole purpose of generating a profit.

spot: The current price of a commodity.

spread (1): The difference between the bid and offer price.

spread (2): Simultaneously buying and selling two options of differing strike price or maturity.

stock: A listed company or a number of shares.

stock borrowing: To temporarily obtain the right to sell stock short and pay a fee to the beneficial owner of that stock.

stock exchange: An organisation established for the purpose of buying and selling shares in listed companies

stock index: A collective measurement of the value of a number of stocks.

stock index arbitrage: To simultaneously buy/sell stocks and sell/buy stock index futures.

stock market: A market in which the shares of listed companies are bought and sold.

stockbroker: A person authorised to buy and sell shares in listed companies on behalf of clients.

straddle: A combination of the at-the-money put and call.

strangle: A combination of the out-of-the-money put and call.

strike price: See 'exercise price'.

swap: An agreement between two parties to swap two interest rates or the return on two instruments between themselves.

swaption: An option to enter into a swap.

theta: A measurement of the time decay of option value.

time decay: The loss of value of an option premium as it approaches maturity.

time to maturity: The remaining time before the maturity of a financial instrument.

tracking error: The discrepancy in return between a market-tracking portfolio and the index.

trade-weighted index: A currency index used to compare the value of the Australian dollar with the value of Australia's major trading partners' currencies.

underlying instrument: That commodity or financial product from which the price of a derivative instrument is determined.

vega: The change in the value of option premium with respect to a change in volatility.

warrant: An option over an existing stock issued by a third party.

yield: The return on an investment.

Index